MotoGP™

Season Review 2012

Julian Ryder

Published in November 2012

A catalogue record for this book is available
from the British Library

ISBN 978 0 85733 252 3

Library of Congress catalog card no 2012940565

Haynes Publishing, Sparkford, Yeovil,
Somerset BA22 7JJ, UK
Tel: +44 (0) 1963 442030
Fax: +44 (0) 1963 440001
E-mail: sales@haynes.co.uk
Website: www.haynes.co.uk

Haynes North America, Inc.,
861 Lawrence Drive, Newbury Park,
California 91320, USA

Printed and bound in the UK by
Gomer Press Limited, Llandysul Enterprise Park,
Llandysul, Ceredigion SA44 4JL

This product is officially licensed by Dorna SL,
owners of the MotoGP trademark (© Dorna 2012)

Managing Editor Mark Hughes
Design Lee Parsons, Richard Parsons, Dominic Stickland
Sub-editor Kay Edge
Special Sales & Advertising Manager
David Dew (david@motocom.co.uk)
Photography Front cover, race action and portraits by
Andrew Northcott/AJRN Sports Photography; technical
images pp17-33, 198, 206-207 by Neil Spalding

Author's acknowledgements

Thanks to:

Toby Moody, Neil Spalding, Dave Dew, Nick Harris,
Martin Raines, Venancio Luis Nieto, Andrew Northcott,
Frankie Parrish, Dean Adams, Nereo Balanzin, Martin
Finnegan and The Rainband

www.motogpbook.com

CONTENTS
MotoGP 2012

FOREWORD
BY CARMELO EZPELETA, CEO OF DORNA,
THE MotoGP RIGHTS HOLDERS
7

THE SEASON
MAT OXLEY LOOKS BACK ON THE FIRST
YEAR OF CRT AND THE LAST YEAR OF
CASEY STONER IN MotoGP
9

RIDERS' RIDER OF THE YEAR
EVERY MotoGP RIDER WHO HAS
RIDDEN IN MORE THAN ONE RACE
VOTES IN OUR POLL
14

TECHNICAL REVIEW 17
NEIL SPALDING EXAMINES HOW YAMAHA
GOT THEIR BIKE SO RIGHT FOR THE FIRST
YEAR OF THE 1,000CC FORMULA

THE BIKES 23
BEAUTIFUL BIG DOUBLE-PAGE IMAGES OF
THE FACTORY BIKES PLUS SINGLE PAGES
ON THE CRT MACHINERY

THE RIDERS 35
HOW THE SEASON UNFOLDED FOR EVERY
RIDER FROM THE WORLD CHAMPION TO
THE WILD CARDS

THE RACES 45
EVERY RACE IN DETAIL, FROM FREE
PRACTICE ON FRIDAY TO THE PODIUM
ON SUNDAY

Moto2 CHAMPIONSHIP 192
HOW MARC MARQUEZ WON
THE TITLE AND AMAZED US
ALONG THE WAY

Moto3 CHAMPIONSHIP 200
KTM'S FIRST ROAD RACING WORLD TITLE
AND THE FIRST RIDERS' CHAMPIONSHIP
FOR GERMANY SINCE 1993

RED BULL ROOKIES 208
ANOTHER QUICK YOUNG GERMAN,
FLORIAN ALT, WINS THE SERIES THAT
PRODUCES FUTURE CHAMPIONS

RIDERS FOR HEALTH 212
WHAT ALVARO BAUTISTA SAW WHEN HE
JOINED RIDERS FOR HEALTH IN ZAMBIA,
BY BARRY COLEMAN

Game,
Set
& Match

MotoGP
Jorge Lorenzo
WORLD CHAMPION
YAMAHA
FACTORY RACING
2012

YZF-R1 Race Blu

YZF-R6 Race Blu

YZF-R125 Race Blu*

2012 MotoGP World Champion Jorge Lorenzo and his Yamaha YZR-M1. A victory defined in blue.
The Yamaha Race Blu Series are now available at your authorised Yamaha dealer.

Race Blu Series
www.yamaha-motor.co.uk

YAMAHA

FOREWORD
CARMELO EZPELETA

The 2012 MotoGP™ season has proved to be a year with much emotion, excitement, drama, controversy and spectacular racing, during which champions of the future have emerged while another has bowed out in style.

It will not only be remembered as the year when Dani Pedrosa pushed countryman Jorge Lorenzo close for the World Championship, or Casey Stoner defied the odds to put in a breathtaking performance in his swansong at Phillip Island, but also as the season that saw the start of a new chapter for motorcycle racing as we know it.

The adaptation to 1,000cc machinery proved an instant hit with fans and riders alike, and the CRT class has shown that with innovation, skill and determination the factory bikes can ultimately be challenged. In addition to this, the inaugural Moto3™ class, which took over from the incredibly popular 125cc bikes, has delivered edge-of-the-seat racing at its best, at almost every single round.

And now I'm pleased once again to introduce this latest edition of the *MotoGP Season Review* from Haynes Publishing, which will take the reader on a journey through a season that has offered so much to the motorcycle racing enthusiast. Relive the year that Lorenzo stormed to his second world title on board his Yamaha, fending off the Repsol Honda duo of Pedrosa and Stoner, who proved an ever-formidable team throughout.

On this note it is with great sadness that I bid farewell to one of the best riders to have graced the FIM World Championship since its introduction in 1949. An injury may have stopped Stoner from challenging for his third title, but he chose to end his season in style with a truly exceptional ride in front of his home crowd in Australia. He will be dearly missed by fans around the globe, and by riders and paddock alike.

Yet while in this instance we may be losing a star, the Moto2™ intermediate class has produced what can only be described as many special talents to watch for in the future, with the likes of Marc Marquez, Andrea Iannone, Pol Espargaro, Scott Redding and Tom Luthi sending fans' hearts racing on more than a dozen occasions this year. Marquez's season has been nothing short of stunning, and I for one cannot wait to see him challenge the best in the premier class next year when he steps up, along with Iannone.

In Moto3 we saw the youngest-ever German rider crowned in the lightweight class in the shape of Sandro Cortese who, under tremendous pressure, held off pre-season favourite Maverick Viñales. And with race-winning rookies like Romano Fenati having already set the 2012 season alight, I can safely say that the future of MotoGP looks bright, and the stars of years to come are already well on their way.

So enjoy reading about the 2012 season, and I look forward to welcoming you all next year.

CARMELO EZPELETA
DORNA SPORTS CEO
NOVEMBER 2012

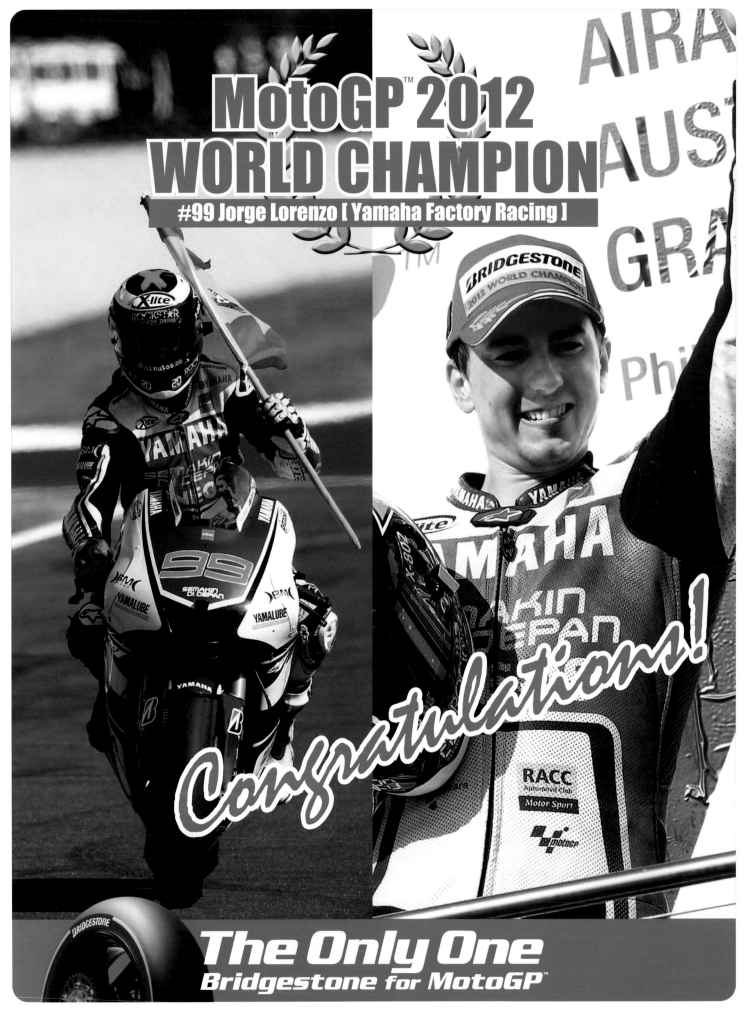

MotoGP™ 2012 WORLD CHAMPION

#99 Jorge Lorenzo [Yamaha Factory Racing]

Congratulations!

The Only One
Bridgestone for MotoGP™

OFFICIAL MotoGP® CLASS TYRE

BRIDGESTONE *Motorsport*

FULL SPEED TO THE FUTURE

MotoGP is a fast-changing World Championship in a fast-changing world. Mat Oxley looks back at the big happenings of 2012, both on and off the track

The 2012 MotoGP season was full of tremors and transformations. The biggest era of change the sport has experienced continued apace, with the 125 class (the last of the original Grand Prix categories from 1949) replaced by Moto3, the arrival of CRT machines in MotoGP, endless talk of further cost-cutting measures in the shape of an rpm limit and control ECU, the departure of disgruntled 2011 World Champion Casey Stoner and a looming showdown between the factories and rights-holders Dorna. Then finally, in October, the earthquake: that Dorna will also take control of MotoGP's rival series, the World Superbike Championship.

It was hard to take it all in, and sometimes it was almost possible to forget that there was racing going on amid all the hot air and negotiations. We live in a fast-changing world, so perhaps it's only to be expected that motorcycle racing should also be evolving at a dizzying rate. The sport needs to change in the face of huge financial challenges, largely brought on by the global economic crisis which seems to be one of the few unchanging features of modern life. The crisis appears no closer to its end now than it seemed back at its beginning in late 2007.

That may explain why Dorna isn't merely sticking to its chosen course of drastic cost-cutting measures. During 2012 the company steered an even sharper route that brought it into collision with some of the factories. For many years Dorna CEO Carmelo Ezpeleta had seen the factories as the foundation of MotoGP racing, but more recently he has come to realise that in fact the

factories could just bring the entire edifice tumbling down through their addiction to ruinously expensive technology. Ezpeleta's big push is to transform MotoGP from a factory R&D operation into a global sports entertainment business.

When he tabled his idea of a control ECU he met with fierce opposition, especially from Honda, who announced that electronics R&D was so central to their racing involvement that they would withdraw their factory team from MotoGP and defect to World Superbike, which at that time had no plans to introduce a control ECU. In years past this threat might have shaken Ezpeleta to the core – but not now. In late 2011 London-based private equity company Bridgepoint bought InFront Sports, a Swiss-based sports marketing business, mainly for its lucrative World Cup TV rights. Also part of InFront's portfolio was the World Superbike series. Since Bridgepoint already owned Dorna, and therefore MotoGP, this deal was rightly put before the EU commission for monopolies. In February 2012 the EU cleared the deal.

Notwithstanding factory opposition, Ezpeleta's plan to reduce costs in MotoGP should have been straightforward. All he had to do was write a new set of technical regulations. Inevitably, these new rules would also slow down the motorcycles. This wouldn't be a problem either, since most fans wouldn't worry if the pace dropped by a second or two, as long as the grids were full and the racing was thrilling. The difficulty was World Superbike. MotoGP's slower pace certainly would matter if lap times were no faster, or even slower, than those in the rival championship. Bridgepoint's decision to amalgamate both series under Dorna's rule solved that problem and substantially increased Dorna's market value, the holy grail of all private equity businesses. Now Dorna can apply cost-cutting measures to both championships, slowing MotoGP bikes and Superbikes at a similar rate to preserve the status quo of the prototypes lapping faster than the production bikes.

The Bridgepoint deal also took away the factories' ability to play one championship off against the other, although HRC vice-president Shuhei Nakamoto announced that if Dorna applied a control ECU to both championships, then Honda would go and race in the All-Japan Superbike series. It is far too early even to guess at how the Bridgepoint deal will change racing, but hopefully it will be for the better because MotoGP and World Superbike can be run in parallel, instead of constant collision.

Five months before the Bridgepoint bombshell, Casey

Stoner dropped one of his own. At May's French GP the Australian announced that he would retire at the end of 2012, making him the first reigning premier-class champion to quit in half a century. Only two others have decided to retire while wearing the crown: John Surtees at the end of 1960 and Gary Hocking a year later.

Stoner's reason was simple. At the age of 27 he had already been racing for 24 years, so he'd had enough, plus he didn't favour MotoGP's new direction. He wanted GP racing to stay strictly prototype – prototype engines in prototype chassis – so he didn't like the CRT concept. Like many fans, Stoner believes that GP racing should be about fire-breathing prototypes, about motorcycles that are as fearsome to ride as the old 500cc two-strokes. He likened allowing CRT bikes into MotoGP to allowing touring cars into Formula 1.

CRT had been under development for more than a year by the time the first bikes hit the tracks during 2011. The concept was simple – to create a new breed of lower-cost motorcycles that didn't belong to the factories. Previously the usual way to put a MotoGP bike on the grid was to lease a machine from one of the factories, for a fee of more than a million Euros per bike, which had to be returned to the factory at the end of the year. That system worked when MotoGP was awash with tobacco cash, but when cigarette sponsorship was banned it failed.

CRT rules don't specify road-bike engines, but engines taken from the latest 200 horsepower-plus superbikes powered every CRT bike on the grid during 2012. However, companies like Cosworth have studied the rules, wondering if they might be able to build CRT engines.

The new bikes certainly swelled the grid – and just in time. MotoGP had been thinning out for years. After the bountiful early seasons, Aprilia, Kawasaki, Ilmor, Team Roberts, Team Pons, WCM and others had all fallen by the wayside, unable to afford the spiralling costs of four-stroke prototype racing. At the end of 2011 Suzuki also quit and Pramac Ducati downsized to one rider. That left a dozen prototypes for 2012 – not a proper grid by any stretch of the imagination.

CRT bikes almost doubled that figure, with an intriguing selection of machinery from Aprilia's ART to the Suter BMW and the FTR Kawasaki and FTR Honda. The Aprilia was the most popular and comfortably the best performer, though also the most expensive, at 1.2 million Euros for two bikes, with enough engine rebuilds for two seasons. Money well spent, however, because on a good day ART riders like Aleix Espargaro and Randy de Puniet were fast enough to leave the slower prototype riders like

Karel Abraham and Hector Barbera red-faced. That must have had the AB Cardion and Pramac teams wondering why they'd bothered spending more than double the money for their rare-groove Desmosedicis. Significantly, both Barbera and Abraham will ride CRT machines in 2013.

The Suter BMW and the FTR Kawasaki and FTR Honda cost less than 400,000 Euros each, a bargain-basement price for a GP bike. All three were works in progress, especially on the electronics side of things. Colin Edwards' Suter used an ECU that had started life in a German DTM touring car; no wonder it took a long while to get the anti-wheelie sorted. The FTR Kawasakis run by the Spanish Avintia Blusens outfit used a basic Motec ECU, which lacked lean-angle sensors. This is why Dorna want a control ECU – to reduce the gap between the CRT bikes and the factory machines with their NASA-like electronics.

Honda believe they have a better idea than CRT. They are considering manufacturing a limited run of MotoGP bikes based closely on their RC213V, but without its more costly technologies like pneumatic valves and slick-shifter gearboxes. The RCV replica wouldn't be as cheap as a CRT bike – HRC mentioned a million Euros for a bike, including a season's engine supply – but it would be faster; perhaps a second slower than the fastest, which would make it considerably quicker than the best CRT bikes, which were usually around 2.5 seconds off the front-running pace.

Oh yes, we had indeed almost forgotten about the racing. Amid all the change and talk of change, only one thing stayed truly consistent during 2012 and

that was Jorge Lorenzo. The Spaniard rode a season of unerring regularity, never finishing a race outside the top two. Ever since he quit his crashing habit for the 2009 season, Lorenzo has had the consistency of a metronome, clocking one identical lap after another and leaving most of his rivals in awe of his ability to use the same inch of racetrack, lap after lap after lap. It's a talent that pays handsomely in an era when the bikes, and even more so the tyres, demand an ultra-smooth approach to cornering. Lorenzo made it all look easy, even though it obviously wasn't. Securing the 2012 crown was certainly a bigger challenge than winning the 2010 championship, the year when Dani Pedrosa was inconsistent on the still below-par Honda, Valentino Rossi broke a leg and Stoner was wrestling the tricky Ducati.

'This year has been even tougher than the first time because I knew the competition was stronger and more consistent than in 2010, so I had to be even more consistent than that,' said the Spaniard. 'It wasn't easy because I also had to be very strong and very fast, so I was taking a lot of risks but I couldn't make any mistakes. Also, Yamaha made me a much, much better bike than last year. For these reasons we were the best in 2012.'

Most people expected Lorenzo's main challenge to come from 2011 World Champion Stoner, but the Aussie was beset by two problems that blunted the start to his campaign and ultimately ended his chances of a third title. Arm pump bothered him at the first few races, but it was tyre chatter which really played havoc with his chances. Bridgestone's softer-construction 2012 slicks had been designed to make the tyres more forgiving, in the hope of ending the rash of cold-tyre crashes that had blighted the

BELOW Jorge Lorenzo prepares to go out and win his second MotoGP title

previous two seasons. The tyres were certainly friendlier for most, but they didn't work so well with the factory Repsol Honda RC213V, creating massive chatter at pretty much every track.

'When I first tested the RC213V last year it was probably the best bike I've ever ridden,' said Stoner. 'But now it's one of the worst and most difficult bikes I've had to ride and it's all because of tyres.'

Notwithstanding the problems, Stoner won two of the first three races, but then his season began to unravel. He was given a reprieve when Lorenzo was taken out by a wayward Alvaro Bautista at Assen, but he then threw it all away with a rash 'win it or bin it' move on team-mate Dani Pedrosa at the penultimate corner at Sachsenring. Three races later a nasty highside at Indianapolis ended his title challenge.

But as Stoner faded, so Pedrosa came on strong. His first win of the year at July's German GP was the start of a relentless push for the title that netted him a further six victories by the end of the season. Using a new anti-chatter chassis (which Stoner didn't like), Pedrosa chipped away at Lorenzo's championship lead, whittling it down from 38 points, after his ill-fated San Marino outing, to 23 points going into the penultimate race in Australia. In his seventh season in MotoGP, Pedrosa had never looked better. He even scored his first wet-weather GP win at Sepang, having exorcised his fear of the rain by training in sand aboard a slick-shod dirt bike.

Like Lorenzo, Pedrosa's forte has always been smoothness, though his consistency didn't quite match that of his compatriot. His start to the season was hardly poor, but two thirds and a fourth at the first five races were enough to leave him lagging behind his rival. The year might well have turned out very differently if it hadn't been for the chaos of Misano, which ended with Pedrosa being punted off by the hapless Hector Barbera. At least that put the two Spaniards equal on blameless DNFs, because Lorenzo had already been taken out by Alvaro Bautista at Assen.

Pedrosa's charge ended on the second lap at Phillip Island, where he was going for his fourth straight win. He knew he had to take risks to stand a chance of beating Lorenzo to the title, and finally the risks caught up with him. 'I pushed hard and I have no regrets – I'm very proud of my performance this year,' he said after the race.

The best of the rest was Andrea Dovizioso. He certainly had the right machinery – Yamaha's new 1,000 was without doubt the best motorcycle in MotoGP, even if it lacked some of the Honda's outright speed. Dovi's podium score rate on his Tech 3 YZR-M1 was pretty much as good as it had been when he was riding a factory Honda. The reward for his speed and intelligence aboard a satellite-team M1 was to fill a berth at the Ducati factory, vacated by the departing Valentino Rossi. Is that a dream job or a nightmare? Rossi certainly knows which. After two years of trying to race competitively on the fickle Desmosedici he gave up and went running back to Yamaha, replacing Ben Spies, who had such horrible luck throughout 2012 that it was tempting to believe his occasional mutterings about voodoo. 'Has anyone got a chicken we can sacrifice?' asked the Texan before one race.

The Rossi/Ducati dream team failed because Ducati's

renouncement of its carbon-fibre chassis technology only partially cured the Desmosedici's problems. Rossi continued to struggle with lack of front-end feel, understeer and the ferocious V4 engine, just as he had done in 2011. He had many miserable races – far from the front – and at Indianapolis he even admitted that an earlier crash at Laguna Seca had deterred him from taking further risks. And who could blame him – his accident rate had increased three-fold with Ducati.

'I had two or three moments with the front, and after that I didn't want to crash another time, so I just cruised,' he said at Indy.

By the end of his two years with Ducati the factory hardly seemed any closer than it had at the beginning. Rossi finished his first race with Ducati 16 seconds behind the winner. At Phillip Island, his penultimate ride on the GP12, he was a whopping 37 seconds down on the winner. After that ride Rossi was even more sombre than usual.

'We more or less have the same problems we had when I first tested the bike at the end of 2010,' he said. 'Sometimes you have the feeling that you've wasted your time.'

Rossi will go into 2013 a (slightly) humbler man. No-one knows what his real expectations might be. Does he merely want to have fun fighting at the front once again, as he has claimed in recent months, or does he think he can rekindle his former glories and retake the crown that has already been his on seven occasions? Have Lorenzo and Pedrosa moved things on since he was last at the front, or will he have enough speed to win a few races or even challenge for the title?

Stoner's exit introduces a new teenager to MotoGP next season. The arrival of Marc Marquez is an enthralling prospect. The 2012 Moto2 World Champion reminds one of Rossi in his younger years and it will be fascinating to see the old master lock horns with the young apprentice. Marquez has many attributes similar to the young Rossi – he is fast, brave, a great strategist and he has great mental agility. His 2012 Moto2 season was something special, even if he sometimes attracted the wrong kind of attention for dangerous manoeuvres that had the mark of the backstreet brawler. And yet rivals who rightly criticised Marquez did admit that he calmed down during the second half of the season, once he had secured his golden ticket to MotoGP with a factory Honda.

Moto2 continued to supply thrills and spills aplenty, though the class is less manic than it was in 2010, when it seemed like there was a different winner every weekend. During 2012 only five riders were regularly battling for the lead, though it was usually Marquez who was out front when it mattered. The man has a magical ability to be in the right place at the right time – he's often happy to jostle in the lead pack until he knows the chequered flag is being unfurled.

The only men who could regularly run with Marquez the Magical (or Marquez the Merciless, if you prefer) were Pol Espargaro, Tom Luthi, Scott Redding and Andrea Iannone. The last-named rider goes to MotoGP in 2013 with Ducati, while Yamaha already have their eyes on Espargaro.

Moto3's inaugural season went splendidly well, with breathtaking racing that brought back memories of the 125 class at its height, a decade or so ago. The category's complex and long-winded technical

regulations were written specifically to keep costs under control and to prevent richer manufacturers building hi-tech missiles that would leave the others way behind. The rules worked. The factory Red Bull KTM of inaugural Moto3 World Champion Sandro Cortese may have been faster than the Hondas – which had minimal support from the factory – but the racing was nearly always thrilling and intense. No wonder Dorna want to apply the Moto3 philosophy to MotoGP.

There will be more racing next year and just as much talk about rules, politics and business. In that way MotoGP has become like any other big-time sport, such as Formula 1 cars and Premiership football. Love it or hate it, that's just the way it is. Dorna knows where it is taking the sport. Hopefully its twin aims of reduced costs and better racing will be realised for the benefit of everyone.

ABOVE Romano Fenati, Maverick Viñales and Sandro Cortese – three of the young stars of Moto3

BELOW Marc Marquez added the Moto2 title to his 125cc championship and moves up to MotoGP for 2013

RIDERS' RIDER
OF THE YEAR 2012

The Riders' Rider of the Year poll asks every rider who has ridden in more than one MotoGP race to name his six toughest rivals. The scrutineers then count up the votes and award six points for a first place down to one for sixth. Here are the results.

VOTED FOR BY

Karel Abraham, Hiroshi Aoyama, Hector Barbera, Alvaro Bautista, Stefan Bradl, Cal Crutchlow, Andrea Dovizioso, Colin Edwards, Toni Elias, James Ellison, Aleix Espargaro, Nicky Hayden, Yonny Hernandez, Jorge Lorenzo, Katsuyuki Nakasuga, Mattia Pasini, Dani Pedrosa, Danilo Petrucci, Michele Pirro, Randy de Puniet, Jonathan Rea, Roby Rolfo, Valentino Rossi, David Salom, Ivan Silva, Ben Spies and Casey Stoner

There is no doubt who the MotoGP riders consider the best in the world this year. Jorge Lorenzo's astonishing consistency meant that 16 of the 25 riders who could have put him first on their list did so, and the rest had him second but for one rebel who put him fourth. The only other name to appear on every ballot paper was second-placed Dani Pedrosa, with four firsts, 13 seconds and four thirds. Surprisingly, Casey Stoner was a distant third with only three first places, and several voters ignored him completely.

Two riders did conspicuously better in our poll than in the final points table: Cal Crutchlow and Aleix Espargaro. Crutchlow jumps from seventh to fourth, Espargaro from 12th to an amazing sixth. He and his team-mate Randy de Puniet were the only two CRT riders to garner any votes at all. The level of recognition for Espargaro, named on 11 ballot papers, was a surprise and a sign that the CRT riders are not completely off the radar of the factory men.

2nd
DANI PEDROSA
114 POINTS

3rd
CASEY STONER
85 POINTS

4th
CAL CRUTCHLOW
64 POINTS

5th
ANDREA DOVIZIOSO
57 POINTS

6th=
ALEIX ESPARGARO
23 POINTS

6th=
STEFAN BRADL
23 POINTS

8th
ALVARO BAUTISTA
19 POINTS

9th
VALENTINO ROSSI
8 POINTS

10th
NICKY HAYDEN
5 POINTS

Espargaro's inclusion in our top ten was the only difference in personnel from the top ten in the championship. Ben Spies was the man who made room; the unlucky Texan was named by only two voters, another indication of a racer's attitude to a competitor who's having a tough time. The same could be said for Valentino Rossi; sixth in the championship but only ninth in the vote, with only five of his rivals choosing to include him. One rider, however, made a point of mentioning that he was voting for a lot of Ducati riders because he knew how difficult their bikes were to deal with.

There appeared to be no particular pattern in the voting; there was no noticeable solidarity with fellow countrymen or team-mates, and only a couple of instances of what looked like voting for a mate. If objectivity was ignored, it was usually to settle a score. Casey Stoner's surprisingly uncompetitive showing compared to the other race winners can certainly be explained by the fact that quite a few of

his competitors chose to ignore him or, worse still, rank him well down the order.

As you'd expect, the Riders' Rider of the Year quite closely mirrors real life, but where the two differ is very informative and tells us a little about attitudes within the paddock. Everyone agrees that the two Spaniards are the best and there's no mercy for the old champions who are seen to be in decline.

PREVIOUS WINNERS

VALENTINO ROSSI	2004, 2005, 2008, 2009
LORIS CAPIROSSI	2006
CASEY STONER	2007
JORGE LORENZO	2010

Yamaha use two three-axis gyroscopes to let the bike know where it is in space

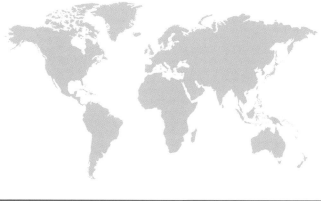

THE REGENERATION OF A RACER

Yamaha's 800 reigned supreme for three years... could Yamaha stretch it to a fourth... as a 1,000?

Yamaha's M-1 struggled through its last year as an 800, yet it was the most successful bike of the five years of the formula. Redeveloped in a hurry after being trounced by Stoner and the Ducati in 2007, the Yamaha went on to win three triple crowns (rider, constructor and team titles) in 2008, '09 and '10.

Yamaha had given up any real thought of winning the final 800cc MotoGP championship in 2011 in the face of a massive attack by the Honda Motor Company, desperate to win at least one 800cc title. It was Honda's for the taking, because Yamaha had another battle in mind: they were preparing their machines for the first of the 1,000cc titles.

Yamaha did their homework carefully. They could take their 800cc bike, by far the most successful of the series, and carefully boost it to 1,000cc. By doing so a year early they would have an advantage in the first few races of 2012 while Honda sorted their bikes out. Honda's main focus was winning in 2011, but it didn't stop them making two completely different bikes for Stoner and Pedrosa to test. It did, though, stop them beginning 2012 with the best bike.

Yamaha didn't have a big budget, but in concentrating on their 1,000cc bike they used their brains. The new engine is a clone of the 800, but with modifications to improve reliability, a bigger sump, and a different oil supply for the gearbox. The handling is taken care of by a further derivation of the same chassis concept they have been developing for the past five years. It's long and quick and, from the start of the year, it's what the tyres – the components that make all the difference – needed.

By mid-season Honda had caught up. Their '2013' bike, introduced at the Mugello test, was their second attempt at the 1,000cc formula. Different frame flexibilities and a smoother, easier-to-control engine have made their mark.

Add those improvements to Honda's already unbelievably high level of technology and the result was a bike that, by Brno in the middle of the season, was better than the Yamaha. What had mattered to Yamaha, however, was to take the lead in the early rounds and preserve it for as long as possible.

PRIORITISING HANDLING OVER POWER

The history of the Yamaha has been well recorded. It has always been an across-the-frame water-cooled four, and it has always had the crankshaft rotating backwards. Back in 2004 Yamaha started adding some really nice twists to the design: longer front engine mounts, four-valve heads and an 'irregular fire' cross-plane crankshaft – ideas that allowed them to use some of the advantages already enjoyed by the then all-conquering V5 Honda RC211V.

Yamaha added new stuff too. A swingarm with most of its mass below the centreline added both stability and lateral flex for grip. Later on, in response to Ducati's 2007 commando raid, Yamaha developed the finest electronics package of the 800cc generation. But it's in its basic construction that the Yamaha displays the company's priorities. The engine may not be the powerhouse of the Honda, but it's quick and is designed to materially affect the handling of the bike.

The reverse-rotating crankshaft was probably initially specified so that power could be taken from the centre of the crankshaft, thus reducing the propensity of the crank to twist under high loads. That concept requires an engine-speed jackshaft to transfer drive across the back of the engine to the primary gear and the clutch basket. This is the same concept that Yamaha used in their TZ700/750s; it's an idea that they have understood well. And that's where Yamaha's focus on handling becomes quite interesting because that crankshaft has several other effects.

We have discovered that high-speed changes of direction are much easier with the crank turning backwards; it cancels out some of the gyroscopic stability that keeps the bike upright and charging forward, making direction changes physically easier. The torque reaction is also quite helpful. We now have electronic throttles that hold the bike at a certain maximum wheelie. If the engine is forcing the front down as the rider accelerates, even by just a couple of kilograms, the bike will be accelerating faster than one where the action is the other way. The same happens in corners; theoretically, a bike with a counter-rotating crank will hold its line in a corner better than one with a crank that turns forward. Over the years we have also discovered that an engine-speed jackshaft is the perfect place to put a balancer weight to counteract the rocking couple generated by a cross-plane crank. All in all, that's not a bad payback for a shaft that probably costs eight to ten horsepower.

We have noted that Yamaha designed their engine power take-off to be from the centre of the crank. That's handy, because they also placed their cam-drive gear train on the back of the cylinder block, taking its drive off that same jackshaft. This centralisation of rotating mass is good for cornering as well, helping the bike to hold a line. All these design decisions are intended to counteract the problems caused by the bike's wide in-line four-cylinder engine, and they very nearly succeed. The benefit of that in-line four, however, is that it's

BELOW The 800 stripped: note the unused bolthole in the middle of the main spar and the way the front engine mounts are braced

far easier to get it to pitch forwards and backwards under braking and acceleration. On a V4 the two cylinder banks act as dampers, slowing the bike's desire to pitch back and forth. Those bikes therefore need softer suspension to encourage pitch.

Yamaha's preoccupation with their engine's ability to influence handling did not leave them well placed to deal with the sudden imposition of a six-engine limit in the MotoGP class. Before the rule came into effect they would commonly use, including rebuilds, more than 25 engines per season. The 800 was modified to survive this much higher reliability requirement, with improved material quality as well as plating and coating technology inside the engine. The 2012 season provided the first real opportunity to do a full redesign, so it's hardly surprising that the 1,000cc version of the bike has been redesigned with robustness in mind.

What is obvious from the outside is the much larger oil sump, and a sudden increase in the number of oil filler holes. More oil means it is easier to keep fresh oil on stressed parts, but the much lower-revving 1,000s are considerably easier to keep in one piece in any event. The rash of oil fillers is evidence of a separate oil supply for the gearbox. Unchanged in concept, it's a sliding dog-ring design, unlike the super-high-tech seamless-shift gearboxes of Honda and Ducati. The whole engine is a simple and thoughtful upgrade of the 800; they have kept the good points and added reliability plus 200cc.

CHASSIS

Yamaha did not start out well on the chassis front – their original M-1 had the main beams bolted directly to the top of the cylinder head. It took the arrival of Masao Furusawa to head up the race department in mid-2003 before the bike sprouted the elongated front engine mounts that were a feature of the then all-conquering Honda RC211V. Since then the bike has been carefully tuned in terms of its lateral, torsional and vertical stiffness. These changes reflect the tyres that the bike rolls on. As the stiffer Bridgestones replaced the fairly soft Michelins of yore, the bikes have reduced lateral rigidity for better high lean angle grip, but Yamaha have simultaneously had to maintain as best as possible torsional and vertical strength to maximise, respectively, braking and handling performance. They have to achieve this using only one piece of metal, so the shape, thickness and sections have changed.

The initial changes were quite dramatic, but now the pace has slowed. Back in 2002 the main frame was a simple beam; now it's a complex web of welded-up CNC-machined aluminium sections providing strength where needed and flex where appropriate. Back in 2005 the cross-member in the rear of the chassis above the gearbox was removed, and since then the beams have been reduced in section and the material thinned right down. The front engine mounts now go all the way down to a point just in front of the crankshaft. Over the years those mounts have progressively been braced more and more, all without increasing the bike's lateral strength. The side beams are themselves very thin, probably with a skin thickness of about 1mm, and they are milled from solid using CNC machines.

ABOVE Yamaha partially blanked off the water and oil radiator exhausts from Catalunya onwards

AERODYNAMICS

As with the rest of the bike, Yamaha didn't change anything unnecessarily. The basic fairing and aerodynamics are almost identical to the last of their 800s, with any differences mostly appearing to be 'bolt on'. Initially the bike had two added sections, both designed to cover the rider's shoulders at high speed. Closer inspection revealed that the actual overall shape was little changed, but that Yamaha had given themselves the ability to remove two outer sections to reduce susceptibility to side winds. Further examination showed that the method of joining the 'side fairings' was a raised shoulder, and one clearly designed to be raised at that.

Halfway through the year, at the first of the circuits with a really fast straight, Yamaha uncovered another new modification, this time flat plates partially obscuring the oil and water radiator exhaust ducts. These ducts had been gradually growing over the previous four years to increase cooling as the 800 revved ever higher, generating ever more internal friction and heat as it did so. Now, however, the friction levels are down, and although piston speeds might remain quite extreme, all the other components that spin and move in a racing engine are doing them a lot slower this year. That means less heat is being generated, and Yamaha decided it would cause less drag if they reduced the airflow through the radiator to a level that was necessary for good cooling. Like the 'shoulder guards', however, the edges of these plates sit proud of the fairing sides.

One would normally think of raised edges causing drag, but in both these cases the raised edge is just before a duct or an open space. The most likely explanation is that the raised edge prevents the boundary layer separating from the fairing, so helping prevent the increase in drag that that would cause. The radiator exhaust ducts are particularly interesting; their presence would cut radiator exhaust airflow, thus forcing air that would have gone through the radiator and created drag as it did so around the outside. In addition, the raised edge might help reduce the pressure in the exhaust duct itself, reducing drag as it does so. Yamaha say the plates are there to assist top speed, but they probably do it by being better at cooling.

Every once in a while Yamaha run prototype chassis without the ubiquitous black paint, and then it's also possible to see the whereabouts of the internal reinforcement. In the middle of 2011 Yamaha brought two 1,000cc prototypes to Brno. The main obvious difference between them was the air intake: one bike followed the current 'air through the headstock' approach, the other routed it underneath. Yamaha opted for the same concept that they had followed for the previous six years, and the air through the headstock design stayed. They also experimented with fuel-tank height as a way of testing different positions for the centre of gravity.

The latest 1,000 chassis is very similar to the last of the 800s; one unused engine mount has been left off, and the front-to-rear weight balance has been changed to get the best out of the latest Bridgestone tyres. Softer in construction than the previous generation, these tyres need less pressure on them than last year's versions. The 800-generation Bridgestones were extremely rigid and required a bike that put a lot of weight on to the rear tyre to maximise grip. The newer tyres are deliberately softer in basic construction, designed to flex and build up heat, and they would simply slide away if they were subject to the same pressure as the old ones. Longer swingarms are the answer here; in Yamaha's case the wheelbase has stretched almost 40mm. This has had the happy side-effect of raising the point at which the bike starts to wheelie, definitely a problem with the new, torquey 1,000cc motors.

ELECTRONICS

When we think about electronics we are usually comparing different throttle responses and traction-control strategies. However, this year it was something else that made a difference. Both Jorge Lorenzo and Dani Pedrosa were taken out by other riders during the course of the year; both lost a race and in points terms both suffered equally. But Lorenzo's crash was far more damaging to his hopes. Yamaha does not have the best 'decide when to switch off the engine when crashing' strategy in MotoGP, so Lorenzo lost engines in the Bautista crash at Assen this year and in warm-up at Le Mans last year. It's normal to change the amount of time the engine will run when it's on its side after a crash between practice and the race. If the bike is on its side the oil doesn't get picked up properly and in 10–15 seconds the lack of oil can ruin the bearings inside the engine.

In a race series where riders are only allowed six engines for the season one really does not want to take any more risks than are necessary. Chasing a good result in a race, however, means one might be prepared to take a few risks to allow the rider to pick the bike up and continue, so the engine might run for 10–15 seconds before switching off.

BELOW The M-1's frame may look unchanged but Yamaha have continually experimented with torsional, vertical and lateral stiffness

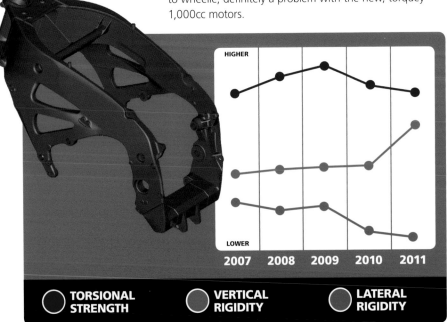

HIGHER

LOWER

2007   2008   2009   2010   2011

● TORSIONAL STRENGTH   ● VERTICAL RIGIDITY   ● LATERAL RIGIDITY

LEFT Andrea Dovizioso's 2012 1,000cc Yamaha M-1

In practice it's better not to take any risks at all. It's clear from both of Lorenzo's crashes, mentioned above, that the throttle stuck open, and it's also clear the Yamaha doesn't have a quick enough electronic strategy for detecting that the bike is on its side, that it's not moving and that the throttle is wide open. If they had, the bike would have automatically shut down to a tickover once it was at 90 degrees to the vertical and switched off all together as soon as it knew it was in the gravel on its side. The difference between Lorenzo's crash and Pedrosa's was that Jorge lost an engine; Dani's bike stopped in time and didn't rev itself to death.

Yamaha would not thank anyone for saying their bikes are not as reliable as Honda's, but that is not their main focus. Using an engine for three races is

normal, while four races is a stretch. The engine that was lost at Assen was new, and to make up for its loss a lot of very careful engine management was necessary. Lorenzo used an older engine for the Sachsenring race, immediately after Assen, and that took its total number of races to four. Each Yamaha rider this year has had to do that at least once.

Yamaha pulled off a very clever trick in 2012. Faced with Honda throwing resources at their V4 – a gearbox that costs more than most houses, a totally new bike halfway through the season – they looked at their old design, tweaked it in all the right places, and turned up with the best bike on the grid. It may even still be the best bike at the end of the season. But what else could they do when they haven't got serious money to spend?

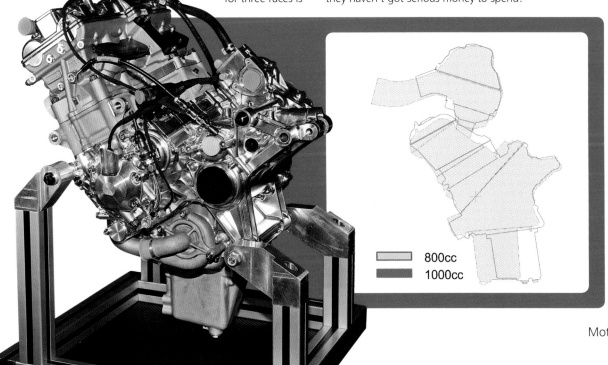

800cc	
1000cc	

LEFT The 800 engine out of its frame, and its dimensions compared to this year's 1,000

THE BIKES

YAMAHA
YZR M1 2012

24

HONDA
RC213V

26

DUCATI
DESMOSEDICI GP12

28

APRILIA
ART GP12

30

FTR HONDA
FTR MGP12

31

FTR KAWASAKI
BQR-FTR

32

SUTER BMW
SUTER CRT

33

YAMAHA
YZR M1 2012

Yamaha took their time during 2011 to build a good and effective 1,000cc machine based closely on their very successful 800. That early preparation paid dividends immediately. The Yamaha could hold the Honda off on the straights, and it could also do all the other things expected of Yamahas, like deal with corners. The early part of the season saw a battle between the Yamahas and Casey on the Honda.

Yamaha kept improving things, too. After the season started new, longer swingarms were introduced and, just as importantly, it only took a few races for all four riders to have them. It was the same with the engine set-up. At least three exhaust systems were obvious, and that usually means three different stages of engine set-up. They also made their way quickly right the way through the Yamaha squads. It was a very good example of a factory knowing what would need to be done to take, and then maintain, an early lead in the series.

Taking an early lead did not mean that Yamaha were without problems, however. The new 1,000s still only had 21 litres of fuel to use in the race, but they effectively made more power with it simply because internal friction levels reduced as the revs came down, with lower frictional losses ultimately equalling more power at the tyre. But that didn't mean that the fuel mapping was accurate, or that the latest version of the software made it from the works team to Tech 3 as quickly as it should have done. Neither Tech 3 bike finished their cooling-down lap at Brno, and at Motegi two months later Cal Crutchlow ran out of fuel while contesting a podium position.

Then there was the strange case of Ben Spies, who had a really miserable season. There were problems with the bike and there were clearly problems with confidence and trust. There were several racing crashes that simply looked unfortunate and there were others that perhaps should not have happened. After a practice crash at Laguna Seca Ben had his rear suspension linkage collapse in the middle of the ultra-high-stress Corkscrew corner during the race; a cracked steel joint took the blame. At Indy Spies had taken the lead only for his engine to self-destruct on the main straight. And at Motegi he managed to heat up his brakes more than anyone else and crash on only the second lap because of brake fade. Some of these problems reflect how close to the edge MotoGP racing is; some make you wonder about the level of preparation.

1 Ben Spies's M-1 with blanking plates fitted. Note the flat sections reducing the radiator exhaust duct area; compare with the main pic

2 Rear lights became mandatory for use in the wet

3 Yamaha's top cowling with removable extensions. The ridges are there to disturb airflow

4 Yamaha technicians carefully measured the track and the gradient of the tarmac on each corner before every major test to help fine-tune their bikes' electronics

HONDA
RC213V

Honda brought their first attempt at the new bike to Brno in August 2011, when both works riders rode it: Casey Stoner was faster and Dani Pedrosa hated it. The new bike was very narrow, with air intakes over the main chassis beam. Clearly a lot of work had gone into making it so narrow, with several major components like the water pump moving position. When the bike was seen again it resembled the last of the Honda 800s, wider and with air intakes through the main beams. And this time Dani liked it more and he went faster.

At the end of the year, however, a meeting of the Grand Prix Commission added 4kg to the intended starting weight of the new bikes, taking them from 153kg to 157kg. For Honda, who had already built their new bikes, this was not good news. At the same time changes were occurring in tyre provision. The riders liked Bridgestone's new softer carcass, with its quicker-heating rear tyre, and they asked for a similar front. Again, unfortunately for Honda, their bike was designed with Bridgestone's 'old' tyres in mind, which had seriously rigid carcasses requiring heavy loads to make them work.

Yamaha seemed to be able to respond quickly and change their bikes to suit the new rubber, while Ducati and the CRT bikes had their own difficulties to sort out. It was, though, a problem for Honda. The new softer rear brought chatter, and that was to cause problems for the whole year. Even worse for Honda, a new 'softer' front tyre became compulsory from the Silverstone race and it was quite clear that the Honda was having stability issues with it.

Immediately after Mugello, however, Honda unveiled their revised '2013' bike, with a new frame and an easier to use engine. The 'new' bike was really just a new frame and engine set-up, but the engine impressed both riders and Dani liked the frame too. Casey, in classic Stoner style, decided to stick with the older chassis and ride around the issues. While Dani found his confidence in the new bike becoming ever stronger, Casey unfortunately crashed at Indianapolis and effectively put himself out of title contention.

1 Stoner's mechanics warm up his bike. Note the weld along the main beam that acts as a stiffener, which was first tested at Sepang in February. Casey used the same frame all year

2 Pedrosa's '2013' bike at the Mugello test, showing the different main beams. Dani used his bike with increasing confidence from then on

3 Casey had a different dash to the other Honda riders. Real-time tyre-temperature readouts told him when he had grip, while additional data on his triple clamp reminded him of the various traction-control map settings

4 Honda's swingarm was longer than in 2011, but was never lengthened as much as Yamaha's

DUCATI
DESMOSEDICI GP12

Ducati brought a new bike to the first test at Valencia. It looked smaller and more aggressive than the final bike of 2011 and it contained a 'new engine' – supposedly. It turned out that Ducati had indeed built a new chassis, but they had managed to make their 'old' 1,000cc L4 engine into a V4 by the simple expedient of rolling it backwards 28 degrees. Once all the variables were considered, from front sprocket position to centre of gravity height, they made an amazingly good job of it.

It went well initially, but it soon became apparent that it still didn't hold a line in a corner. Settings could be moved around, but in the end the old problem remained: the only way to hold a line in a corner was to hold the brakes on. All it actually needed was a second version, with redesigned crankcases and the correct internal weight distribution, but it never materialised.

An aluminium swingarm was tried at tests in Mugello and Catalunya but discarded when it brought chatter with it. At Misano, way after the mid-point of the season, a revised frame and swingarm did turn up. The headstock had been moved back 10mm, and the swingarm pivot forward by the same amount. Two new swingarms came with it, both 10mm longer to make up for the change in their pivot point, one the same stiffness as before and one less stiff laterally. The change at the front allowed different geometry and more weight to be tried over the front, helping to balance the grip levels. It seemed to help, but when the softer swingarm was tried the additional side grip it provided unbalanced the bike again, so it was back to the front tyre being pushed.

The bike is getting there slowly, but the path could have been a lot smoother and the outcome very different if internal politics had not stood in the way of change for so long.

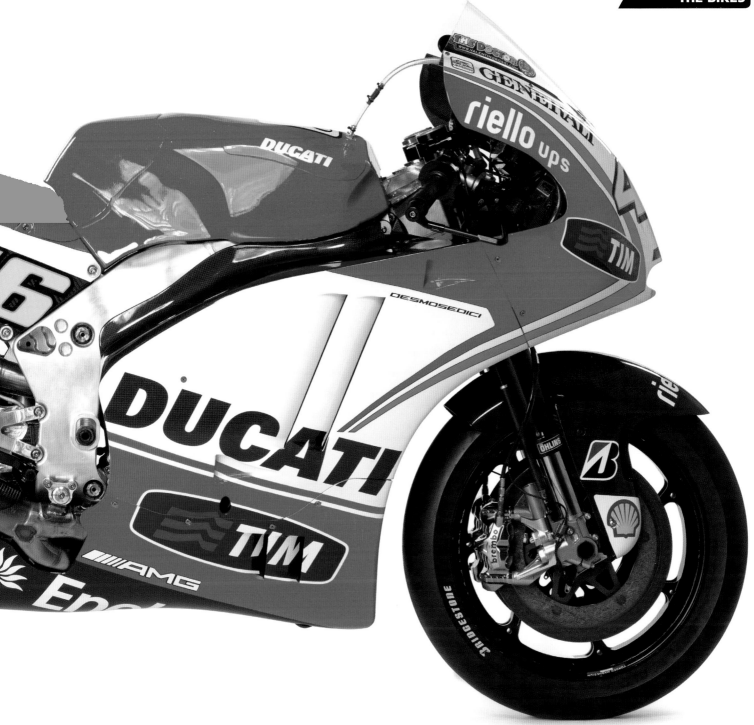

1 Hayden's bike at Catalunya clearly showing the angled sump, rolled-back engine and substantial airbox

2 An aluminium swingarm almost identical to Honda's was tested at Mugello and Catalunya, but was found to bring grip and chatter. It didn't return

3 The 2012 bike brought a new dash with loads more info, including a helpful COLD! warning

4 Rossi tested a new engine design with external flywheel at Mugello. He used it as often as possible after that

APRILIA
ART GP12

Aprilia built eight 'ART' bikes, all basically RSV4 superbikes with detuned superbike engines and 'prototype' chassis with superbike-level electronics. The project was completed in a mere two months and, as a measure of just how rushed they were, several teams received one bike with a new swingarm and a second with a visually very similar but second-hand World Superbike swingarm. They worked well, but with their 'Pirelli-style' stiff chassis they always struggled with the Bridgestone tyres. The bikes used Aprilia's own ECU and software: it wasn't MotoGP level but it was top World Superbike level and, as such, was way ahead of any of the other CRT bikes.

Chatter was virtually a permanent problem, however. Some of it was classic 'harmonic resonance' chatter, but some was created by the Aprilia's traction control getting into a feedback loop, and overreacting to high lean angle throttle openings. Extending the electronics built-in limitations helped, as did standing the bike up quicker before nailing the throttle on corner exits. Half-way through the year upgraded engines were available with gear-driven cams and a raised 15,500rpm rev limit. The next version of this bike could be very good – a year's experience of the tyres and Aprilia's undoubted chassis skills should make a big difference to the redesigned Mk2 bike.

1 New engines for de Puniet and Espargaro. Note the machined heads, signifying they were lightened heads with gear-driven cams

2 Aprilia brought a customer version of their World Superbike electronics

FTR HONDA
FTR MGP12

Pre-season everyone thought Gresini's adventure into building a CRT bike would prosper, because the team was supported by Honda Europe and would be using a Ten Kate World Superbike-tuned Honda Fireblade, complete with Ten Kate standard Cosworth electronics and even Johnny Rea's throttle map and settings for Qatar. The bike was surprisingly quick, even with little pre-season preparation, but it never really improved.

The bike's chassis was an FTR frame similar in concept to the Avintia Blusens Kawasaki; indeed, the swingarm was almost identical. Problems occurred with several mysterious rear chain failures – something virtually unheard of these days – and, in some cases, rider inexperience. The bike's best showing was at Assen, home circuit for its engine builder, while the second-best result was at the team's home circuit in Misano.

Given that no independent chassis manufacturer except Suter had had any direct experience of Bridgestone's quirky but effective race tyres before the end of the 2011 season it was not surprising that some changes to geometry, weight distribution and flexibility should be required during the year. The FTR chassis were modified several times, with the main frame being altered to be stronger under braking, and the swingarm made less stiff laterally as the year went on.

1 The FTR frame was constantly being strengthened for additional help with braking. This is the first version

2 Cosworth provided the electronics and attended the initial tests to make sure everything worked

FTR KAWASAKI
BQR-FTR

FTR made chassis for two teams in the CRT category, the first being for the Avintia Blusens ZX10-engined bikes. Their year started painfully and ignominiously when, at the first Sepang test, they destroyed all their engines and had to borrow one off a local Malaysian dealer just to stay on track.

Early problems with their Motec electronics systems were solved by recruiting an ex-Alstare Suzuki World Superbike engineer, but it took until the test at Mugello before the bike really started to improve.

The initial suspension settings were very stiff, to stop the bike

pitching; a change to a much softer Ohlin's rear unit allowed the rider to weight the rear tyre on acceleration, improving grip and 'feel'. This relatively simple change improved the throttle response simply because it now took far more power to upset the rear grip and the bike's ability to drive out of corners.

Ultimately the team gained a lot of respect by building a simple, quick and very usable bike on which Yonny Hernandez and Ivan Silva could display their talents. During the year it was the Avintia Blusens bikes that improved the most, and by mid-season the FTR Kawasakis were arguably the best of the 'non-factory' CRTs.

1 As expected, the FTR Kawasaki was very similar in concept to the FTR Honda. Against all expectations it ended the year as a far better package

2 Avintia started the year on Showa and transferred to Ohlins after a successful test at Mugello. The much more compliant settings in the rear shock made a big difference, but the forks less so

SUTER BMW
SUTER CRT

The Suter BMW had been on track, and infuriatingly slow, for a full year. At the first round it actually looked quite good, but as the year progressed the other bikes put it in its place. Although equipped with BMW superbike engines of various different specs, severe problems were encountered in making the Bosch throttle system 'rider friendly' and it simply never delivered good 'rider feel'.

The Suter chassis remained unchanged until mid-season despite a contract that called for regular development. In Mugello, however, a new development chassis finally appeared with longer front engine mounts. This was quite difficult to achieve as, in the absence of low-down BMW engine mounts, steel plates had to be attached to the engine to act as front engine mounts. Designed to allow many frame flex options, the chassis was used in the most flexible 'set-up' for the rest of the year.

There was a near falling-out towards the end of the season, with Suter staff effectively accusing Edwards of not trying. Suter himself took the bike to the Bosch test track to try to improve things but ended up in hospital as a result. Danilo Petrucci used a Suter BMW for the last few races of the season, posting similar lap times to Edwards. It would have been interesting to see the bike on track with BMW's superbike electronics, which were clearly a lot more developed by the end of 2012.

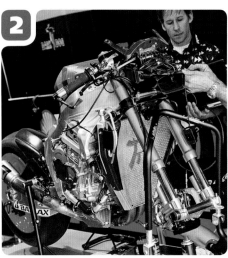

1 The mid-year short front engine mount version of the Suter. The 2012 bike had an upside-down swingarm for a better balance of torsional and lateral stiffness. This bike has had the carbon reinforcing removed from the headstock area

2 The problematic Bosch throttle system is flash loaded before the first Qatar practice

Producers of World Championship race winning machinery

Experienced and qualified motor sports design team

First year victories in all classes; Moto2, Moto3 and MotoGP (CRT)

Best finish for a CRT machine in inaugural year, fifth

Award winning design and fabrication

MOTOGP MOTO2 MOTO3

1st	1st	1st	1st	1st	1st	1st
2010 Moto2	2010 Moto2	2010 Moto2	2010 Moto2	2010 Moto2	2012 Moto3	2012 Moto3
Andrea Iannone	Andrea Iannone	Andrea Iannone	Karel Abraham	Alex de Angelis	Maverick Vinales	Romano Fenati
Mugello	Assen	Aragon	Valencia	Sepang	Qatar	Jerez

1st	1st	1st	1st	1st	1st	1st
2012 Moto3	2012 Moto3	2012 Moto3	2012 Moto3	2012 Moto3	2012 MotoGP (CRT)	2012 MotoGP (CRT)
Louis Rossi	Maverick Vinales	Maverick Vinales	Maverick Vinales	Maverick Vinales	Yonny Hernandez	Michele Pirro
Le Mans	Catalunya	Silverstone	Assen	Mugello	Indianapolis	Valencia

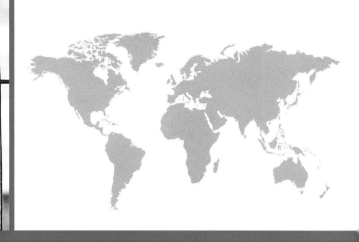

THE SEASON IN FOCUS

Every MotoGP rider's season analysed, from the World Champion to the wild-card entry whose race lasted less than a lap

1	Jorge Lorenzo	350
2	Dani Pedrosa	332
3	Casey Stoner	254
4	Andrea Dovizioso	218
5	Alvaro Bautista	178
6	Valentino Rossi	163
7	Cal Crutchlow	151
8	Stefan Bradl	135
9	Nicky Hayden	122
10	Ben Spies	88
11	Hector Barbera	83
12	Aleix Espargaro	74
13	Randy de Puniet	62
14	Karel Abraham	59
15	Michele Pirro	43
16	James Ellison	35
17	Yonny Hernandez	28
18	Katsuyuki Nakasuga	27
19	Danilo Petrucci	27
20	Colin Edwards	27
21	Jonathan Rea	17
22	Mattia Pasini	13
23	Ivan Silva	12
24	Toni Elias	10
25	Hiroshi Aoyama	3
26	Steve Rapp	2
27	David Salom	1

1 JORGE LORENZO
YAMAHA FACTORY RACING

Just as in his first championship year, 2010, Jorge proved that consistency wins titles. It wasn't just that he was ever-present on the rostrum when he finished a race, but he also qualified on the front row 15 times and his ability to put together long runs at race pace in practice was unparalleled.

With the guidance of crew chief Ramon Forcada he took full advantage of the Yamaha's strengths early in the year. After winning the first race of the season, he was only headed once in the points table – after Stoner won in Portugal – retook the lead at the next race and wasn't headed again.

Of his six wins, five came before the summer break. From Laguna Seca onwards he had to protect his lead from the much-improved Hondas. Stoner's crash at Indianapolis and Pedrosa's misfortune at Misano certainly helped, but that could be viewed as Fate stepping in to even things up. The lead Jorge built up in the first third of the year was demolished at the first corner of the Dutch race by an errant Alvaro Bautista.

The only other time Jorge didn't finish first or second was when he got a little anxious at the final race of the year, after the title had been won, and crashed. But for that he surely would have set a new mark for the number of podiums in a MotoGP season. Instead he had to be content with equalling the record that he holds jointly with Rossi and Stoner.

Apart from a bit of a wobble after the Assen incident and in Japan when a run of five second places in six races got to him, Jorge looked and sounded in control all year.

NATIONALITY Spanish
DATE OF BIRTH 4 May 1987
2012 SEASON 6 wins, 16 rostrums, 7 pole positions, 5 fastest laps
TOTAL POINTS 350

2 DANI PEDROSA
REPSOL HONDA TEAM

By far his best season and also – no coincidence, this – the only season in which Dani hasn't suffered a serious injury or been recovering from one. It wasn't just his fitness, though. Even HRC boss Nakamoto-san was gleefully making jokes about his 'new rider' after the last-lap win in the Czech Republic. There was a new willingness in Dani to fight and lead the team – a trait we hadn't seen before.

After the events of Misano, which effectively ended his hopes of a title challenge, Dani called a team meeting at which he delivered the message that he wasn't going to give up and he didn't expect his team to.

In the second half of the year, using the new bike first seen at the Mugello test, Dani set six of his eight fastest laps and took five of his seven wins. The other races were a third at Laguna Seca (with the new bike not yet fully understood) and crashes at Misano and Phillip Island. The first crash wasn't his fault. The second came as he abandoned his usual tactic of stalking Lorenzo for half a race before pouncing; he knew he had to win and he went for it. There was no apology, just pride in his season and his championship challenge.

Like his team-mate, Dani didn't like the new Bridgestone tyres and was afflicted with chatter for much of the season. Things were better with the advent of the 2013 bike, but not perfect. To close to within 18 points of Lorenzo when the gap had got up to 38 after Misano was testament to Dani's motivation in his seventh season in MotoGP.

NATIONALITY Spanish
DATE OF BIRTH 29 September 1985
2012 SEASON 7 wins, 15 rostrums, 5 pole positions, 9 fastest laps
TOTAL POINTS 332

3 CASEY STONER
REPSOL HONDA TEAM

His championship challenge may have been blunted by injury, but Casey's hopes of retiring as a triple champion were already pretty slim after his crash at Indianapolis. The biggest highside anyone could remember made a mess of Casey's right ankle and he missed three races, but the damage had already been done. The last-lap crash in Germany followed by an eighth place in Mugello had dropped him to third overall, 37 points behind leader Lorenzo.

Those misfortunes ensured that Casey would retire with his two championships, 2007 and 2011, for Ducati and Honda respectively, as one of just five men to have won the title on two different makes of motorcycle. The others are Geoff Duke (Norton and Gilera), Giacomo Agostini (MV and Yamaha), Eddie Lawson (Yamaha and Honda) and Valentino Rossi (Honda and Yamaha). Not bad company.

Casey's announcement on the Thursday before the French GP that he would be retiring at the end of the season shocked the paddock and shook up the rider market for 2013. Honda offered Stoner more than they've ever paid any rider (or driver) to stay for one more year, but his mind was made up.

Why did he retire? Even he finds it difficult to explain. The bottom line is the things that annoy him about MotoGP now outweigh the things he enjoys. In Casey's case, the enjoyment was always confined to those 45 minutes on track on Sunday afternoon.

One thing is certain, it's going to take a while for anyone to beat his race and lap records at Phillip Island.

NATIONALITY Australian
DATE OF BIRTH 16 October 1985
2012 SEASON 5 wins, 10 rostrums, 5 pole positions, 2 fastest laps
TOTAL POINTS 254

4 ANDREA DOVIZIOSO
MONSTER YAMAHA TECH 3

After ten years on Hondas, the last three on factory MotoGP machinery, this was Andrea's first year on a Yamaha, and in a satellite team too.

In his usual unobtrusive manner, he put together the best season we've seen from a satellite team rider in MotoGP, with six rostrum finishes. All but one of them came in a seven-race sequence from Catalunya to Indianapolis, and three of them were in consecutive races. Not surprisingly, given that sort of form, Andrea was a clear fourth in the championship well ahead of the other satellite riders and a few factory guys as well.

His worst dry-weather finish was fifth in the first race of the year, and there was only one race crash, at Silverstone, though he also fell at Sepang but remounted to finish in the points. More often than not he found himself racing his team-mate Cal Crutchlow on track, and their intra-team struggle was one of the best sub-plots of the year.

Andrea still doesn't get the most out of the bike in qualifying, and he started from the front row only three times this year; he didn't set a fastest race lap either. However, his fast starts, experience and consistency make him a very difficult man to out-pace over race distance.

For 2013 Andrea returns to being a factory rider, this time with Ducati. It seems a risky move – the recent track record for Italian riders of Ducatis hasn't been good. However, there are those who think his set-up preferences might suit the Desmo.

NATIONALITY Italian
DATE OF BIRTH 23 March 1986
2012 SEASON 6 rostrums
TOTAL POINTS 218

5 ALVARO BAUTISTA
SAN CARLO HONDA GRESINI

Alvaro picked up a heavy burden at the start of the season. He moved from the Suzuki team to a satellite Honda team on the bike that would have been ridden by Marco Simoncelli. It started the season in black livery and the team didn't dispense with the mourning weeds until Mugello. To make things even more complicated, he was the only man on the MotoGP grid using Showa suspension. The time it takes to achieve workable settings when you have no data may help to explain some of Alvaro's lowly qualifying positions.

After an underwhelming start to the year, Alvaro took his first MotoGP pole at Silverstone and backed that up with a career-best fourth place, only two seconds away from the rostrum. Then came his torpedoing of Lorenzo at Assen.

After that it took a while for Alvaro's confidence to return but he then scored two rostrums in three races. The first, fittingly, was at Misano, the closest circuit to the team's HQ and only a few kilometres from Marco Simoncelli's home. You'd have needed a heart of stone not to be affected by the emotion of the team and the local fans when 'Marco's bike' came into *parc fermé*.

It was a well-timed rostrum. There had been stories that he would be replaced by either Jonathan Rea or Ben Spies, but those fell by the wayside and Alvaro re-signed for Team Gresini. He could have fought for another rostrum at Valencia but by then the priority was to finish fifth overall. When Crutchlow crashed and Rossi was struggling, the team instructed him to settle for fourth place.

NATIONALITY Spanish
DATE OF BIRTH 21 November 1984
2012 SEASON 2 rostrums, 1 pole position
TOTAL POINTS 178

6 VALENTINO ROSSI
DUCATI TEAM

So the two-year marriage between two Italian national icons ended without any fanfares, with Valentino Rossi and Ducati separating quietly after another lack-lustre season.

The only real high spot of Valentino's season was a well-deserved rostrum at home in Misano to back up the wet-weather one in France. At times it was sad to watch him. The denouement at Valencia was particularly downbeat, and the sight of Rossi and his team-mate circulating together, well off the pace, at Phillip Island, a track they both love and where they have stood on the rostrum together, was particularly painful.

The usual post-race refrain was 'this was our potential' – and unfortunately Vale was usually referring to seventh place. A bewildering number of

chassis changes, including a complete redesign, didn't appear to help the situation. The problem that wouldn't go away was understeer – and the associated lack of confidence in the front tyre.

When things got particularly bad, Rossi was unable to resist criticising the factory. At the end of the year he was openly lamenting that he felt he was in the same situation as he'd been when he first arrived at Ducati. Nothing significant had changed.

Given time, Audi's takeover of Ducati may change the situation at Ducati's Bologna factory but Valentino won't be hanging about to find out. For 2013 he's returning to Yamaha, for whom he rode from 2004 to 2010. Is the magic still there? Vale wants to find out, too.

NATIONALITY Italian
DATE OF BIRTH 16 February 1979
2012 SEASON 2 rostrums, 1 fastest lap
TOTAL POINTS 163

7 CAL CRUTCHLOW
MONSTER YAMAHA TECH 3

NATIONALITY
British

DATE OF BIRTH
29 October 1985

2012 SEASON
2 rostrums, 1 fastest lap

TOTAL POINTS
151

Without doubt the most improved rider in MotoGP. After a difficult first year, Cal was a different person in 2012. British fans were able to enjoy the first rostrum by a British rider in 12 years, and the sort of consistent qualifying and finishing they hadn't seen since the mid-1980s heyday of Mackenzie and Haslam.

Cal was fourth in the championship up to Assen and could so easily have had two more rostrums, but he ran out of gas in Japan and crashed at Valencia. Seventh overall doesn't do his season justice.

8 STEFAN BRADL
LCR HONDA MotoGP

NATIONALITY
German

DATE OF BIRTH
29 November 1989

TOTAL POINTS
135

The reigning Moto2 champion came up to MotoGP on a satellite Honda with the LCR team. As the only rookie on a satellite bike he won Rookie of the Year easily but also impressed in his own right. Stefan was sixth in the championship up until Aragon but then a trio of uncharacteristic crashes dropped him two places.

His best ride was at Mugello, where he looked as if he might get his first rostrum but had to settle for a close fourth. Both Honda and Lucio Cecchinello's team are delighted with him and Stefan continues on a V4 in 2013.

9 NICKY HAYDEN
DUCATI TEAM

NATIONALITY
American

DATE OF BIRTH
30 July 1981

TOTAL POINTS
122

For the first time since he came to MotoGP in 2003, Nicky suffered the indignity of not finishing on the rostrum all season. He had a good go at it in Italy but lost out on the last lap when he was pushed wide. His chances of racing to the top three with his team-mate at Misano were ruined by the injury he suffered at home in Indianapolis. Misano was his comeback and the broken bones in his hand were still giving trouble. Nicky also survived a bizarre crash at Aragon that could have been a lot worse. As Scott Redding was moved to observe when Nicky didn't miss a race, 'That dude is hard core.'

10 BEN SPIES
YAMAHA FACTORY RACING

NATIONALITY
American

DATE OF BIRTH
11 July 1984

TOTAL POINTS
88

Has a rider ever had a more varied collection of bad luck and weird failures in one season? Ben would be forgiven for thinking someone had it in for him.

Machinery problems, tyre failure and illness afflicted him at almost every race. The worst were on home ground: the failed suspension bolt that put him on the floor at Laguna Seca and the blow-up that stopped him at Indianapolis when he was odds-on for a rostrum at the very least. Somewhere along the line he also fell out with Yamaha and for 2013 he will ride for Ducati's new Junior Team, where he will surely have better luck.

11 HECTOR BARBERA
PRAMAC RACING TEAM

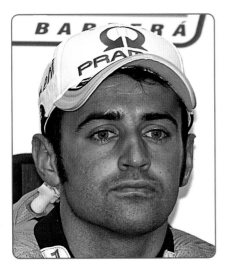

NATIONALITY
Spanish

DATE OF BIRTH
2 November 1986

TOTAL POINTS
83

The lone Pramac team man, like other Ducati riders, did not have an easy year. The usual problems – lack of feel and confidence in the front end plus lack of traction at the rear – made life tough.

The highlight of Hector's season was his front-row start at Mugello, the first by a Ducati satellite team rider. The low point was the spate of injuries that followed the Italian race. After a motocross training accident broke his leg, Hector came back at Indy only to suffer a nasty neck injury. He returned at Misano, only to tag Dani Pedrosa on the first lap and end his championship chances. Next year, CRT.

12 ALEIX ESPARGARO
POWER ELECTRONICS ASPAR

NATIONALITY
Spanish

DATE OF BIRTH
30 July 1989

TOTAL POINTS
74

Returned to MotoGP after a season in Moto2 as team-mate to de Puniet in Jorge Martinez's CRT team on Aprilias. Aleix tussled all season long with de Puniet but came out on top of the CRTs nine times to Randy's four with a best finish of eighth in Malaysia. No other CRT team or rider finished first in their class more than once.

He enjoyed every moment, whether harassing the satellite bikes, teasing his team-mate or leading the Valencia race for two laps. Aleix rejoins Aspar's team for 2013 with his reputation enhanced, not something everyone expected when he signed up to ride a CRT bike. And his little brother is quite quick too...

13 RANDY DE PUNIET
POWER ELECTRONICS ASPAR

NATIONALITY
French

DATE OF BIRTH
14 February 1981

TOTAL POINTS
62

Started the season as strong favourite to finish top of the CRT entries, but lost out to his younger team-mate Espargaro by 12 points. Randy was top CRT rider five times to Aleix's eight as the Aspar team and their Aprilias dominated the class.

De Puniet's personal highlights were two eighth places, in Assen and Brno, both in the dry, and a stunning qualifying lap in Australia that put him ninth on the grid. Both Randy and Aleix stay with the Aspar team for the 2013 season and will again be favourites for top CRT honours.

14 KAREL ABRAHAM
CARDION AB MOTORACING

NATIONALITY
Czech

DATE OF BIRTH
2 January 1990

TOTAL POINTS
62

The youngest rider on a prototype, Karel endured a tough second season in MotoGP following his promising debut in 2011 when he ran Cal Crutchlow close for Rookie of the Year honours.

In 2012 the recalcitrant Ducati caused him serious problems and Karel didn't score a point until Catalunya. He then suffered a very nasty hand injury in testing and missed four races. It took him time to find his confidence again but he finished the season with his best result, seventh. In 2013 Karel's AB Cardion team will run CRT Aprilias.

15 MICHELE PIRRO
SAN CARLO HONDA GRESINI

NATIONALITY
Italian
TOTAL POINTS
43

Problems with the Honda-engined CRT bike stopped Michele challenging for top CRT honours, but he was rewarded with a splendid fifth place at Valencia when he was brave enough to start on slicks.

16 JAMES ELLISON
PAUL BIRD MOTORSPORT

NATIONALITY
British
TOTAL POINTS
35

Twelve points-scoring rides and top CRT finisher at the French GP, with a highest finishing position of ninth place at both Malaysia and Valencia – not bad for the only Brit in the CRT class on his return to GPs.

17 YONNY HERNANDEZ
AVINTIA BLUSENS

NATIONALITY
Colombian
TOTAL POINTS
28

Always entertaining to watch while making the only Kawasaki-engined bike in MotoGP go faster than anyone else who rode it. Delighted with his top CRT finish at Indianapolis when he was ninth overall.

18 KATSUYUKI NAKASUGA
YAMAHA FACTORY RACING

NATIONALITY
Japanese
TOTAL POINTS
27

Yamaha's test rider rode as a wild card at Motegi and came ninth. Then he replaced Spies at Valencia, where he scored the most unexpected rostrum of the season with second place the day after the birth of his second son.

19 DANILO PETRUCCI
CAME IODARACING PROJECT

NATIONALITY
Italian
TOTAL POINTS
27

Started with the team's own chassis housing an Aprilia motor before changing to a Suter BMW. Danilo will be back on the same bike for the Ioda team in 2013. His ride to 11th place at Assen was a little gem.

20 COLIN EDWARDS
NGM MOBILE FORWARD RACING

NATIONALITY
American
TOTAL POINTS
27

Top CRT rider in the first race of the year, but after that it was a season of struggle with the Suter BMW's under-developed Bosch electronics. Best finish was 11th at Misano. Nevertheless, he'll be back.

21 JONATHAN REA
REPSOL HONDA TEAM

NATIONALITY
British
TOTAL POINTS
17

Rode Casey Stoner's bike as a replacement at Misano and Aragon, finishing eighth and seventh. Was in the running for a Team Gresini ride in 2013 but elected to return to World Superbikes.

22 MATTIA PASINI
SPEED MASTER

NATIONALITY
Italian
TOTAL POINTS
13

Rode the Speed Master team's CRT Aprilia for the first 14 races of the year, scoring a best finish of 12th at Le Mans. Replaced, amid some acrimony, for the final part of the season by Roby Rolfo.

23 IVAN SILVA
AVINTIA BLUSENS

NATIONALITY
Spanish
TOTAL POINTS
12

Started the year as the team's regular rider before being dropped to test rider role for two races in favour of David Salom. Five points-scoring rides with a brace of 12th places being the highlights.

24 TONI ELIAS
PRAMAC RACING TEAM

NATIONALITY
Spanish
TOTAL POINTS
10

Replaced the injured Hector Barbera for the two American races and Brno after parting company with his Moto2 team, scoring two 11th places. Returned to Moto2 with a different team to finish the year.

25 HIROSHI AOYAMA
AVINTIA BLUSENS

NATIONALITY
Japanese
TOTAL POINTS
3

The last 250cc champion replaced the injured Yonny Hernandez at the last race of the year, in Valencia, and will return for the Avintia team as a full-time rider in 2013.

26 STEVE RAPP
ATTACK PERFORMANCE

NATIONALITY
American
TOTAL POINTS
2

Scored his points as a wild card at Indianapolis on a bike built by his team. Also entered Laguna Seca but didn't qualify – not surprisingly since the bike hadn't turned a wheel before first practice.

27 DAVID SALOM
AVINTIA BLUSENS

NATIONALITY
Spanish
TOTAL POINTS
1

Came into the Avintia team for the Misano and Aragon races as a replacement for Ivan Silva. One 15th place obviously didn't impress the team and he was promptly dropped and Silva reinstated.

AARON YATES
GPTECH

NATIONALITY
American
TOTAL POINTS
0

The veteran of the American Superbike Championship raced at Indianapolis as a wild card on a Suzuki-engined bike built by his team. It was his first race since he badly broke his leg early in 2010.

ROBERTO ROLFO
SPEED MASTER

NATIONALITY
Italian
TOTAL POINTS
0

The ex-250 Grand Prix winner rode the last four races of the year for the Speed Master team after they had parted company with Mattia Pasini. He finished one, retired in one and crashed in the other two.

CLAUDIO CORTI
AVINTIA BLUSENS

NATIONALITY
Italian
TOTAL POINTS
0

Having been sacked by his Moto2 team despite running tenth in the championshp and finishing on the rostrum in France, he rode the Inmotec-chassis Kawasaki for Avintia at Valencia.

THE RACES

ROUND 1 — **46**
COMMERCIALBANK
GRAND PRIX OF QATAR

ROUND 2 — **54**
GRAN PREMIO bwin
DE ESPAÑA

ROUND 3 — **62**
GRANDE PRÉMIO DE PORTUGAL
CIRCUITO ESTORIL

ROUND 4 — **70**
MONSTER ENERGY
GRAND PRIX DE FRANCE

ROUND 5 — **78**
GRAN PREMI APEROL
DE CATALUNYA

ROUND 6 — **86**
HERTZ BRITISH
GRAND PRIX

ROUND 7 — **94**
IVECO TT
ASSEN

ROUND 8 — **102**
eni MOTORRAD GRAND
PRIX DEUTSCHLAND

ROUND 9 — **110**
GRAN PREMIO
D'ITALIA TIM

ROUND 10 — **118**
RED BULL
U.S. GRAND PRIX

ROUND 11 — **126**
RED BULL
INDIANAPOLIS GRAND PRIX

ROUND 12 — **134**
bwin GRAND PRIX
ČESKÉ REPUBLIKY

ROUND 13 — **142**
GRAN PREMIO APEROL DI SAN
MARINO E DELLA RIVIERA DI RIMINI

ROUND 14 — **150**
GRAN PREMIO IVECO
DE ARAGÓN

ROUND 15 — **158**
AIRASIA GRAND
PRIX OF JAPAN

ROUND 16 — **166**
MALAYSIAN MOTORCYCLE
GRAND PRIX

ROUND 17 — **174**
AIRASIA AUSTRALIAN
GRAND PRIX

ROUND 18 — **182**
GRAN PREMIO GENERALI DE
LA COMUNITAT VALENCIANA

COMMERCIALBANK GRAND PRIX OF QATAR

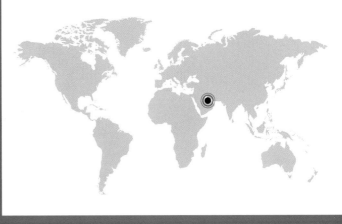

STRANGELY STRANGE BUT ODDLY NORMAL

New rules, new class, new bikes, but the usual suspects stood on the rostrum

If it's ever possible to call a win by Jorge Lorenzo a shock, then this one was it. All the indicators, all the records, pointed to a Casey Stoner rampage. Last year he got the full set: pole, fastest lap and the victory, the first time he raced the Honda 800. With his record here – wins in 2007, '08, '09 and '11 – plus the Honda revealing itself as the best of the new generation of 1,000cc MotoGP bikes, anything apart from Stoner domination would have been more than a surprise.

Two serious obstacles got in the Aussie's way. First, the chatter that had afflicted the Hondas in some, but not all, pre-season testing returned with a vengeance. Although Pedrosa's expression of disbelief at his post-qualifying debrief spoke volumes, the team did manage to damp it down for Sunday warm-up. When Dani got the holeshot from the third row it looked like business as usual. Lorenzo immediately bit back but only led for two laps before Stoner went past and started what looked like an inexorable progress towards victory. It wasn't easy, though. Lorenzo refused to concede and it took Stoner ten laps to increase the lead to over two seconds, after which the gap remained constant for a couple of laps before suddenly shrinking.

Casey had encountered his second obstacle. This time it was arm pump, which severely affected his control of both throttle and brake. A new pair of gloves didn't help – Alpinestars had finally got his favourite pair off him as there was a hole in one palm – and neither did the nature of the many right-hand corners which effectively gave him repetitive strain injury. He said it made him feel like a backmarker, getting in everyone's way, but only the other Repsol Hondas and Lorenzo's Yamaha were close enough to pass him. Dani did try to push through

first but Lorenzo held him off, took Casey and then had two laps to open up a gap of nearly a second before Pedrosa found a way past. That delay, said Dani, cost him the win. He didn't seem too upset; rather, given the traumas of practice and qualifying, which included a big crash, he seemed mildly shocked to have been in with a chance.

A long way behind the top three, the two Tech 3 Yamahas spent the whole race in close company. Cal Crutchlow, starting from the front row for the first time in his MotoGP career, was, according to his team-manager, a different person. He now seemed sure of his status, and at press conferences it was obvious that the top men now considered him one of them. Cal's new team-mate, Andrea Dovizioso, had finished third in the championship in 2011 only to be passed over by Honda. He led the British rider for 18 of the 22 laps, although the gap was never above half a second once the race had settled down. Then Cal slipped past with a clean outbraking move six laps from the flag and held Dovi off by a similarly small margin. Team-boss Hervé Poncharal was suitably impressed by both his riders and grateful that neither had had a rush of blood and done something they – and the team – might regret.

There was another big stretch of empty tarmac behind the Tech 3 duo before a third absorbing battle came into sight. For most of the race the only rookie on a satellite bike, Stefan Bradl, had a firm grip on sixth place, only losing it when he made a mistake late on. That error put him into the hands of Hayden, Barbera and Bautista.

Bradl's seriously impressive debut highlighted the

problems still being suffered by Valentino Rossi and Ducati. In particular, there was a TV shot in qualifying showing Bradl being held up by the nine-times champion. Whatever the new aluminium chassis had done, it hadn't fixed the old problems. Valentino

'I PUT EVERYTHING I HAVE, ALL MY ENERGY INTO THE TRACK'
JORGE LORENZO

ABOVE The new Tech 3 team mates, Andrea Dovizioso and Cal Crutchlow, got to know each other a little bit better

LEFT Lorenzo versus the factory Hondas, the battle for the lead that set the pattern for the season

OPPOSITE Casey Stoner focuses on the task in hand

ABOVE Valentino Rossi's
second season with Ducati
started no better than the
first one – he wasn't happy

OPPOSITE Nicky Hayden's
Ducati follows the satellite bike of
Hector Barbera and the satellite
Hondas of Bradl and Bautista

BELOW The honour of being
the first CRT entry home went to
Colin Edwards and the Forward
Racing Suter-BMW

qualified twelfth, the slowest of the prototype bikes, and only managed tenth in the race. He'd got up to tenth before having a coming-together with Hector Barbera at Turn 1 on lap five that put him off the track. The Spaniard was later heard to whisper to his friends that he'd had no alternative; Rossi was slower than he was, and he had to push past. The incident lost Rossi not much more than five seconds yet he finished over 33 seconds behind the winner. Those five seconds would have put him in the fight for sixth, the place finally occupied by team-mate Nicky Hayden, which tended to back up Valentino's assessment of the potential of the Desmosedici.

It was just like the previous season: understeer and aggressive power delivery were blamed, while Rossi assured the press that everyone was working hard. Then he marched off to give an interview with Italian TV that opened up a new front. For the first time he was directly critical of the factory, saying that his requests had not been met and that he couldn't ride the bike as he wanted, so he 'couldn't make the difference'. At this point, everybody remembered that the only MotoGP rider with a contract for 2013 was Stefan Bradl.

As expected, the new CRT bikes only threatened the prototypes when the factory bikes had a problem. Colin Edwards and the Forward Racing Suter BMW surprised by being the best CRT, however you measured them. He qualified 13th, less than a second slower than the slowest prototype, and finished 12th, just over a second behind Spies. Over a lap, Edwards was on average 2.5s off the quickest bike out there, but it's worth remembering that Stoner's fastest lap of the race was 0.4s faster than anyone else managed. The real surprise was the ease with which Edwards dealt with the Aprilias, although a rash of front-end crashes in practice suggested that they had problems getting heat into the Bridgestone fronts.

Anyone expecting the new 1,000cc bikes to change the order of things would have been disappointed. The three men who'd been expected to finish on the rostrum duly did so, although not necessarily in the order predicted. A little digging uncovered a few issues, however. Could Stoner really afford to give away those places on what is historically his track, given that he'd never won at the next two venues? And just what would happen at Ducati now that Valentino had gone public with his criticism?

NEW ORDER

The bikes may have looked the same as in 2011, but this year was a brand-new start. The capacity limit was raised from 800 to 1,000cc but the fuel allowance was kept at 21 litres for the race and the engine allowance for the season remained at six. Bridgestone introduced a new family of rear tyres in response to riders' worries about the difficulty in getting them up to, and keeping them at, operating temperature. A new-design front tyre was scheduled for introduction at Silverstone.

The biggest change to the established order was the relaxing of the technical regulations to get more teams on to the grid. Known as Claiming Rule Teams (CRT), these new squads are allowed an extra three litres of fuel for the race and twelve engines for the season. The Grand Prix Commission essentially decides if a team qualifies for CRT and is also able to withdraw that status. There is no definition of a CRT team in the rules, but if they have factory or leased bikes they do not qualify. If a team buys its bikes, it's in. This inevitably means using production-based engines, something that's not new to GPs and was only specifically forbidden by the first MotoGP regulations for 2002.

Three teams – Aspar, Paul Bird Motorsport and Speed Master – bought Aprilias; Ioda put an Aprilia engine in their own chassis; Avintia put Kawasaki motors in FTR frames; Gresini also used an FTR frame, but with a Honda engine; Forward Racing picked up the Suter BMW project initiated by the Marc VDS team in 2011. Between them, those teams put nine new bikes on the grid.

The whole CRT project can be viewed as Dorna's response to the unrealistic costs involved in leasing factory bikes. When a team as well supported as Aspar's could not afford them any more it was clear something had to be done. Dorna's CEO Carmelo Ezpeleta is keen to reduce costs even further, with an rpm limit and a control ECU being mooted.

COMMERCIALBANK GRAND PRIX OF QATAR
LOSAIL INTERNATIONAL CIRCUIT

ROUND 1
March 20

RACE RESULTS

CIRCUIT LENGTH 3.343 miles
NO. OF LAPS 22
RACE DISTANCE 73.546 miles
WEATHER Dry, 24°C
TRACK TEMPERATURE 23°C
WINNER Jorge Lorenzo
FASTEST LAP 1m 55.541s, 104.159mph, Casey Stoner
LAP RECORD 1m 55.153s, 104.510mph, Casey Stoner, 2011

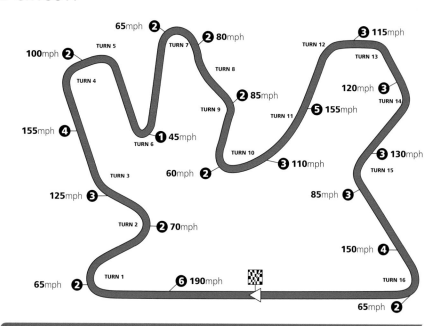

QUALIFYING

	Rider	Nationality	Team	Qualifying	Pole +	Gap
1	Lorenzo	SPA	Yamaha Factory Racing	1m 54.634s		
2	Stoner	AUS	Repsol Honda Team	1m 54.855s	0.221s	0.221s
3	Crutchlow	GBR	Monster Yamaha Tech 3	1m 55.022s	0.388s	0.167s
4	Spies	USA	Yamaha Factory Racing	1m 55.512s	0.878s	0.490s
5	Hayden	USA	Ducati Team	1m 55.637s	1.003s	0.125s
6	Dovizioso	ITA	Monster Yamaha Tech 3	1m 55.858s	1.224s	0.221s
7	Pedrosa	SPA	Repsol Honda Team	1m 55.905s	1.271s	0.047s
8	Barbera	SPA	Pramac Racing Team	1m 55.983s	1.349s	0.078s
9	Bradl	GER	LCR Honda MotoGP	1m 56.063s	1.429s	0.080s
10	Abraham	CZE	Cardion AB Motoracing	1m 56.198s	1.564s	0.135s
11	Bautista	SPA	San Carlo Honda Gresini	1m 56.521s	1.887s	0.323s
12	Rossi	ITA	Ducati Team	1m 56.813s	2.179s	0.292s
13	Edwards	USA	NGM Mobile Forward Racing	1m 57.644s	3.010s	0.831s
14	De Puniet	FRA	Power Electronics Aspar	1m 58.266s	3.632s	0.622s
15	Espargaro	SPA	Power Electronics Aspar	1m 58.520s	3.886s	0.254s
16	Hernandez	COL	Avintia Blusens	1m 58.795s	4.161s	0.275s
17	Pirro	ITA	San Carlo Honda Gresini	1m 59.085s	4.451s	0.290s
18	Pasini	ITA	Speed Master	1m 59.195s	4.561s	0.110s
19	Petrucci	ITA	Came IodaRacing Project	1m 59.664s	5.030s	0.469s
20	Silva	SPA	Avintia Blusens	2m 00.493s	5.859s	0.829s
21	Ellison	GBR	Paul Bird Motorsport	2m 00.757s	6.123s	0.264s

FINISHERS

1 JORGE LORENZO Pole and the win makes it look like an easy weekend; it wasn't. Jorge had to work hard to hang on to Stoner in the early stages, time his pass, and then hold off Pedrosa. The victory made Lorenzo the first rider to win in all three classes at the Losail circuit.

2 DANI PEDROSA After suffering terrible chatter, flu, a crash and disastrous qualifying, Dani managed to get the holeshot from the third row, but taking a lap to get past Stoner in the closing stages put him out of range of the win – a fact which seemed to surprise him more than a little.

3 CASEY STONER The serious chatter that dogged him in practice was at least tamed for the race, but it was arm pump that prevented him from winning. He'd only suffered from it once before, at Silverstone in 2010, and was sure he could get rid of the problem without surgery.

4 CAL CRUTCHLOW Qualified on the front row for the first time, then followed his team-mate for 16 of the 22 laps before making a perfectly timed pass and holding off Dovizioso to the flag. Equalled his best MotoGP finish, but this was easily his best race so far.

5 ANDREA DOVIZIOSO Relatively happy with the result of his first race on a Yamaha, but not pleased with how long it took him to get past Spies. Blamed this for his inability to go with the leading group, and losing out on fourth to his team-mate.

6 NICKY HAYDEN Handily faster than his team-mate all weekend. Couldn't race the Tech 3 Yamahas, probably because he took too long to get past Spies. Won the fight for sixth which, considering his close-season injuries and lack of testing, was not a bad start to the year.

7 ALVARO BAUTISTA Rescued a fraught weekend with a fine race. Only top man to use the softer rear tyre. Never got to the bottom of his problems with front grip, and had a cold-tyre crash in warm-up, but gave Hayden a good fight for sixth. This was his first race finish since Aragon the previous season.

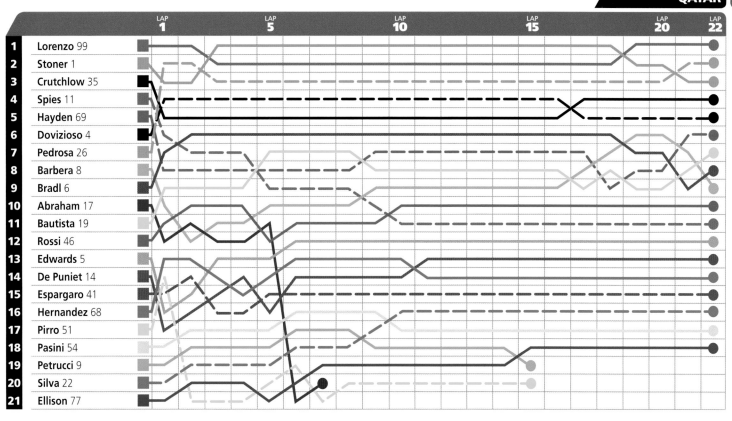

		LAP 1	LAP 5	LAP 10	LAP 15	LAP 20	LAP 22
1	Lorenzo 99						
2	Stoner 1						
3	Crutchlow 35						
4	Spies 11						
5	Hayden 69						
6	Dovizioso 4						
7	Pedrosa 26						
8	Barbera 8						
9	Bradl 6						
10	Abraham 17						
11	Bautista 19						
12	Rossi 46						
13	Edwards 5						
14	De Puniet 14						
15	Espargaro 41						
16	Hernandez 68						
17	Pirro 51						
18	Pasini 54						
19	Petrucci 9						
20	Silva 22						
21	Ellison 77						

RACE

	Rider	Motorcycle	Race Time	Time +	Fastest Lap	Av Speed	B
1	Lorenzo	Yamaha	42m 44.214s		1m 56.067s	103.253mph	XH/H
2	Pedrosa	Honda	42m 45.066s	0.852s	1m 56.001s	103.219mph	XH/H
3	Stoner	Honda	42m 47.122s	2.908s	1m 55.541s	103.136mph	XH/H
4	Crutchlow	Yamaha	43m 01.328s	17.114s	1m 55.984s	102.568mph	XH/H
5	Dovizioso	Yamaha	43m 01.634s	17.420s	1m 56.208s	102.556mph	XH/H
6	Hayden	Ducati	43m 12.627s	28.413s	1m 56.881s	102.122mph	XH/H
7	Bautista	Honda	43m 12.660s	28.446s	1m 56.796s	102.120mph	XH/M
8	Bradl	Honda	43m 13.678s	29.464s	1m 56.466s	102.080mph	XH/H
9	Barbera	Ducati	43m 15.598s	31.384s	1m 56.639s	102.005mph	XH/H
10	Rossi	Ducati	43m 17.879s	33.655s	1m 57.144s	101.915mph	XH/H
11	Spies	Yamaha	43m 41.121s	56.907s	1m 56.958s	101.011mph	XH/H
12	Edwards	Suter	43m 42.302s	58.088s	1m 58.153s	100.966mph	XH/H
13	De Puniet	Art	43m 54.864s	1m 10.650s	1m 58.363s	100.484mph	XH/H
14	Hernandez	BQR-FRT	44m 00.157s	1m 15.943s	1m 58.996s	100.283mph	XH/H
15	Espargaro	Art	44m 10.947s	1m 26.733s	1m 59.191s	99.875mph	XH/H
16	Silva	BQR-FRT	44m 27.541s	1m 43.327s	1m 59.956s	99.253mph	XH/H
17	Pasini	Art	44m 31.633s	1m 47.419s	1m 59.983s	99.101mph	XH/M
18	Ellison	Art	44m 36.096s	1m 51.882s	2m 00.246s	98.936mph	XH/M
NF	Petrucci	Ioda	30m 29.288s	7 laps	2m 00.142s	98.683mph	XH/M
NF	Abraham	Ducati	14m 40.447s	15 laps	1m 57.051s	95.682mph	XH/H
NF	Pirro	FTR	43m 46.733s	7 laps	1m 59.543s	68.724mph	M/H

CHAMPIONSHIP

	Rider	Team	Points
1	Lorenzo	Yamaha Factory Racing	25
2	Pedrosa	Repsol Honda Team	20
3	Stoner	Repsol Honda Team	16
4	Crutchlow	Monster Yamaha Tech 3	13
5	Dovizioso	Monster Yamaha Tech 3	11
6	Hayden	Ducati Team	10
7	Bautista	San Carlo Honda Gresini	9
8	Bradl	LCR Honda MotoGP	8
9	Barbera	Pramac Racing Team	7
10	Rossi	Ducati Team	6
11	Spies	Yamaha Factory Racing	5
12	Edwards	NGM Mobile Forward Racing	4
13	De Puniet	Power Electronics Aspar	3
14	Hernandez	Avintia Blusens	2
15	Espargaro	Power Electronics Aspar	1

8 STEFAN BRADL A very impressive MotoGP debut by the reigning Moto2 champion. Easily achieved his target of a third-row start, began well, ran in sixth early on, but was caught by Hayden, Bautista and Barbera at the end after making a mistake adjusting his brake lever.

9 HECTOR BARBERA Involved in the fight for sixth for most of the race but lost two places when he ran on at the start of the last lap. But for that he might have achieved his ambition of being top Ducati.

10 VALENTINO ROSSI A shocking weekend given the hopes invested in the new bike. It was the same old story – difficulties going into corners, peaky engine – but this time he followed up with a pointed attack on Ducati in an interview with Italian TV.

11 BEN SPIES Two big crashes in practice were followed by the most enormous chatter problem in the race. Some of this was later traced to an invisible crack in the rear sub-frame.

12 COLIN EDWARDS Top CRT bike in qualifying and the race. Colin reported none of the chatter that had afflicted the bike in testing and just one problem at Turn 3 in the race when he 'confused the electronics'.

13 RANDY DE PUNIET Two big crashes in practice affected the French rider's confidence and a gearbox problem in the race nearly sent him straight on at Turn 1. Made six overtaking moves in the first half of the race, recovering from his problems.

14 YONNY HERNANDEZ The surprise of the race. Should have been blown into the weeds by the Aprilias, but Yonny split the Aspar team's bikes.

15 ALEIX ESPARGARO Unable to deal with the chatter that had afflicted him all weekend. Happy to take the last point on his return to the premier class.

16 IVAN SILVA Like his team-mate, the Spanish rider did better than expected by finishing in front of two Aprilias.

17 MATTIA PASINI Not happy with the result but content with the work done, track time and his consistent pace in the race. Given his almost total lack of winter testing, maybe it's no surprise that he sounded like he was talking about a test session.

18 JAMES ELLISON A fraught return to MotoGP. Qualified at the back of the grid and was last finisher. Like other CRT riders, he had trouble getting heat into the front tyre.

NON-FINISHERS

DANILO PETRUCCI Fighting with Pasini after a bad start when the pit-lane speed limiter cut in going into a corner. The bike then became nervous and Petrux decided it was best to retire.

KAREL ABRAHAM Eliminated by a problem with his brakes. Felt a lack of stopping power on the second lap, then ran on next time round. The problem was clearly visible on the data but the cause was a mystery.

MICHELE PIRRO Despite having to retire because of a rear-grip issue in the race, Pirro showed enough pace to give the team hope that he can compete with the top CRT men. He said later it was more like a test than a race.

GRAN PREMIO bwin DE ESPAÑA

EXPECT THE UNEXPECTED

After being beaten at Losail, where he usually wins, Stoner got his revenge by taking victory at the track where he'd never won before

Casey Stoner doesn't much care for the Jerez circuit. It's not surprising, really, as he'd only had one rostrum finish there in any class before 2012. It is the place where, pro rata, he has had by far the least success. And even after he'd won, extending his unbroken run of rostrum finishes to 17, he still didn't care for it much. 'I'm not like some riders who only like tracks they win on.'

He couldn't have chosen trickier circumstances to break his Jerez duck. Practice and qualifying were dogged by rain, while the Moto2 and Moto3 races were seriously affected by the weather. Stoner missed morning warm-up to conserve a set of wet tyres in case they were needed for the race, so he started from fifth on the grid with untried chassis settings. It was his worst qualifying since he'd joined Honda. The race started on a track dotted with damp patches. Casey hung back from the frenzied activity on the first couple of laps before suddenly materialising at the front, finding a way between Lorenzo and Pedrosa on the run down to the first corner at the start of the third lap. He'd been fifth for most of the second lap but took advantage of some fairing bashing to line up a perfect drive down the straight that took him past Lorenzo on acceleration and Pedrosa on the brakes. Early leader Pedrosa had been watching the earlier races and taken note of the plethora of crashes, which, he said, made him too cautious in the opening stages of his own race.

There was a definite lack of caution about the Tech 3 Yamaha riders. Cal Crutchlow refused to moan about not having the latest Brembos but used Nicky Hayden's Ducati to help him get round the right at the end of the back straight, thus making the point that he was having

LEFT Despite qualifying on the front row, Nicky Hayden did not have an enjoyable race as Ducati's old problems made themselves felt

OPPOSITE Jorge Lorenzo made the wrong tyre choice for the race; he could hang on to Stoner but never looked like being able to make a pass

BELOW As usual, Pedrosa led the charge to the first corner; no surprise, now, to see Cal Crutchlow up there, too

difficulty stopping in a different way. Andrea Dovizioso shoved Jorge Lorenzo out of the way, drawing a gesture of reprimand and the subsequent pointed remark that he did not expect that sort of risky manoeuvre from a fellow Yamaha rider.

Hayden was the surprise of qualifying: he started from the front row for the first time since Estoril 2010, and was by far the best Ducati. The other three Ducatis started behind the top CRT man, Randy de Puniet, with Valentino Rossi the slowest of them in 13th. It was also the first Ducati front-row start since Stoner left the team. The Italian press had been rumbling for a while, questioning Valentino's attitude and comparing it to Fernando Alonso's efforts in Formula 1 in another Italian motorsport icon whose product wasn't quite as competitive as it should be. 'It is Valentino's luck that Hayden is always so polite and so correct,' whispered one Italian journalist. He also has to put up with every question he's asked starting with the words 'Valentino says…'. It happened again when a lady from a Spanish national daily asked the American why the other side of the garage was in such trouble. Nicky flashed her his most disarming smile and said: 'I haven't thought about it too much.'

Everybody else had, though. Rossi denied that he was now using Hayden's settings, but he did say he was having to make the bike longer and lower than he usually would. Despite the two factory Ducati riders starting ten places apart on the grid, they finished eighth and ninth, six seconds apart. Nicky lost out in a fight with the very impressive Stefan Bradl, while Valentino had to fend off Hector Barbera.

pre-event press conference about 'having to pay to get in' the previous year, then went on to keep everyone entertained with a story about some rodent driving him out of his motorhome.

Crutchlow backed up the comedy act with a tenacious ride. He sank his teeth into Pedrosa's Honda and didn't let go, using the new-construction front tyre with hard tread compound (see inset story) and the extra stability that gave on the brakes to threaten Dani in the closing stages. There was no way through, however. 'He doesn't make mistakes,' said Cal, with more than a hint of admiration. There was plenty of admiration coming Cal's way too. He set the fastest lap of the race, the first time a British rider had done so since Barry Sheene at the opening race of the 1984 season in Kyalami.

The only thing that troubled Stoner was a return of the arm pump that had ruined his chances in Qatar. Thankfully, it was nowhere near as serious as in the previous race; a spectator at the side of the track would have been hard pushed to tell he was in any trouble. Casey reported that he'd had a problem with his throttle control which caused him to run wide a couple of times. When Jorge did get close to the Honda, though, he was the one who could be seen to run wide. It was enough to persuade the Yamaha man to settle for second place.

Despite several invitations, Casey refused to change his opinion of the circuit. However, he did have to admit that, considering how fast Dani and Jorge are at this track, 'to win here is something very special for me.' It also balanced the championship up nicely, after Lorenzo's win in Qatar.

ABOVE Like all the other CRT riders, James Ellison was much happier with the new, softer construction front Bridgestone and was unlucky not to finish

OPPOSITE Crutchlow shadowed Pedrosa for most of the race and set the fastest lap

Once everyone had calmed down Stoner pulled away, taking Lorenzo with him. Pedrosa had to find his way back past Dovizioso while Hayden tried to establish himself in third place, but then found he was being harassed by Crutchlow. The Englishman was definitely impressive in Qatar, but here in Spain he announced he'd joined the elite. It was very noticeable that his interaction with the other top MotoGP riders was now as an equal. Cal made a knowing joke at the

'THERE WERE A LOT OF WET PATCHES AND IT WAS EASY TO MAKE A MISTAKE'
CASEY STONER

SOFTLY SOFTLY

Over the close season Bridgestone responded to riders' concerns by introducing a new family of tyres. Riders didn't like, and got hurt, by the way the old tyres took time to get up to operating temperature but then lost heat very quickly if not being ridden at race pace. The 2012 designs feature a much more compliant and softer construction, which warms up more quickly thanks to internal friction generated by flexing of the carcass, as well as new tread compounds.

All rear tyres used this season, including during the pre-season tests, were of this new construction. The plan was to introduce the new-spec fronts at Silverstone, but pressure from the riders meant two of the new fronts, in the hard compound, were added to the allocation for Jerez. Stoner thought this was ridiculous: how could they be tested? However, only Casey and his team-mate at Repsol Honda, Pedrosa, wanted to keep the old tyre; everyone else was anxious to get their hands on the new one, the '33'. It certainly helped the CRT and satellite team riders, who never had the power or speed to force enough energy into the old stiff-construction Bridgestones. All bar one of them used the new front. Of the works riders, only Rossi used the new design. No surprise there, because he suspected the old front was one of the reasons for the uncertain feedback from the front of his Ducati. It had been much rumoured that he was the leader of the gang who didn't want to wait for the 33s to get into full production.

Ironically, all the rostrum men used the old front, although Jorge thought afterwards that if he had used the new one he could have won. This wasn't anything to do with the new construction; it was that the hard compound tread rubber would have given him the stability he lacked.

ABOVE Rossi used the new softer construction front tyre which, he said, at least enabled him to ride the way he wanted. It was another tough weekend, though

TYRE OPTIONS
FRONT SOFT (S) / MEDIUM (M) / HARD (H) / HARD-New Spec (Hn)
REAR SOFT (S) / MEDIUM (M)

OFFICIAL TIMEKEEPER

GRAN PREMIO bwin DE ESPAÑA
CIRCUITO DE JEREZ

ROUND 2
April 28

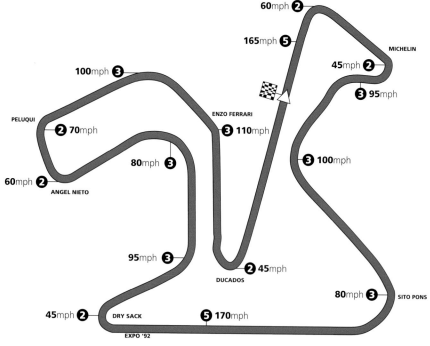

RACE RESULTS

CIRCUIT LENGTH 2.748 miles
NO. OF LAPS 27
RACE DISTANCE 74.205 miles
WEATHER Dry, 14°C
TRACK TEMPERATURE 15°C
WINNER Casey Stoner
FASTEST LAP 1m 40.019s, 98.920mph, Cal Crutchlow
LAP RECORD 1m 39.731s, 99.206mph, Dani Pedrosa, 2010

QUALIFYING

	Rider	Nationality	Team	Qualifying	Pole +	Gap
1	Lorenzo	SPA	Yamaha Factory Racing	1m 39.532s		
2	Pedrosa	SPA	Repsol Honda Team	1m 39.667s	0.135s	0.135s
3	Hayden	USA	Ducati Team	1m 40.563s	1.031s	0.896s
4	Crutchlow	GBR	Monster Yamaha Tech 3	1m 40.570s	1.038s	0.007s
5	Stoner	AUS	Repsol Honda Team	1m 40.577s	1.045s	0.007s
6	Spies	USA	Yamaha Factory Racing	1m 41.090s	1.558s	0.513s
7	Dovizioso	ITA	Monster Yamaha Tech 3	1m 41.180s	1.648s	0.090s
8	Bautista	SPA	San Carlo Honda Gresini	1m 41.447s	1.915s	0.267s
9	Bradl	GER	LCR Honda MotoGP	1m 41.550s	2.018s	0.103s
10	De Puniet	FRA	Power Electronics Aspar	1m 41.700s	2.168s	0.150s
11	Abraham	CZE	Cardion AB Motoracing	1m 41.724s	2.192s	0.024s
12	Barbera	SPA	Pramac Racing Team	1m 41.871s	2.339s	0.147s
13	Rossi	ITA	Ducati Team	1m 42.961s	3.429s	1.090s
14	Espargaro	SPA	Power Electronics Aspar	1m 43.135s	3.603s	0.174s
15	Pirro	ITA	San Carlo Honda Gresini	1m 43.363s	3.831s	0.228s
16	Pasini	ITA	Speed Master	1m 44.308s	4.776s	0.945s
17	Hernandez	COL	Avintia Blusens	1m 44.467s	4.935s	0.159s
18	Petrucci	ITA	Came IodaRacing Project	1m 44.645s	5.113s	0.178s
19	Silva	SPA	Avintia Blusens	1m 44.717s	5.185s	0.072s
20	Ellison	GBR	Paul Bird Motorsport	1m 45.724s	6.192s	1.007s
21	Edwards	USA	NGM Mobile Forward Racing	1m 46.200s	6.668s	0.476s

FINISHERS

1 CASEY STONER After his worst qualifying since joining Honda, and trying to keep out of trouble in the first two laps, took the lead at the start of the third lap and was never headed; mind you, he was never a second ahead. Amazingly, it was his first win and only his second rostrum at Jerez.

2 JORGE LORENZO Started from pole and mildly irked with his tyre choice – used the old construction and regretted it. Lacked the confidence he'd had in practice and it was all he could do to match Casey's pace. Did close the gap in the closing stages but ran wide on the penultimate lap.

3 DANI PEDROSA Too cautious at the start – he'd seen all the crashes in the earlier races – which lost him the chance to race for the win. Got the holeshot but was pushed back to fifth and had to repass Hayden and Dovizioso; then had to worry about defending third rather than attacking the leaders.

4 CAL CRUTCHLOW Combative at the start, then spent most of the race glued to Pedrosa's rear wheel. Delighted to be so close to the rostrum and to be able to match Dani's pace at his home track. Used the new-spec front tyre with hard tread compound, unlike his team-mate.

5 ANDREA DOVIZIOSO Not happy with his decision to use the old-spec front tyre, which he blamed for his inability to compete with Crutchlow. The almost total lack of dry

track time as he tried to understand the Yamaha M1 didn't help, but very aggressive in the opening laps.

6 ALVARO BAUTISTA A little cautious at the start, after the mixed conditions of practice and qualifying, so although able to recover and pass Bradl and Hayden, he was too far back to attack the Tech 3 Yamahas.

7 STEFAN BRADL For a guy who didn't like the wet a couple of years ago ninth on the grid followed by a fight with Hayden made it a pretty good weekend. Swapped to a clear visor after track conditions worried him on the warm-up lap, and suffered mild arm pump mid-race.

8 NICKY HAYDEN Happy to be involved with the early skirmishes at the front, thanks

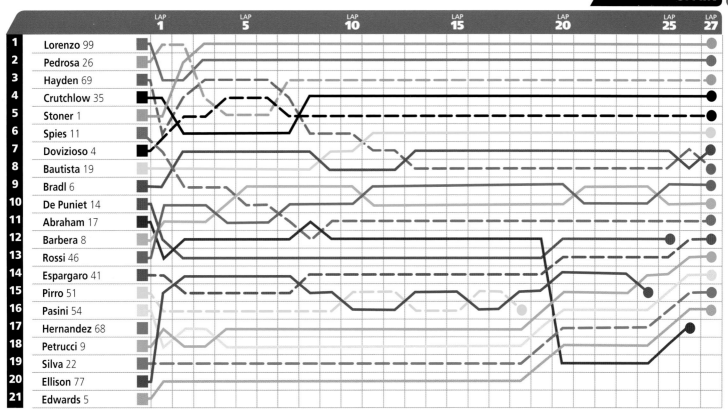

		LAP 1		LAP 5		LAP 10		LAP 15		LAP 20		LAP 25	LAP 27
1	Lorenzo 99												
2	Pedrosa 26												
3	Hayden 69												
4	Crutchlow 35												
5	Stoner 1												
6	Spies 11												
7	Dovizioso 4												
8	Bautista 19												
9	Bradl 6												
10	De Puniet 14												
11	Abraham 17												
12	Barbera 8												
13	Rossi 46												
14	Espargaro 41												
15	Pirro 51												
16	Pasini 54												
17	Hernandez 68												
18	Petrucci 9												
19	Silva 22												
20	Ellison 77												
21	Edwards 5												

RACE

	Rider	Motorcycle	Race Time	Time +	Fastest Lap	Av Speed	B
1	Stoner	Honda	45m 00.000s		1m 40.151s	97.712mph	M/S
2	Lorenzo	Yamaha	45m 00.000s	0.947s	1m 40.350s	97.679mph	M/S
3	Pedrosa	Honda	45m 00.000s	2.063s	1m 40.062s	97.639mph	M/S
4	Crutchlow	Yamaha	45m 00.000s	2.465s	1m 40.019s	97.625mph	Hn/S
5	Dovizioso	Yamaha	45m 00.000s	18.100s	1m 40.548s	97.070mph	M/S
6	Bautista	Honda	45m 00.000s	21.395s	1m 41.009s	96.954mph	Hn/S
7	Bradl	Honda	46m 00.000s	28.637s	1m 41.195s	96.670mph	Hn/S
8	Hayden	Ducati	46m 00.000s	28.869s	1m 41.363s	96.692mph	M/S
9	Rossi	Ducati	46m 00.000s	34.852s	1m 41.062s	96.483mph	Hn/S
10	Barbera	Ducati	46m 00.000s	35.103s	1m 41.047s	96.474mph	Hn/S
11	Spies	Yamaha	46m 00.000s	38.041s	1m 41.521s	96.372mph	M/S
12	Espargaro	Art	46m 00.000s	1m 12.728s	1m 42.742s	95.180mph	Hn/S
13	Petrucci	Ioda	46m 00.000s	1m 18.669s	1m 42.989s	94.980mph	Hn/S
14	Pasini	Art	47m 00.000s	1m 29.142s	1m 43.419s	94.627mph	Hn/S
15	Silva	BQR	47m 00.000s	1m 32.478s	1m 43.300s	94.516mph	M/S
16	Edwards	Suter	47m 00.000s	1m 40.577s	1m 43.034s	94.245mph	Hn/S
17	Abraham	Ducati	45m 00.000s	1 lap	1m 41.569s	93.567mph	M/S
NF	De Puniet	Art	43m 00.000s	2 laps	1m 41.996s	95.479mph	Hn/S
NF	Ellison	Art	41m 00.000s	3 laps	1m 42.975s	94.889mph	Hn/S
NF	Pirro	FTR	31m 00.000s	9 laps	1m 43.1430s	94.830mph	Hn/S
NF	Hernandez	BQR					Hn/S

CHAMPIONSHIP

	Rider	Team	Points
1	Lorenzo	Yamaha Factory Racing	45
2	Stoner	Repsol Honda Team	41
3	Pedrosa	Repsol Honda Team	36
4	Crutchlow	Monster Yamaha Tech 3	26
5	Dovizioso	Monster Yamaha Tech 3	22
6	Bautista	San Carlo Honda Gresini	19
7	Hayden	Ducati Team	18
8	Bradl	LCR Honda MotoGP	17
9	Rossi	Ducati Team	13
10	Barbera	Pramac Racing Team	13
11	Spies	Yamaha Factory Racing	10
12	Espargaro	Power Electronics Aspar	5
13	Edwards	NGM Mobile Forward Racing	4
14	Petrucci	Came IodaRacing Project	3
15	De Puniet	Power Electronics Aspar	3
16	Pasini	Speed Master	2
17	Hernandez	Avintia Blusens	2
18	Silva	Avintia Blusens	1

to the facility with which the Ducati gets heat into its tyres. Once the opposition got their tyres working he was already noticing grip dropping off at the front, which meant the old Ducati problem of understeer returned.

9 VALENTINO ROSSI Despite starting ten places behind his team-mate, he finished the race one place and less than 6s behind Hayden. After a weekend of depression the bike was lowered and lengthened for race day, and although unable to ride the way he wanted to, he could at least ride it.

10 HECTOR BARBERA Not a fan of the Andalusian track, and even less so when there were damp patches on it – by his own admission lacked confidence for the race. Drew more than a little solace from being able to fight with Rossi almost throughout.

11 BEN SPIES A worrying repeat of his Qatar result, but without the mitigating circumstances. Started well but didn't have any feeling from, or confidence in, the front.

12 ALEIX ESPARGARO Inherited top CRT spot after his team-mate's bike stopped two laps from the flag. Admitted he was too cautious in the early stages, but matched de Puniet's pace later on.

13 DANILO PETRUCCI Short straights and tricky conditions meant his lack of horsepower wasn't as much of a handicap as at Losail, so Danilo delighted his team with their first World Championship points.

14 MATTIA PASINI The first points of the season for the Italian, and the first

time the team felt they were starting to understand the bike. Changes made on Sunday morning had the desired effect, and Mattia lapped consistently.

15 IVAN SILVA Tried the new Inmotec carbon beam frame in practice, but reverted to the FTR chassis for the race.

16 COLIN EDWARDS A very different race from Qatar, where Edwards dominated the CRTs. This time, with hardly any dry weather in practice or qualifying, the set-up was way off. The bike was run shorter than at the Jerez test, which got rid of some of the chatter.

17 KAREL ABRAHAM Running in eighth when he lost the front, remounting to finish outside the points. Had a good wet-weather

setting but lost out when the track dried; was over-achieving when he crashed.

NON-FINISHERS

RANDY DE PUNIET Dominant CRT rider of the weekend. Qualified in tenth ahead of three prototypes and was running in 12th, and top CRT, when the engine shut down. The electronics sensed that the bike had run out of petrol, but there was plenty in the tank.

JAMES ELLISON Running with the top CRT riders when his Aprilia went into safety mode, because of low oil pressure. Much happier with the new Bridgestone front, which helped with the chatter, as did turning off the traction control.

MICHELE PIRRO Another rider going well and looking to score his first points of the year when he had to retire with an electronics problem while running behind the two Aspar Aprilias.

YONNY HERNANDEZ His bike stopped on the grid and Yonny therefore started from pit lane, only to pull in at the end of the first lap.

GRANDE PRÉMIO DE PORTUGAL CIRCUITO ESTORIL

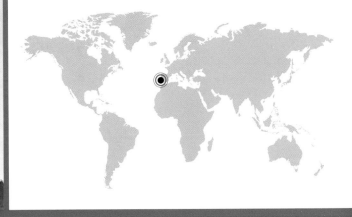

THE FULL SET

Stoner had his share of problems but he still held off a race-long challenge from Lorenzo

One week after winning for the first time at Jerez, Casey Stoner underlined just what a complete rider he was by winning for the first time at Estoril. Those two victories meant he had now won at every circuit on the calendar, plus the other three he raced on which are no longer on the schedule – Donington Park, Shanghai and Istanbul. It was the 42nd win of his career, putting him level with Max Biaggi and Toni Mang, and his 18th successive podium. Only two riders have a longer run of top-three finishes, Valentino Rossi and Giacomo Agostini.

It's worth bearing in mind that from 2007 to 2009 Stoner rode the Ducati, a bike that became increasingly more difficult to handle, so perhaps his stats since joining Honda give a more realistic picture of Casey's achievements. This was his 20th race for the Repsol Honda team, for which he has notched up 12 wins, 19 podiums and 13 pole positions. Since his move to Honda, only four riders have finished in front of Casey: Lorenzo, Pedrosa, Spies and Dovizioso. The Spaniards have beaten him six and five times respectively, the other two just once. The one time he didn't finish on the podium for Honda was the time he was knocked down by Valentino Rossi, at Jerez in 2011.

If you're an up-and-coming rider, like Cal Crutchlow, it isn't just Stoner you have to deal with. As Cal noted, after following Dani Pedrosa for most of the Spanish Grand Prix, the top men don't make any mistakes. For the third race running we were left in no doubt as to the identity of those top men. Only three riders – the three aliens? – got to stand on the rostrum in the first three races of the year, and they were Casey, Jorge Lorenzo and Pedrosa. Their domination is illustrated by the fact that this was the 16th time they had shared the rostrum, four times more

GRANDE PRÉMIO DE PORTUGAL
CIRCUITO ESTORIL

corner where he started running up the inside kerb with the rear tyre spinning. It was impossible to escape the conclusion that anyone else trying that would have had a very big crash, and led Shuhei Nakamoto of HRC to remark that Casey was making their bike look better than it actually was.

Pedrosa's race was compromised by some scary slides as he had difficulty warming his tyres up and was then troubled by chatter. He had to try to make up the difference on the brakes, something that he wasn't comfortable with. It was enough to see him between 1s and 1.5s adrift of the leading duo throughout the race. He could console himself with another statistic; it was his 100th podium in all classes of GP racing, although he did mention that it 'shows how fast the time goes'.

In between the two Hondas, Lorenzo overcame what he called a 'nightmare' – qualifying fourth – to become the first man to set a new lap record on the 1,000cc bikes. Despite his speed he never managed to make a serious challenge for the lead. Going deep at Turn 1 late in the race ended any thoughts he had of going for the win.

The other Yamahas maintained their good form. Ben Spies looked more like his old self but a couple of errors shuffled him back behind the Tech 3 pair, who, as in the first two outings of the year, circulated in close company for the whole race. This time it was Dovizioso who came home first, although an entertaining little intra-team spat about Crutchlow's riding style and Dovi's alleged purchase of the latest specification Brembo brakes livened things up. It was

ABOVE Casey Stoner savours the win that gave him a full set of victories at every track in the MotoGP calendar

BELOW Valentino Rossi was again racing with the satellite Hondas but he was much happier with the bike than in the first two races

than the next-best triumvirates: Stoner/Rossi/Pedrosa, Lawson/Gardner/Mamola and Rainey/Schwantz/Doohan.

All three of the top men had problems over the weekend, however. Casey had to deal with chatter, which brought on arm pump. He got round the problems by juggling engine maps and adjusting his riding style, all the while dealing with Jorge Lorenzo, who spent most of the race a quarter of a second behind the Honda. The Australian again contributed an unforgettable image, this time at the long, long final

LEFT Jorge Lorenzo ahead of Pedrosa but behind Stoner, on a track he has dominated on in the past

BELOW Colin Edwards was scooped up by Randy de Puniet during qualifying; he broke a collarbone

the first time Dovi had beaten Cal in a race this year, despite the Englishman qualifying on the front row. The Italian was clearly coming to terms with the M1 after spending his whole career on Hondas.

Over at Ducati, Nicky Hayden had his race ruined by something interfering with his ECU, which put the traction control and other systems a half-lap out of sync with reality. Similar problems afflicted both Rossi and Pedrosa throughout practice. Valentino's results didn't look too different from previous races but he

'THEY DON'T MAKE ANY MISTAKES, THEY'RE MACHINES'
CAL CRUTCHLOW

seemed much happier than at Jerez, where he had completely failed to hide his mood. The fact that Claudio Domenicali, Ducati CEO, was present for some lengthy meetings might have helped. What didn't help was the

RAPID RESPONSE

The unfortunate collision between Randy de Puniet and Colin Edwards saw the first deployment of MotoGP's new medical intervention vehicles. Two BMWs, each carrying a doctor from Barcelona's Instituto Universitario USP Dexeus along with comprehensive medical equipment, will be at every GP to supplement existing emergency staff.

MotoGP's protocols already stipulate that a doctor must be able to reach a fallen rider in a very short time anywhere on a circuit. Similarly, an ambulance must be accessible within a given, short space of time. Each circuit on the calendar has a detailed plan to ensure it complies with all requirements of the protocol. That means a considerable number of doctors, other medical

staff and ambulances at strategically selected access points around the circuit access road.

The deployment of the medical rapid intervention vehicles is controlled by the Race Director, in the event of a red flag, on the recommendation of and in consultation with the Chief Medical Officer, Medical Director and the Clerk of the Course, depending on the circuit, and the nature and location of the incident.

The doctors and other staff from the Dexeus Institute will give a sense of continuity and familiarity to riders and teams but, as previously, they cannot be in overall charge. Local law always requires a doctor qualified to practise in that country to be in charge. As per existing practice, the first intervention will come from a doctor from one of the posts around the circuit, who may then request assistance from the doctors in the intervention vehicles to stabilise the patient for transport to the circuit's medical centre.

LEFT The new MotoGP medical intervention vehicles and their crews

test of a new engine being washed out on Monday. To add to Ducati's worries, the performance of their satellite bikes was not impressing either, with the top CRTs getting uncomfortably close.

One thing all the riders did agree about was that Estoril is, as Stoner said, 'a complete circuit with all types of corners, lots of opportunities for overtaking – and to make a mistake'. The fact that we didn't see

much of either only underlines the level at which those top men are riding. Such a shame, then, that this was probably the last time for the foreseeable future that MotoGP will race there. The economic situation has seen to that. The event was propped up by the local authorities, thus enabling ticket prices to be as low as a couple of Euros, so at least there was a record crowd to bid the riders goodbye.

OPPOSITE Andrea Dovizioso was getting to grips with the Yamaha, he beat his team mate for the first time

BELOW Stoner on his way to the win from pole position

GRANDE PRÉMIO DE PORTUGAL
CIRCUITO ESTORIL
ESTORIL

ROUND **3**
May 6

RACE RESULTS

CIRCUIT LENGTH 2.599 miles
NO. OF LAPS 28
RACE DISTANCE 72.772 miles
WEATHER Dry, 17°C
TRACK TEMPERATURE 35°C
WINNER Casey Stoner
FASTEST LAP 1m 36.909s,
96.532mph, Jorge Lorenzo (Record)
PREVIOUS LAP RECORD 1m 36.937s,
96.505mph, Dani Pedrosa, 2009

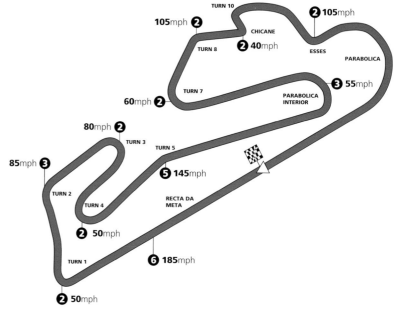

QUALIFYING

	Rider	Nationality	Team	Qualifying	Pole +	Gap
1	Stoner	AUS	Repsol Honda Team	1m 37.188s		
2	Pedrosa	SPA	Repsol Honda Team	1m 37.201s	0.013s	0.013s
3	Crutchlow	GBR	Monster Yamaha Tech 3	1m 37.289s	0.101s	0.088s
4	Lorenzo	SPA	Yamaha Factory Racing	1m 37.466s	0.278s	0.177s
5	Spies	USA	Yamaha Factory Racing	1m 37.723s	0.535s	0.257s
6	Bautista	SPA	San Carlo Honda Gresini	1m 37.917s	0.729s	0.194s
7	Dovizioso	ITA	Monster Yamaha Tech 3	1m 37.943s	0.755s	0.026s
8	Barbera	SPA	Pramac Racing Team	1m 38.006s	0.818s	0.063s
9	Rossi	ITA	Ducati Team	1m 38.059s	0.871s	0.053s
10	Hayden	USA	Ducati Team	1m 38.253s	1.065s	0.194s
11	Bradl	GER	LCR Honda MotoGP	1m 38.265s	1.077s	0.012s
12	Espargaro	SPA	Power Electronics Aspar	1m 39.353s	2.165s	1.088s
13	Abraham	CZE	Cardion AB Motoracing	1m 39.398s	2.210s	0.045s
14	De Puniet	FRA	Power Electronics Aspar	1m 39.586s	2.398s	0.188s
15	Hernandez	COL	Avintia Blusens	1m 40.029s	2.841s	0.443s
16	Pirro	ITA	San Carlo Honda Gresini	1m 40.225s	3.037s	0.196s
17	Pasini	ITA	Speed Master	1m 40.387s	3.199s	0.162s
18	Edwards	USA	NGM Mobile Forward Racing	1m 40.964s	3.776s	0.577s
19	Ellison	GBR	Paul Bird Motorsport	1m 41.394s	4.206s	0.430s
20	Petrucci	ITA	Came IodaRacing Project	1m 41.486s	4.298s	0.092s
21	Silva	SPA	Avintia Blusens	1m 41.490s	4.302s	0.004s

FINISHERS

1 CASEY STONER Led all the way but pressured by Lorenzo and had to cope with chatter on the warmer track and losing the front twice in the early stages. Experimented with electronics settings, worked out how to ride round the problem and got on the pace again for his first win here. Now had a full set of wins on every circuit in the calendar.

2 JORGE LORENZO Happy to be second despite this, historically, being one of his best tracks. Got over trouble in practice, dealt with overheating the clutch off the start and spent most of the race within a second of Stoner. Set the fastest lap and tried to attack late on, only to run wide.

3 DANI PEDROSA The second-youngest rider, after Rossi, to reach the milestone of 100 podiums in GPs. A major moment early on lap one lost the advantage of the holeshot, then struggled with mid-corner speed. Like Stoner, played with engine maps and riding style to equal the lap times of those ahead of him, but couldn't close the gap.

4 ANDREA DOVIZIOSO Beat his team-mate for the first time this season, although they again spent all the race in very close company. Gave himself a lot to do starting from the third row – no chance to go with the leaders – but was pleased to be able to run a better pace than in qualifying.

5 CAL CRUTCHLOW Qualified on the front row for the second time this season.

Reckoned he was having to work harder than the men in front of him to conserve grip and to stop. Happy to retain fourth in the championship, and impressed with his team-mate who refused to make a mistake despite race-long pressure.

6 ALVARO BAUTISTA His best result so far, but Alvaro wasn't happy. Thought he should have been able to get closer to the Tech 3 Yamahas, but lack of feeling with the front made turning the bike difficult, in addition to the regular problem with braking.

7 VALENTINO ROSSI Much happier than at Jerez, despite the results not looking too different. Pleased he was able to run the lap times he expected after gaining a couple of places early on.

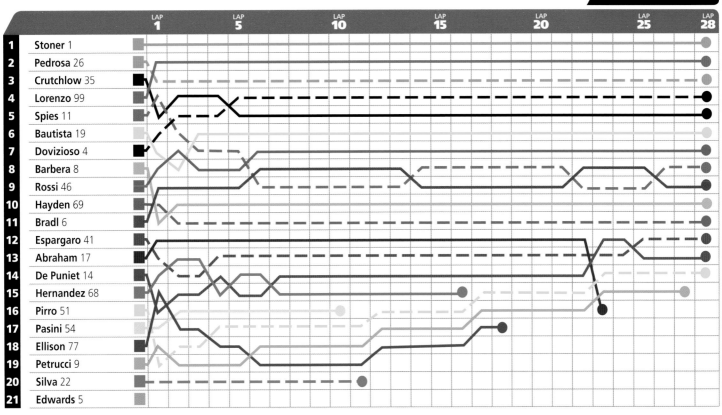

		LAP 1	LAP 5	LAP 10	LAP 15	LAP 20	LAP 25	LAP 28
1	Stoner 1							
2	Pedrosa 26							
3	Crutchlow 35							
4	Lorenzo 99							
5	Spies 11							
6	Bautista 19							
7	Dovizioso 4							
8	Barbera 8							
9	Rossi 46							
10	Hayden 69							
11	Bradl 6							
12	Espargaro 41							
13	Abraham 17							
14	De Puniet 14							
15	Hernandez 68							
16	Pirro 51							
17	Pasini 54							
18	Ellison 77							
19	Petrucci 9							
20	Silva 22							
21	Edwards 5							

RACE

	Rider	Motorcycle	Race Time	Time +	Fastest Lap	Av Speed	B
1	Stoner	Honda	45m 37.513s		1m 37.091s	95.684mph	M/M
2	Lorenzo	Yamaha	45m 38.934s	1.421s	1m 36.909s	95.634mph	Mn/M
3	Pedrosa	Honda	45m 41.134s	3.621s	1m 37.178s	95.558mph	M/M
4	Dovizioso	Yamaha	45m 51.359s	13.846s	1m 37.513s	95.202mph	Mn/M
5	Crutchlow	Yamaha	45m 54.203s	16.690s	1m 37.461s	95.104mph	Mn/M
6	Bautista	Honda	45m 59.397s	21.884s	1m 37.846s	94.925mph	Mn/M
7	Rossi	Ducati	46m 04.310s	26.797s	1m 38.146s	94.756mph	M/M
8	Spies	Yamaha	46m 10.775s	33.262s	1m 38.077s	94.535mph	Mn/M
9	Bradl	Honda	46m 13.380s	35.867s	1m 38.207s	94.447mph	Mn/M
10	Barbera	Ducati	46m 30.876s	53.363s	1m 38.162s	93.854mph	Mn/M
11	Hayden	Ducati	46m 40.143s	1m 02.630s	1m 38.834s	93.544mph	M/M
12	Espargaro	Art	46m 58.249s	1m 20.736s	1m 39.838s	92.943mph	Mn/M
13	De Puniet	Art	47m 00.996s	1m 23.483s	1m 39.5690s	92.852mph	Mn/M
14	Pirro	FTR	47m 15.418s	1m 37.905s	1m 40.454s	92.380mph	Mn/M
15	Petrucci	Ioda	46m 01.358s	1 lap	1m 41.072s	91.470mph	Mn/M
NF	Abraham	Ducati	39m 52.674s	5 laps	1m 38.853s	89.925mph	M/M
NF	Ellison	Art	30m 51.198s	10 laps	1m 41.309s	90.961mph	Mn/M
NF	Hernandez	BQR	26m 59.749s	12 laps	1m 40.214s	92.408mph	Mn/M
NF	Pasini	Art	18m 33.107s	17 laps	1m 40.170s	92.447mph	M/M
NF	Silva	BQR	19m 10.392s	17 laps	1m 42.396s	89.451mph	M/M

CHAMPIONSHIP

	Rider	Team	Points
1	Stoner	Repsol Honda Team	66
2	Lorenzo	Yamaha Factory Racing	65
3	Pedrosa	Repsol Honda Team	52
4	Crutchlow	Monster Yamaha Tech 3	37
5	Dovizioso	Monster Yamaha Tech 3	35
6	Bautista	San Carlo Honda Gresini	29
7	Bradl	LCR Honda MotoGP	24
8	Hayden	Ducati Team	23
9	Rossi	Ducati Team	22
10	Barbera	Pramac Racing Team	19
11	Spies	Yamaha Factory Racing	18
12	Espargaro	Power Electronics Aspar	9
13	De Puniet	Power Electronics Aspar	6
14	Edwards	NGM Mobile Forward Racing	4
15	Petrucci	Came IodaRacing Project	4
16	Pirro	San Carlo Honda Gresini	2
17	Pasini	Speed Master	2
18	Hernandez	Avintia Blusens	2
19	Silva	Avintia Blusens	1

Still complaining about the aggressive engine characteristics making corner exits difficult.

8 BEN SPIES Qualified and started well but ran wide on the second lap and was shuffled back three places, then made more mistakes and was as low as ninth. Spent the second half of the race dicing with Bradl, finally coming out on top.

9 STEFAN BRADL Struggled with rear grip from the start of practice, then found he couldn't get on the throttle early in the race. Still managed to put up a good fight in his dice with Spies and, despite the problems, impressed again.

10 HECTOR BARBERA Disappointed to lose places off the start and couldn't make any up, apart from passing Hayden's misbehaving factory bike. Blamed trouble with his shoulder which didn't allow him to take advantage of what he thought was a competitive set-up on a track he likes.

11 NICKY HAYDEN Bitterly disappointed. Radio-frequency interference got to the bike's ECU, resulting in engine management being a half-lap out of alignment with reality. Had to deal with some truly scary variations in power delivery – like the bike refusing to accelerate out of the final corner.

12 ALEIX ESPARGARO Delighted to be top CRT man, although he did acknowledge that his team-mate wasn't 100% fit.

13 RANDY DE PUNIET Crashed hard on Saturday, when his bike took Edwards down and put the American out of the race. Randy hurt his ribs in the incident and was in no fit state to challenge his team-mate for top CRT honours from the tenth lap onwards.

14 MICHELE PIRRO Happy to finish without being lapped. Pushed hard for the last eight laps when he saw Casey was getting close, and was rewarded with his first MotoGP points on what had been a difficult weekend.

15 DANILO PETRUCCI There were enough retirements to allow him to score his and the Ioda team's first MotoGP points, so on this occasion he was not really bothered about being lapped.

NON-FINISHERS

KAREL ABRAHAM The awful start to the season continued with a crash six laps from home. Still no points for the young Czech.

JAMES ELLISON After the encouragement of Jerez the chatter was back with a vengeance, seemingly generated by the electronics, specifically the traction control. It was so bad that James felt forced to pull in.

YONNY HERNANDEZ His usual entertaining self. Qualified well, in 15th, but crashed without injury just after half-distance.

MATTIA PASINI Running with the Aspar Aprilias and planning a late attack when he slid off. Still happy that he and the team were learning fast.

IVAN SILVA Used the carbon chassis Inmotec, but a big fall in warm-up left the Spanish rider hurting. Tried to race but had to pull in before half-distance.

NON-STARTERS

COLIN EDWARDS Just minding his own business when scooped up by de Puniet's Aprilia. Never knew what hit him: went down hard on his left side and broke his collarbone.

MONSTER ENERGY
GRAND PRIX DE FRANCE

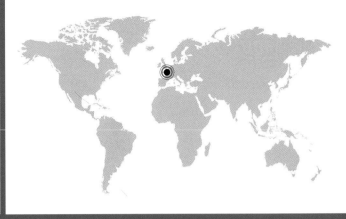

SHOCK
AND AWE

Stoner dropped a bombshell, Rossi was back on the rostrum and Lorenzo showed both of them how to win in the wet

One fact slipped past most people's notice after the landscape-altering events of the French Grand Prix: Jorge Lorenzo left Le Mans back on top, with a very handy championship lead of eight points. Meanwhile, the paddock was in a frenzy over the implications of Casey Stoner's retirement announcement. The always lively Le Mans crowd first enjoyed a true home win in Moto3, then got behind Valentino Rossi's charge to second place – a timely reminder of his worth in the now-turbulent rider market.

Casey's announcement also gave a major boost to Lorenzo's market value, which he underlined with a quite brilliant and controlled ride. His rush past the Repsol Hondas on the first lap was not without risk, but he saw they were spinning their rear tyres excessively and went past Stoner and Pedrosa on the run to Garage Vert. After that it was a matter of building and then controlling the lead without giving in to the temptation to push too hard when the Aussie closed in.

The race illustrated perfectly the current strengths and weaknesses of the bikes on the grid. All the Yamahas had the pace to be at the front; the Hondas were finicky, prone to chatter and very sensitive to conditions; the Ducatis worked in the wet in a way they haven't done in the dry – and no, no-one understands why. All of the Yamahas had the speed to contend for a rostrum finish, but Jorge did what he's been doing all season and rode the perfect race under the most difficult of conditions, while Spies had another slice of the uncommonly bad luck that has afflicted the start to his season. The Tech 3 duo both fell and remounted while fighting with Rossi.

The factory Hondas both struggled. Despite his

LEFT Both Tech 3 Yamahas were in the hunt for a rostrum finish but both crashed and both riders remounted to finish the race

OPPOSITE Valentino Rossi took advantage of the conditions to get on the rostrum for the second year in a row at Le Mans

BELOW Not a good weekend for the Spaniards on the satellite bikes – Barbera attacks Bautista just like in their 250 days

traditional holeshot, Pedrosa was never in with a chance and benefited from the misfortune of others in finishing fourth. Stoner's race was governed by his tyres. At the start there was too much water and he couldn't get any heat into them. Then conditions eased and he took big lumps out of Lorenzo's four-second lead. And finally it became a bit too dry and the rear started spinning. Casey was sitting up on the straight with his weight as far back as he could get it and he still couldn't get the power down – and that put him in Rossi's clutches. For the first time since Jerez 2011 they came together on track. Valentino was content to follow at first, mindful of that debacle, and Casey knew it. He also knew that later in the race Valentino would have forgotten all about it. Once Rossi had recovered from a misting visor he did indeed attack late on and the two swapped places twice at the Dunlop chicane before the Honda man conceded the position. Both agreed it had been a good dice, with Stoner making a point of saying it had been clean racing.

Rossi later made it clear that this was not a turning point but a fortunate combination of circumstances that had enabled him to ride the bike in the way he wanted for the first time this year. In normal conditions the understeer and vicious power delivery remained serious problems. 'When you want the rain, you are usually in the shit,' said Vale, jovially. It is doubtful if the conversations in Bologna were as flippant.

James Ellison had also had a few less than amicable exchanges with his team-boss, Paul Bird, who had intimated that he might be replaced. The British rider responded by coming home as top CRT after a frantic

last few laps dicing with Petrucci and Pasini. To make it even more enjoyable, Bird was watching at the track for the first time this season.

The crowd went home happy. Two guys called Rossi had seen to that (the other one being Louis Rossi, born in Le Mans, who won the Moto3 race). Paddock people, meanwhile, departed in turmoil, trying to calculate the implications of Casey Stoner's announcement in light of the fact that the only current MotoGP rider

with a contract for 2013 was Stefan Bradl. First, it was obvious that the market value of Jorge Lorenzo and Valentino Rossi had just shot up. Second, Honda now had a serious dilemma. The man they'd brought in, they thought and hoped, for a long career at the top would be leaving after just two seasons. What to do? The answer was obviously to go after Lorenzo and to continue campaigning for the Rookie Rule to be repealed, to enable Marc Marquez to be signed directly to the factory team.

And what about Rossi? HRC said they couldn't see him back in the factory team, but their satellite teams could employ whoever they wished. As for Yamaha, would they need Valentino, given the strength of their four current riders? And what would be the knock-on effects for Ducati, Dani Pedrosa and Nicky Hayden?

As usual, none of these questions would be answered until the main player in the game had made his decision, and that man was now indubitably Jorge Lorenzo.

ABOVE Stefan Bradl impressed again with his best finish of the season so far

BELOW James Ellison came out on top of a lively last-lap battle for top CRT honours

THE LONG GOODBYE

Casey Stoner, looking haggard and red-eyed, with his wife sitting in the audience of the press conference for the first time this year, announced that he would be retiring at the end of the 2012 season. Nobody was expecting that. He said he'd made the final decision only the previous week, but the subject had been seriously on his mind since 2009, the year when his lactose intolerance was diagnosed and he took a sabbatical for three races. That, said Casey, was 'a big eye-opener' when he 'realised what really mattered'.

Looking back with the benefit of hindsight, it's hard to recall him looking and acting as if he was really enjoying himself much in the last couple of years. What happens in the mind of a kid who's uprooted from home at the age of fourteen to live in a cold and distant land in pursuit of his career? Roberts used to talk about 'ten years in your tank' when competing at the top level; Casey's first GP outing was as a wild card in 2001...

Stoner was keen to point out that his decision wasn't to do with money or the birth of his daughter, but because he didn't like 'the way things in the sport are going'. He castigated the media for talking MotoGP down – he meant by calling a race in which he and Jorge were never more than a second apart 'boring' – but then spent some time telling us what was wrong with the sport. 'This is a prototype championship,' he said, 'but we are going backwards. It's not the championship I fell in love with.' He's been a vociferous opponent of CRT and sees such things as the fastest CRT going to *parc fermé* after qualifying as further evidence that the organisers have no intention of keeping MotoGP as one championship. It was time to get out: 'I don't want to completely lose my passion for bikes.'

The overwhelming impression, as ever, was of a tightly wound sportsman with a selection of grievances that have finally outweighed the things he finds attractive about racing. He displayed more emotion than he'd ever shown before – this was plainly not an easy announcement for him to make in public – and at times it felt like we were intruding on private grief.

Some of those grievances, like the CRT issue, are new; some were old, like the cynics who questioned whether his lactose intolerance was genuine. Nobody has actually talked about that recently, but he brought it up again. The boy has never been anything but straightforward. He has always answered any question, and honestly as well, not caring whether the answer would be popular. No PR man could ever take the edges off Casey.

Of course there have been times when he hasn't done himself any favours, and he can contradict himself. There are no grey areas, but Casey is hardly unique in that respect. Neither is he the only top sportsman who never had a normal childhood, as Jorge Lorenzo would certainly attest. Stoner has always been a loner – there are probably only two people in the paddock who might be described as his good friends. The abiding image of Casey's statement, however, came as he thought about another answer to the 'why are you going?' question. He looked down and muttered to himself 'difficult to explain'. It looked as if the full reason was just that, difficult to explain. Even to himself.

'I WON'T HAVE REGRETS'
CASEY STONER

BRIDGESTONE

TYRE OPTIONS
FRONT WET SOFT (**WS**) / WET HARD (**WH**)
REAR WET SOFT (**WS**) / WET HARD (**WH**)

OFFICIAL TIMEKEEPER

MONSTER ENERGY
GRAND PRIX DE FRANCE
LE MANS

ROUND 4
May 20

RACE
RESULTS

CIRCUIT LENGTH 2.597 miles
NO. OF LAPS 28
RACE DISTANCE 72.812 miles
WEATHER Wet, 24°C
TRACK TEMPERATURE 23°C
WINNER Jorge Lorenzo
FASTEST LAP 1m 44.614s,
89.487mph, Valentino Rossi
LAP RECORD 1m 33.617s,
99.979mph, Dani Pedrosa, 2011

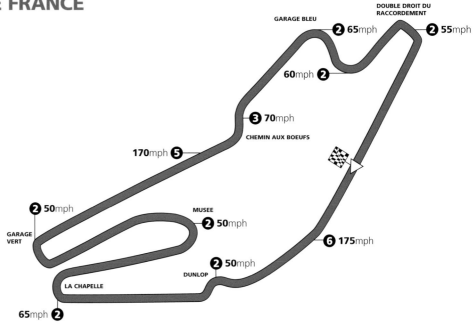

DOUBLE DROIT DU RACCORDEMENT
GARAGE BLEU
2 65mph **2** 55mph
60mph **2**
3 70mph
CHEMIN AUX BOEUFS
170mph **5**
2 50mph
MUSEE
GARAGE VERT
2 50mph
6 175mph
2 50mph
DUNLOP
LA CHAPELLE
65mph **2**

QUALIFYING

	Rider	Nationality	Team	Qualifying	Pole +	Gap
1	Pedrosa	SPA	Repsol Honda Team	1m 33.638s		
2	Stoner	AUS	Repsol Honda Team	1m 33.941s	0.303s	0.303s
3	Dovizioso	ITA	Monster Yamaha Tech 3	1m 33.976s	0.338s	0.035s
4	Lorenzo	SPA	Yamaha Factory Racing	1m 34.104s	0.466s	0.128s
5	Crutchlow	GBR	Monster Yamaha Tech 3	1m 34.178s	0.540s	0.074s
6	Spies	USA	Yamaha Factory Racing	1m 34.669s	1.031s	0.491s
7	Rossi	ITA	Ducati Team	1m 34.907s	1.269s	0.238s
8	Bautista	SPA	San Carlo Honda Gresini	1m 34.922s	1.284s	0.015s
9	Barbera	SPA	Pramac Racing Team	1m 34.950s	1.312s	0.028s
10	Abraham	CZE	Cardion AB Motoracing	1m 35.250s	1.612s	0.300s
11	Hayden	USA	Ducati Team	1m 35.291s	1.653s	0.041s
12	De Puniet	FRA	Power Electronics Aspar	1m 35.694s	2.056s	0.403s
13	Bradl	GER	LCR Honda MotoGP	1m 35.862s	2.224s	0.168s
14	Pirro	ITA	San Carlo Honda Gresini	1m 36.646s	3.008s	0.784s
15	Hernandez	COL	Avintia Blusens	1m 37.202s	3.564s	0.556s
16	Ellison	GBR	Paul Bird Motorsport	1m 37.666s	4.028s	0.464s
17	Espargaro	SPA	Power Electronics Aspar	1m 37.760s	4.122s	0.094s
18	Petrucci	ITA	Came IodaRacing Project	1m 37.767s	4.129s	0.007s
19	Silva	SPA	Avintia Blusens	1m 38.198s	4.560s	0.431s
20	Pasini	ITA	Speed Master	1m 38.511s	4.873s	0.313s
21	Vermeulen	AUS	NGM Mobile Forward Racing	1m 38.658s	5.020s	0.147s

FINISHERS

1 JORGE LORENZO News of Stoner's retirement and Rossi's return to the rostrum made it easy to overlook just what a good race this was. Jorge took a big risk punching past the Hondas on the first lap, didn't panic when Casey started to make inroads, and maintained his concentration all the way: perfection under the most difficult conditions.

2 VALENTINO ROSSI Took advantage of the conditions, which allowed him to ride the Ducati as he wanted, and reminded everyone what he could do. First battled with the Tech 3 Yamahas, then with Stoner. A thrilling ride which really engaged the cold and wet crowd.

3 CASEY STONER Battled problems with his tyres all the way. At first the track was too wet, then when it dried a little he closed down on Lorenzo. Finally it got too dry and he was wheelspinning everywhere. Didn't give up second place easily, though.

4 DANI PEDROSA Knew from the start it was going to be a bad day. No traction coming out of corners, especially in the lower gears. Went the wrong way with a chassis adjustment after warm-up, so was happy to take advantage of the Tech 3 crashes.

5 STEFAN BRADL After a big highside in qualifying this was a superb display, as well as his best result so far. Not bad for a rider who'd never finished a wet race

before he won the Moto2 at Silverstone last year. Gained six places on the first lap and followed Pedrosa from lap four, which he found an education.

6 NICKY HAYDEN Spun up in first gear off the start and was buried in the pack, finishing the first lap in 11th. Got within two seconds of Bradl before he had a major moment and had to try again. On the German's wheel at the flag, but frustrated with sixth on a bike good enough for the rostrum.

7 ANDREA DOVIZIOSO Racing with his team-mate, as usual, and Rossi. Fell at Chemin aux Boeufs after Crutchlow crashed while pressuring the Ducati. Both remounted, with Dovi finding himself in front of Cal and holding the advantage to the flag.

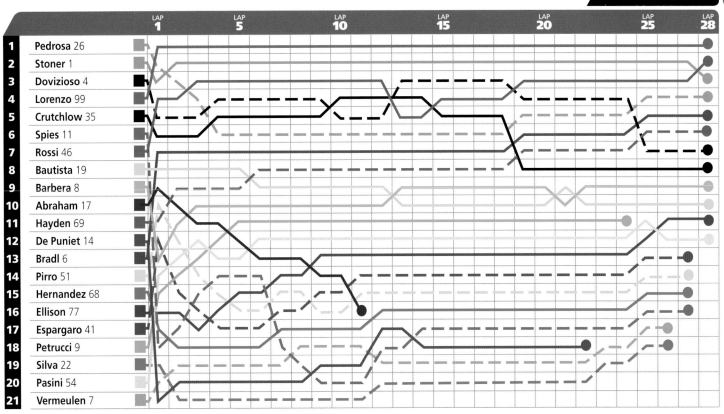

	Rider		LAP 1	LAP 5	LAP 10	LAP 15	LAP 20	LAP 25	LAP 28
1	Pedrosa	26							
2	Stoner	1							
3	Dovizioso	4							
4	Lorenzo	99							
5	Crutchlow	35							
6	Spies	11							
7	Rossi	46							
8	Bautista	19							
9	Barbera	8							
10	Abraham	17							
11	Hayden	69							
12	De Puniet	14							
13	Bradl	6							
14	Pirro	51							
15	Hernandez	68							
16	Ellison	77							
17	Espargaro	41							
18	Petrucci	9							
19	Silva	22							
20	Pasini	54							
21	Vermeulen	7							

RACE

	Rider	Motorcycle	Race Time	Time +	Fastest Lap	Av Speed	B
1	Lorenzo	Yamaha	49m 39.743s		1m 44.947s	87.968mph	ws/ws
2	Rossi	Ducati	49m 49.648s	9.905s	1m 44.614s	87.676mph	ws/ws
3	Stoner	Honda	49m 51.041s	11.298s	1m 45.122s	87.636mph	ws/ws
4	Pedrosa	Honda	50m 09.104s	29.361s	1m 45.693s	87.110mph	ws/ws
5	Bradl	Honda	50m 12.220s	32.477s	1m 46.307s	87.020mph	ws/ws
6	Hayden	Ducati	50m 12.585s	32.842s	1m 45.607s	87.009mph	ws/ws
7	Dovizioso	Yamaha	50m 39.502s	59.759s	1m 44.919s	86.239mph	ws/ws
8	Crutchlow	Yamaha	50m 44.895s	1m 05.152s	1m 45.362s	86.086mph	ws/ws
9	Barbera	Ducati	50m 47.589s	1m 07.846s	1m 46.185s	86.010mph	ws/ws
10	Bautista	Honda	50m 52.936s	1m 13.193s	1m 47.070s	85.859mph	ws/ws
11	Ellison	Art	51m 06.406s	1m 26.663s	1m 46.599s	85.482mph	ws/ws
12	Pasini	Art	51m 07.376s	1m 27.633s	1m 47.378s	85.455mph	ws/ws
13	Espargaro	Art	49m 55.456s	1 lap	1m 48.712s	84.382mph	ws/ws
14	Pirro	FTR	50m 03.709s	1 lap	1m 48.880s	84.150mph	ws/ws
15	Hernandez	BQR	50m 13.248s	1 lap	1m 49.513s	83.883mph	ws/ws
16	Spies	Yamaha	50m 55.642s	1 lap	1m 46.254s	82.719mph	ws/ws
17	Vermeulen	Suter	49m 42.348s	2 laps	1m 47.799s	81.613mph	ws/ws
18	Silva	BQR	51m 28.427s	2 laps	1m 50.041s	78.810mph	wH/ws
NF	Petrucci	Ioda	43m 54.019s	4 laps	1m 47.586s	85.298mph	ws/ws
NF	De Puniet	Art	42m 19.625s	6 laps	1m 48.953s	81.096mph	ws/ws
NF	Abraham	Ducati	20m 45.461s	17 laps	1m 50.272s	82.681mph	ws/ws

CHAMPIONSHIP

	Rider	Team	Points
1	Lorenzo	Yamaha Factory Racing	90
2	Stoner	Repsol Honda Team	82
3	Pedrosa	Repsol Honda Team	65
4	Crutchlow	Monster Yamaha Tech 3	45
5	Dovizioso	Monster Yamaha Tech 3	44
6	Rossi	Ducati Team	42
7	Bradl	LCR Honda MotoGP	35
8	Bautista	San Carlo Honda Gresini	35
9	Hayden	Ducati Team	33
10	Barbera	Pramac Racing Team	26
11	Spies	Yamaha Factory Racing	18
12	Espargaro	Power Electronics Aspar	12
13	Pasini	Speed Master	6
14	De Puniet	Power Electronics Aspar	6
15	Ellison	Paul Bird Motorsport	5
16	Edwards	NGM Mobile Forward Racing	4
17	Petrucci	Came IodaRacing Project	4
18	Pirro	San Carlo Honda Gresini	4
19	Hernandez	Avintia Blusens	3
20	Silva	Avintia Blusens	1

8 CAL CRUTCHLOW Quickest in warm-up, but felt he lacked speed on the straight so was trying to make up for it on the brakes. Battling with Rossi and his team-mate when he slid off at the Dunlop chicane; remounted for some useful points.

9 HECTOR BARBERA Not happy. Went to a stiffer set-up for warm-up, which worked at the time but was far from right for the much wetter race. Had to be content with winning his personal battle with Bautista.

10 ALVARO BAUTISTA Happy in the dry, but this was the first time he'd raced the Honda in the rain and the first time his crew, particularly his Showa suspension technicians, had to deal with a wet race. Had no feeling from the bike so survival was his only ambition.

11 JAMES ELLISON With a fraught start to the season and less than supportive remarks from the team-owner, finishing as top CRT after a good dice with Petrucci and Pasini was just what he needed – a confidence-building race after a difficult start to the year.

12 MATTIA PASINI The Italian only lost top CRT position to Ellison after a close fight in the closing stages.

13 ALEIX ESPARGARO Well beaten on track by two other CRTs and lucky to profit from the problems of others and pick up points after being lapped. Had no weight on the rear tyre and 'was sliding all over the place'. Glad to get this one over and head for his home race.

14 MICHELE PIRRO Distraught at being lapped for the first time in his life. The blame was pinned on the electronics, which simply hadn't had enough development time.

15 YONNY HERNANDEZ Scored a point for the first time since the opening race of the season in conditions that didn't suit either his style or his bike.

16 BEN SPIES Another race disrupted by a large slice of bad luck: flicked out of the saddle early on and hit the screen with his visor. Kept going for five laps with a river running through his helmet before pulling in to change visors. Frustratingly, his lap times were good enough for at least fourth place.

17 CHRIS VERMEULEN Replaced Edwards on the Suter BMW and had a tough return to MotoGP at the circuit where he took Suzuki's only win. Took five laps to get any heat in the tyres, pitted to sort out vision problems and finished two laps adrift.

18 IVAN SILVA The first of many crashers in the race, he went down on the second lap and took a long time to get going, but he did make it to the finish.

KAREL ABRAHAM His awful season continued when he pulled in unable to find any grip with the rear tyre. Still to score a point this season.

Fell before crossing the start-line when he tried to find traction on a white line, then crashed for the second and final time six laps from the flag.

NON-FINISHERS

DANILO PETRUCCI Looked like being top CRT rider, but touched a white line on the exit of Chemin aux Boeufs on lap 25 and fired himself over the bars.

RANDY DE PUNIET Le Mans has never been kind to Randy, but this year it was cruel.

NON-STARTERS

COLIN EDWARDS Recovering from the collarbone broken at Estoril. Replaced by Vermeulen.

GRAN PREMI APEROL
DE CATALUNYA

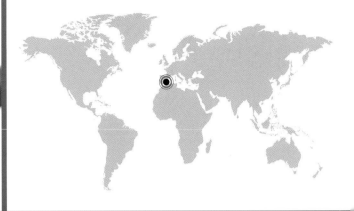

HAMMER TIME

Lorenzo made it two victories in a row after a fight with Pedrosa, and a satellite bike got on the rostrum

Finally, a weekend almost unaffected by the weather. It allowed a clear view of what was really going on in MotoGP, and the big picture was that Jorge Lorenzo and the factory Yamaha were the best combination on the grid. Jorge's fault-free riding and metronomic reliability mesh perfectly with the M1. The bike appears to have no major problems, certainly nothing on the level of the chatter afflicting the Hondas, and it doesn't even suffer from the top-speed deficiency we have become used to seeing. In the race, the joint top speed on the kilometre-long front straight was 208.8mph (336.0km/h); both Rossi's Ducati and Lorenzo's Yamaha hit that mark, and all four Yamahas had a higher top speed than the fastest Honda.

Historically, the top speed of the Yamahas has been traded for the bike's sweet handling and manoeuvrability: no longer. The Hondas, by contrast, continued to struggle with their tyres. The new-for-2012 softer construction rear slick seemed, perversely, to chatter more as it wore, and the new front, the only fitment from the next race onwards but available here alongside the original design, added instability on the brakes. Pedrosa and Stoner were, accordingly, the only factory men to race with the old-spec front tyre and the harder option rear. The contrast between both Repsol team riders and Lorenzo was stark. Jorge looked able to do exactly what he wanted with his bike. Dani's bike was making the sort of shapes not normally associated with the usually smooth Spaniard, and Casey simply never got the hard tyre to work on race day, maybe because Sunday was considerably cooler than Friday and Saturday. It was the first time since he joined the Repsol Honda team that he'd finished a race off the rostrum.

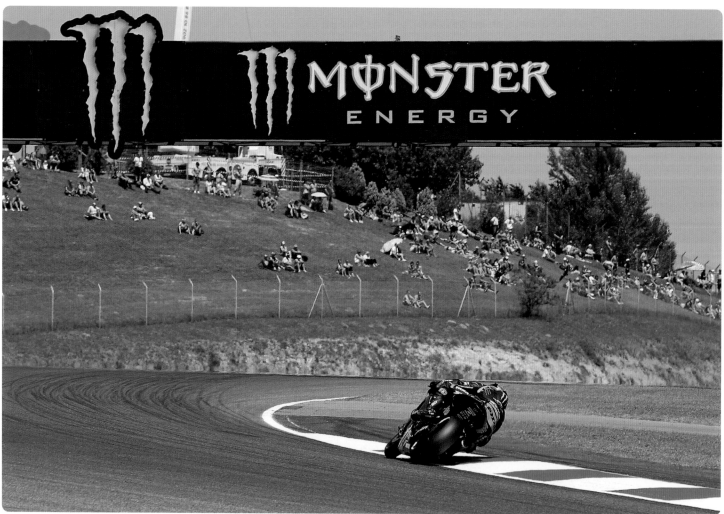

RIGHT Pedrosa leads the first lap with the luckless Spies in second

OPPOSITE Dani Pedrosa, his race engineer Mike Leitner and the men from head office try to work out what to do about Lorenzo

'JORGE IS HAVING THE PERFECT SEASON'
DANI PEDROSA

BELOW Andrea Dovizioso on his way to the rostrum, his first on a Yamaha

Stoner was held at bay in the closing stages by an increasingly impressive Andrea Dovizioso who, as usual, first had to deal with his team-mate. Dovi was promoted to third early in the race when Ben Spies ran on. The Texan had his best qualifying of the year and for the first two and a bit laps reminded us of what had been missing. He harassed holeshot man Pedrosa (who else?) until he became a touch frustrated and ran wide attempting a pass, hitting the edge of the track and toppling off at low speed. Ben remounted and took ten laps to catch and pass all the CRTs and, by the flag, he'd also passed two satellite bikes. It was a timely reminder of what he can do. In the first four GPs of the year his races consisted of inexplicably bad performances in Spain and Portugal, and weird problems in Qatar and France. Factor in that he'd never qualified lower than sixth and his results were even more perplexing. Hopefully his ride, if not his finishing position, marked a return to form.

Dovizioso seemed almost surprised by how well he was getting on with the Yamaha. He recovered from a major moment that delivered him into the claws

ABOVE Yonny Hernandez was always worth watching, even if he couldn't force the BQR into the points this time

BELOW Michele Pirro and Team Gresini's CRT bike, a World Superbike-spec Honda Fireblade engine in an FTR chassis; nearly but not quite competitive with the Aprilias

of Stoner and Crutchlow but, after playing with the mapping, coolly held on for the first rostrum finish by a satellite bike since Colin Edwards at Silverstone the previous season. Judging by the smile on his face, Andrea's insistence that he was still adapting his riding to the strengths of the Yamaha, and that there was more to come, rang true.

There was an even broader smile on the face of Alvaro Bautista. He'd had great pace all through practice but couldn't make any advances in qualifying. He was the only Honda rider to use the softer rear tyre, and despite adding a bad start to third-row qualifying made it up to Crutchlow's back wheel. It was Alvaro's third

sixth place of the year, but by far the closest he'd been to the top three. Fausto Gresini went so far as to suggest that with better qualifying Alvaro would have been a rostrum finisher.

There was some more cautious optimism at Ducati. Again, seventh position for Rossi wasn't something he was prepared to get excited about – 'this is our potential' – but the gap to the leaders and being half a second rather than a full second slower allowed him to point to some positives. Understeer was still the major complaint, leading to over-use of the rear to help turn the bike, which in turn left Valentino with very little grip with which to try and attack Bautista in the closing stages.

Lorenzo had no such problem. He took the lead with a tough pass at Turn 1 on lap seven only for Pedrosa to repay the compliment five laps later. The Honda led until lap 20 when Dani wheelied inadvertently and then went deep at the next corner trying to repair the damage. Lorenzo was alongside with the inside line and momentum. Pedrosa could only hang on for a lap before conceding over a second. Jorge had been observing and knew Dani was struggling. In fact it was even obvious from TV pictures that the Honda was a real handful both going into and coming out of corners. Lorenzo had stayed cool and waited for the right moment. Dani was philosophical; he was having a really good season with no injuries, but he really wanted to win again and his home race would have been a good place to start.

Meanwhile, the politicking over future technical regulations continued without any conclusion. The GP Commission was supposed to resolve such issues as a rev limit and a control ECU, but instead they decided to meet again at Assen.

CRUTCHLOW'S PROGRESS

To success-starved British fans, the start to Cal Crutchlow's season has been as manna from heaven. He ended 2011 on an up, with fourth place at Valencia after a troubled second half of the season. However, he began 2012 in record-breaking form. At Qatar he became the first British rider to start from the front row since James Toseland in 2008. His fourth-place finish in that race made him the first Brit to score back-to-back top-four finishes since Niall Mackenzie in 1989. When he finished fourth again, at Jerez, he achieved the longest sequence of top-four finishes by a British racer since Ron Haslam's four in a row in 1984.

Cal also set the fastest lap of the race at Jerez, the first time a Brit had done that in the 28 years since Barry Sheene's effort at the opening race of the 1984 season. Qualifying in the top five at the first five races of the year gave Cal the best sequence of grid positions since Rob McElnea in 1986, and his tally of 56 points is the best start to a season since Haslam in 1987.

His team-manager Hervé Poncharal described Crutchlow as 'a different person' from the rider of the previous season. His attitude to and body language around the other top riders had also changed. No more deference or forced jokes about paying to get in, Cal looked and acted like their equal. He rode that way, too. Not surprisingly, this attracted the interest of other factories. He has made no secret of the fact he felt he deserved a works bike, and that a works bike is what is needed to win a title. Cal regards it as a point of honour to answer a question honestly; even so, talking

openly about an approach from Ducati and how he felt his style would suit the Italian bike might be regarded as a little too forthright for Japanese corporate taste. None of which alters the fact that with the retirement of Casey Stoner at the end of the year, Cal Crutchlow was on the way to becoming one of the hottest properties on the rider market.

Circuit de Catalunya

RIGHT Stoner had a bad weekend; off the rostrum in a race he won last year

TYRE OPTIONS
FRONT SOFT (**S**) / MEDIUM (**M**) / HARD (**H**) / HARD-New Spec (**Hn**)
REAR MEDIUM (**M**) / HARD (**H**)

OFFICIAL TIMEKEEPER

GRAN PREMI APEROL DE CATALUNYA
CIRCUIT DE CATALUNYA

ROUND 5
June 3

RACE RESULTS

CIRCUIT LENGTH 2.937 miles
NO. OF LAPS 25
RACE DISTANCE 73.431 miles
WEATHER Dry, 27°C
TRACK TEMPERATURE 40°C
WINNER Jorge Lorenzo
FASTEST LAP 1m 42.642s, 103.018mph, Jorge Lorenzo
LAP RECORD 1m 42.358s, 103.304mph, Dani Pedrosa, 2008

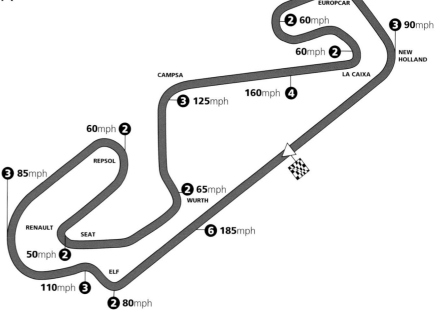

QUALIFYING

	Rider	Nationality	Team	Qualifying	Pole +	Gap
1	Stoner	AUS	Repsol Honda Team	1m 41.295s		
2	Lorenzo	SPA	Yamaha Factory Racing	1m 41.441s	0.146s	0.146s
3	Crutchlow	GBR	Monster Yamaha Tech 3	1m 41.548s	0.253s	0.107s
4	Spies	USA	Yamaha Factory Racing	1m 41.552s	0.257s	0.004s
5	Pedrosa	SPA	Repsol Honda Team	1m 41.656s	0.361s	0.104s
6	Dovizioso	ITA	Monster Yamaha Tech 3	1m 41.687s	0.392s	0.031s
7	Hayden	USA	Ducati Team	1m 42.029s	0.734s	0.342s
8	Bradl	GER	LCR Honda MotoGP	1m 42.065s	0.770s	0.036s
9	Rossi	ITA	Ducati Team	1m 42.175s	0.880s	0.110s
10	Bautista	SPA	San Carlo Honda Gresini	1m 42.356s	1.061s	0.181s
11	Barbera	SPA	Pramac Racing Team	1m 42.375s	1.080s	0.019s
12	Abraham	CZE	Cardion AB Motoracing	1m 43.266s	1.971s	0.891s
13	De Puniet	FRA	Power Electronics Aspar	1m 43.500s	2.205s	0.234s
14	Edwards	USA	NGM Mobile Forward Racing	1m 44.024s	2.729s	0.524s
15	Espargaro	SPA	Power Electronics Aspar	1m 44.041s	2.746s	0.017s
16	Pirro	ITA	San Carlo Honda Gresini	1m 44.356s	3.061s	0.315s
17	Ellison	GBR	Paul Bird Motorsport	1m 44.763s	3.468s	0.407s
18	Pasini	ITA	Speed Master	1m 44.764s	3.469s	0.001s
19	Hernandez	COL	Avintia Blusens	1m 44.833s	3.538s	0.069s
20	Petrucci	ITA	Came IodaRacing Project	1m 45.730s	4.435s	0.897s
21	Silva	SPA	Avintia Blusens	1m 45.962s	4.667s	0.232s

FINISHERS

1 JORGE LORENZO A cool and calculated victory. Stalked Pedrosa before pushing past on lap seven, was then repassed five laps later before taking advantage of a mistake by Dani to pounce and pull away on lap 20 of 25.

2 DANI PEDROSA Certainly made the tyres work better than his team-mate but was still having problems 'keeping the bike straight' both into and out of corners. Wasn't too happy with Lorenzo's first pass but admitted there was nothing he could do to prevent the winning move.

3 ANDREA DOVIZIOSO Really getting to grips with the Yamaha's strengths to put a satellite bike on the podium. Lost touch with the leaders after a big moment on lap 14, then coolly adjusted his electronics and held off Stoner and Crutchlow.

4 CASEY STONER Used the hard tyre, like his team-mate, but it 'never came in'. Dramatically closed the gap on Dovizioso in the final laps, but couldn't find a way past. His rostrum streak ended at 19, the third longest in history, not that Casey was bothered about such trivialities.

5 CAL CRUTCHLOW This was Cal's fourth top-five finish of the season, and again he was very close – less than 3.5s – behind the rostrum finishers. Content, though not happy, to be able to shadow Stoner on a track where the Brit had only raced once before.

6 ALVARO BAUTISTA Could have been a breakthrough if only he'd qualified better. Impressive pace all weekend and, despite a bad start, a good race. His fight with Rossi held him up and put him out of range of the leading group when he got to sixth; delighted to pass Valentino in the final right-hander.

7 VALENTINO ROSSI Vale's best dry-weather race so far this year. Happy that the lap-time deficit was nearer half a second than a whole one, but still handicapped by over-stressing the rear tyre in using it to help turn the bike. Had no rubber left when he wanted to attack Bautista in the final stages.

8 STEFAN BRADL Used the harder rear tyre and never got it working properly. No edge grip at the start so spun a lot. It's a measure of the rookie's progress that he

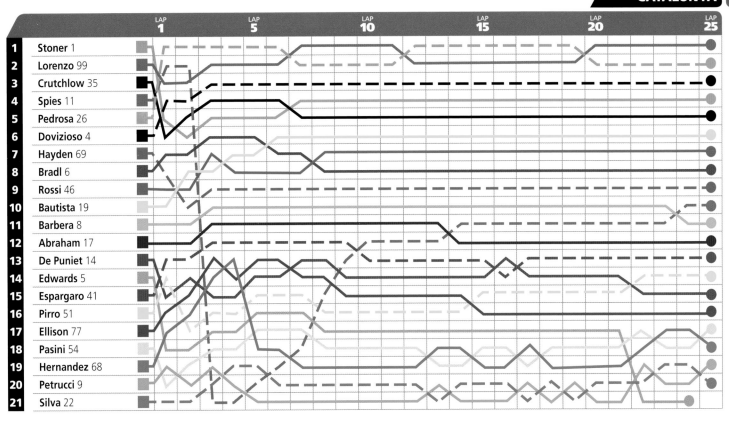

			LAP 1	LAP 5	LAP 10	LAP 15	LAP 20	LAP 25
1	Stoner	1						
2	Lorenzo	99						
3	Crutchlow	35						
4	Spies	11						
5	Pedrosa	26						
6	Dovizioso	4						
7	Hayden	69						
8	Bradl	6						
9	Rossi	46						
10	Bautista	19						
11	Barbera	8						
12	Abraham	17						
13	De Puniet	14						
14	Edwards	5						
15	Espargaro	41						
16	Pirro	51						
17	Ellison	77						
18	Pasini	54						
19	Hernandez	68						
20	Petrucci	9						
21	Silva	22						

RACE

	Rider	Motorcycle	Race Time	Time +	Fastest Lap	Av Speed	
1	Lorenzo	Yamaha	43m 07.681s		1m 42.642s	102.157mph	Hn/M
2	Pedrosa	Honda	43m 12.684s	5.003s	1m 42.667s	101.960mph	H/H
3	Dovizioso	Yamaha	43m 17.042s	9.361s	1m 42.808s	101.789mph	Hn/M
4	Stoner	Honda	43m 17.225s	9.544s	1m 42.816s	101.781mph	H/H
5	Crutchlow	Yamaha	43m 20.187s	12.506s	1m 42.770s	101.666mph	Hn/M
6	Bautista	Honda	43m 21.629s	13.948s	1m 42.852s	101.609mph	Hn/M
7	Rossi	Ducati	43m 25.236s	17.555s	1m 43.198s	101.469mph	Hn/M
8	Bradl	Honda	43m 31.159s	23.478s	1m 43.048s	101.238mph	Hn/H
9	Hayden	Ducati	43m 38.091s	30.410s	1m 43.215s	100.970mph	Hn/M
10	Spies	Yamaha	43m 40.578s	32.897s	1m 43.037s	100.875mph	Hn/M
11	Barbera	Ducati	43m 43.825s	36.144s	1m 43.704s	100.750mph	Hn/M
12	Abraham	Ducati	44m 03.910s	56.229s	1m 44.528s	99.984mph	H/H
13	Espargaro	Art	44m 15.735s	1m 08.054s	1m 45.287s	99.539mph	H/M
14	Pirro	FTR	44m 16.456s	1m 08.775s	1m 45.471s	99.512mph	Hn/M
15	De Puniet	Art	44m 18.164s	1m 10.483s	1m 45.269s	99.448mph	H/H
16	Ellison	Art	44m 20.771s	1m 13.090s	1m 45.241s	99.350mph	Hn/M
17	Pasini	Art	44m 28.584s	1m 20.903s	1m 45.408s	99.060mph	H/M
18	Hernandez	BQR	44m 28.916s	1m 21.235s	1m 45.092s	99.047mph	Hn/M
19	Petrucci	Ioda	44m 48.888s	1m 41.207s	1m 46.s	98.311mph	Hn/M
20	Silva	BQR	44m 49.569s	1m 41.888s	1m 45.998s	98.287mph	Hn/M
NF	Edwards	Suter	44m 55.263s	1 lap	1m 45.427s	94.156mph	Hn/M

CHAMPIONSHIP

	Rider	Team	Points
1	Lorenzo	Yamaha Factory Racing	115
2	Stoner	Repsol Honda Team	95
3	Pedrosa	Repsol Honda Team	85
4	Dovizioso	Monster Yamaha Tech 3	60
5	Crutchlow	Monster Yamaha Tech 3	56
6	Rossi	Ducati Team	51
7	Bautista	San Carlo Honda Gresini	45
8	Bradl	LCR Honda MotoGP	43
9	Hayden	Ducati Team	40
10	Barbera	Pramac Racing Team	31
11	Spies	Yamaha Factory Racing	24
12	Espargaro	Power Electronics Aspar	15
13	De Puniet	Power Electronics Aspar	7
14	Pasini	Speed Master	6
15	Pirro	San Carlo Honda Gresini	6
16	Ellison	Paul Bird Motorsport	5
17	Abraham	Cardion AB Motoracing	4
18	Edwards	NGM Mobile Forward Racing	4
19	Petrucci	Came IodaRacing Project	4
20	Hernandez	Avintia Blusens	3
21	Silva	Avintia Blusens	1

regarded eighth place at one of his favourite tracks as a bad day at the office.

9 NICKY HAYDEN Compromised by numbness in his right hand that came on mid-race and meant he couldn't feel the brake lever at all. Took to shaking his fingers on the straight to get some feeling back and managed to get to the flag.

10 BEN SPIES Harassed Pedrosa for the first two laps but lost patience and ran on trying a pass at the start of lap three. Tipped off, remounted and charged through the field. Not a great result, but it looked more like the old Spies on track.

11 HECTOR BARBERA Never got to grips with Sunday's conditions. Forced to switch to a map that 'took power from my

bike' and had a lonely race until he was caught by Spies three laps from home.

12 KAREL ABRAHAM Very relieved to score his first points of the year, but still unhappy with the Ducati, the main problem being rear grip. Thought about trying to pass Barbera, but settled for a safe 12th.

13 ALEIX ESPARGARO Went with the softer rear tyre, which proved to be the right decision. Top CRT after really picking up the pace mid-race.

14 MICHELE PIRRO Got a good start but couldn't push early on – both as usual. Still managed to split the Aspar Aprilias and was less than three-quarters of a second behind Espargaro at the finish. The Gresini team was delighted.

15 RANDY DE PUNIET Raced with the harder rear tyre, unlike his team-mate, but never had the feel he'd experienced in the much warmer practice sessions.

16 JAMES ELLISON Only five seconds behind the first CRT bike, but out of the points in a race everyone finished. Pleased with his own race, but a gearbox problem had him missing gears on the straight. That, and a sore leg from a warm-up crash, prevented him beating de Puniet for the last point.

17 MATTIA PASINI Lost a lot of time on the first lap, then struggled to get past Petrucci and Silva. Decided to run his own pace and treat the race as a test session.

18 YONNY HERNANDEZ Like his team-mate, Yonny never found a good set-up and was caught on the last lap by the slow-starting Pasini.

19 DANILO PETRUCCI Lots of problems with traction, and with the front when he pushed hard, but was able to pass Silva on the last lap.

20 IVAN SILVA Chatter was the problem in qualifying, but a lack of rear grip in the race led to some spectacular slides. Not the result Ivan wished for at his home race.

NON-FINISHERS

COLIN EDWARDS Nothing but trouble all weekend, culminating in the engine stopping on the last lap and Colin finishing the race by rolling down pit lane.

HERTZ BRITISH
GRAND PRIX

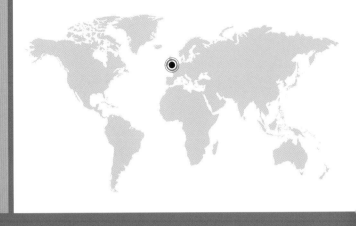

SUNSHINE
SUPERMAN

Lorenzo managed his tyres better than the rest to win a thrilling dice with Stoner and increase his championship lead

It takes quite a lot to get Silverstone buzzing. It's a very big track, the longest of the year, and 50,000 spectators can seem lost in the giant grandstands that seem even more remote from the action than at the new Hermann Tilke-designed circuits. As in the previous two years, since the British GP moved back to Northamptonshire, the weather wasn't kind in the run-up to the event. In fact it was horrible, and the forecast was far from optimistic. But, to the great relief of organisers and spectators alike, race day was the best of the weekend by a distance. Local riders rewarded the 66,000 who turned out with great sport in all three classes – Scott Redding's fighting second place in Moto2 warmed the crowd up nicely for the MotoGP boys, and Cal Crutchlow made their day with an heroic charge from the back of the grid. The noise the crowd made reminded all those of a certain age of the old days at Silverstone, the days of two-strokes, Kenny Roberts and Barry Sheene, and so did the quality of the racing. Silverstone's size may make it feel less intimate than Donington Park, but the upside is the sort of close-quarters high-speed racing that takes the breath away.

Things didn't look good on Saturday morning, however. Moto3 championship leader Sandro Cortese reported that the wind was so strong he couldn't pull top gear down the Hangar Straight. Then Cal Crutchlow crashed in free practice and was taken to hospital for a scan on his left ankle. When he didn't return for qualifying things looked bleak. Alvaro Bautista didn't care; he was on pole for the first time in his career and was keen to point out it was deserved. Sure, rain had affected the last few minutes of the session, but everyone knew the weather was coming and made sure

'WHEN I CAUGHT CASEY WE HAD A WONDERFUL FIGHT'
JORGE LORENZO

they set a good time early on. Besides, said Alvaro, he had a soft tyre left and would have gone out again.

Thankfully, race day dawned bright and without the howling winds that had afflicted Friday and Saturday, and the fans began to flood in. Crutchlow managed to persuade the medical officer he was fit to race, but he had to run and go up on tiptoes repeatedly to convince

him. Once he was out of the medical centre Cal tweeted that he had broken and dislocated the ankle. Everyone assumed that the best he would be able to manage was finishing last of the prototypes.

The other riders were worrying about their tyres. All the front tyres in the allocation were, for the first time, the new, softer carcass design. Casey Stoner and Dani Pedrosa were the only ones against adopting them and they continued to find problems with chatter. The choice of rear tyre was occupying everyone too. If temperatures had continued rising then they would all have gone with the harder option, but a sprinkling of rain on the sighting lap and a sudden drop in track temperature to just over 20°C saw all the riders, with the notable exception of Valentino Rossi, swapping to the softer rubber. What they hadn't bargained for was the track temperature then going up 8°, thus putting the softer tyres rather close to the edge of their performance envelope. Bridgestone brought asymmetric dual-compound tyres to Silverstone. Both choices use their medium tread compound on the right side while the left side uses either the soft or ultra-soft version. In other words, everyone bar Rossi started the race with the softest rubber in the whole spectrum on the left shoulder of their rear slicks.

This may account for some of the problems the fast guys ran into. Ben Spies, the early leader, reported a serious drop-off of grip in his rear tyre after five laps, as did Stoner. After the race he was vehement in his opinion that the tyre had been faulty. All of the prototypes, except walking wounded Crutchlow, set their fastest lap the second or third time round, proving that Bridgestone's objective of quick warm-up

ABOVE Cal Crutchlow missed practice having his injured ankle scanned but made it to the back of the grid on race day

OPPOSITE TOP Lorenzo and Stoner fought an enthralling battle for the win

OPPOSITE Dani Pedrosa attacked his team mate on the last lap but decided that third was a better idea than two Repsol Hondas on the floor

ABOVE Despite the awful weather on Friday and Saturday, a good crowd turned up on race day and made some noise for Cal Crutchlow

OPPOSITE The Aspar Aprilia riders Espargaro and de Puniet fouht over the top CRT placing to the final corner

BELOW Not a good day for Valentino Rossi; lots of chatter on the harder tyre

had certainly been achieved with the new-generation construction. As for degradation, Bridgestone pointed to the way riders were able to increase their pace late in the race, as Stoner did for a couple of laps, proving that levels of grip were predictable.

Casey certainly had to use tight lines, going deep on the brakes, then getting the bike on the centre of the tyre to fire it out of the corner in order to counter Jorge when the Spaniard wore down Stoner's lead. Lorenzo responded with big, sweeping outside lines. The contrast was wonderful to watch and illustrated the differing strengths of two very evenly matched motorcycles as they went side by side through two of Silverstone's high-speed S-bends. That was the move

that put Jorge to the front at half-distance and left Casey seething about his tyres.

Much as the crowd admired the leading pair, their focus was on Crutchlow. Many thought he would pull in after a couple of laps. Instead, he ripped through the CRT bikes in two laps, took four more to get past Rossi, and in four more was up to seventh. A lap from home he caught Nicky Hayden, meaning Cal had passed all four Ducatis and the satellite Honda of Stefan Bradl. His team-mate Andrea Dovizioso also helped by crashing, so the British rider took fourth place in the championship back off him. Cal couldn't have been a bigger hero if he'd finished on the rostrum. Which, if he'd avoided injury in what was an in-lap crash, is where he surely could have been.

JORGE, MARC AND THE ROOKIE RULE

With the news breaking after Catalunya that Jorge Lorenzo had re-signed with Yamaha for the 2013 and '14 seasons there were some serious moves in the rider market at Silverstone. Factor in Stoner's decision to retire and Honda found themselves in a tricky position. They had tried to interest Lorenzo but failed, so they looked to his heir apparent, Marc Marquez. However, the Rookie Rule requires that new MotoGP riders must do a season with a satellite team before going to a factory squad. Hence Ben Spies's first year was with Tech 3.

Those were the days when there were four satellite Hondas, plus two Yamahas and three Ducatis run by satellite squads. In 2013 there will be two each from Honda and Yamaha and one, if any, from Ducati. If the rule were to stand Marquez would have to go to either LCR or Gresini and his career-long sponsorship by Repsol would clash with those teams' well-established relationships with Elf and Castrol, respectively. Thus there is a situation where a rule designed to help satellite teams would effectively lose them a sponsor – hardly helpful. And that's before considering that Marquez would probably come with his own crew.

Dorna CEO Carmelo Ezpeleta was originally adamant that the rule would not be rescinded. He had been taking a hard line with the factories over MotoGP technical regulations, but at Silverstone he conceded that it might no longer be useful. Ezpeleta therefore proposed to the GP Commission that the rule be abolished. As IRTA, the teams' association, MSMA, the manufacturers' body, and the FIM all supported the change, the abolition of the Rookie Rule was now a formality.

It could also be said that it ensured Marc Marquez would be in the Repsol Honda team in 2013.

BRIDGESTONE

TYRE OPTIONS
FRONT SOFT (S) / MEDIUM (M)
REAR MEDIUM-SOFT (MS) / MEDIUM (M)

OFFICIAL TIMEKEEPER

HERTZ BRITISH GRAND PRIX
SILVERSTONE
ROUND 6
June 17

RACE RESULTS

CIRCUIT LENGTH 3.666 miles
NO. OF LAPS 20
RACE DISTANCE 73.322 miles
WEATHER Dry, 15°C
TRACK TEMPERATURE 23°C
WINNER Jorge Lorenzo
FASTEST LAP 2m 02.888s, 107.398mph, Jorge Lorenzo (Record)
PREVIOUS LAP RECORD 2m 03.526s, 105.874mph, Jorge Lorenzo, 2010

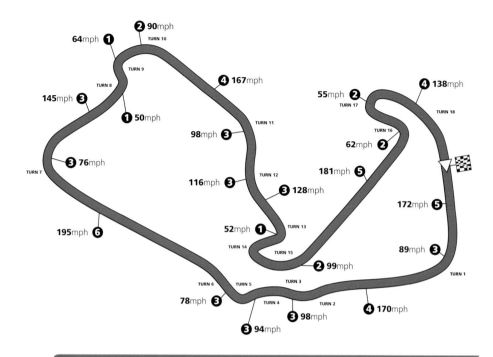

QUALIFYING

	Rider	Nationality	Team	Qualifying	Pole +	Gap
1	Bautista	SPA	San Carlo Honda Gresini	2m 03.303s		
2	Spies	USA	Yamaha Factory Racing	2m 03.409s	0.106s	0.106s
3	Stoner	AUS	Repsol Honda Team	2m 03.423s	0.120s	0.014s
4	Lorenzo	SPA	Yamaha Factory Racing	2m 03.763s	0.460s	0.340s
5	Pedrosa	SPA	Repsol Honda Team	2m 03.835s	0.532s	0.072s
6	Barbera	SPA	Pramac Racing Team	2m 03.876s	0.573s	0.041s
7	Hayden	USA	Ducati Team	2m 04.162s	0.859s	0.286s
8	Dovizioso	ITA	Monster Yamaha Tech 3	2m 04.304s	1.001s	0.142s
9	Bradl	GER	LCR Honda MotoGP	2m 05.035s	1.732s	0.731s
10	Rossi	ITA	Ducati Team	2m 05.416s	2.113s	0.381s
11	Espargaro	SPA	Power Electronics Aspar	2m 06.283s	2.980s	0.867s
12	De Puniet	SPA	Power Electronics Aspar	2m 06.303s	3.000s	0.020s
13	Hernandez	COL	Avintia Blusens	2m 06.814s	3.511s	0.511s
14	Pirro	ITA	San Carlo Honda Gresini	2m 07.016s	3.713s	0.202s
15	Edwards	USA	NGM Mobile Forward Racing	2m 07.376s	4.073s	0.360s
16	Pasini	ITA	Speed Master	2m 07.511s	4.208s	0.135s
17	Ellison	GBR	Paul Bird Motorsport	2m 08.228s	4.925s	0.717s
18	Petrucci	ITA	Came IodaRacing Project	2m 08.686s	5.383s	0.458s
19	Silva	SPA	Avintia Blusens	2m 10.092s	6.789s	1.406s
NF	Abraham	CZE	Cardion AB Motoracing			
NF	Crutchlow	GBR	Monster Yamaha Tech 3			

FINISHERS

1 JORGE LORENZO Another beautifully judged win. Bided his time catching and passing Stoner after dropping to fifth off the start. Nearly crashed four laps from the flag but made it three in a row and extended his championship lead to 25 points.

2 CASEY STONER Blamed an almost instant loss in edge grip on the left side of the rear tyre for not being able to hold off Lorenzo. Led early on but knew that the others, specifically the Yamahas, had better race pace.

3 DANI PEDROSA Happy to be on the podium – had struggled on his only previous appearance here – but had to stay calm after, for once, a bad start and being as low as seventh. Knew he couldn't catch Jorge, had a couple of digs at Casey and was shaping for another at the last chicane, but had a vision of two Repsol Hondas on the ground.

4 ALVARO BAUTISTA His first pole position backed up when he ran with the leaders for the entire race. The post-Catalunya tests helped with settings for the Showa forks and he took advantage, but decided not to take risks, preferring to finish just five seconds behind the winner rather than attack for third place.

5 BEN SPIES Led the first four laps after a good practice and qualifying, then made a small mistake and let Stoner through. Almost instantly, he ran into rear grip problems bad enough to put a second on his lap times. After that, it was damage limitation.

6 CAL CRUTCHLOW An heroic ride from the back of the grid after an ankle injury meant he missed qualifying and threatened to put him out of the race. Passed all the CRTs in two laps, then all the Ducatis and Bradl's Honda.

7 NICKY HAYDEN One of many who swapped to the softer rear on the grid, but the weather didn't co-operate. The track got hotter and the Ducati, as expected, ran out of rubber quicker than the rest. The positives were he was closer to the winner than at any time so far this year.

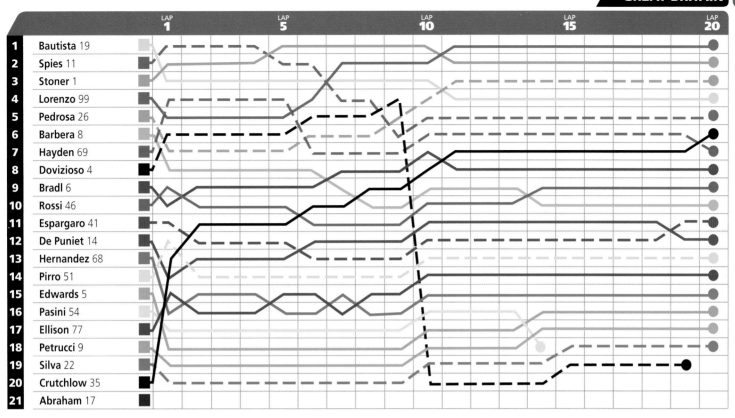

	Rider		LAP 1	LAP 5	LAP 10	LAP 15	LAP 20
1	Bautista	19					
2	Spies	11					
3	Stoner	1					
4	Lorenzo	99					
5	Pedrosa	26					
6	Barbera	8					
7	Hayden	69					
8	Dovizioso	4					
9	Bradl	6					
10	Rossi	46					
11	Espargaro	41					
12	De Puniet	14					
13	Hernandez	68					
14	Pirro	51					
15	Edwards	5					
16	Pasini	54					
17	Ellison	77					
18	Petrucci	9					
19	Silva	22					
20	Crutchlow	35					
21	Abraham	17					

RACE

	Rider	Motorcycle	Race Time	Time +	Fastest Lap	Av Speed	
1	Lorenzo	Yamaha	41m 16.429s		2m 02.888s	106.588mph	M/MS
2	Stoner	Honda	41m 19.742s	3.000s	2m 02.975s	106.446mph	S/MS
3	Pedrosa	Honda	41m 20.028s	3.000s	2m 02.980s	106.433mph	M/MS
4	Bautista	Honda	41m 21.625s	5.000s	2m 03.069s	106.365mph	M/MS
5	Spies	Yamaha	41m 27.960s	11.000s	2m 02.909s	106.094mph	M/MS
6	Crutchlow	Yamaha	41m 31.541s	15.000s	2m 03.500s	105.941mph	M/MS
7	Hayden	Ducati	41m 31.956s	15.000s	2m 02.922s	105.924mph	M/MS
8	Bradl	Honda	41m 38.950s	22.000s	2m 03.907s	105.628mph	M/MS
9	Rossi	Ducati	41m 52.567s	36.000s	2m 04.393s	105.055mph	M/M
10	Barbera	Ducati	41m 57.757s	41.000s	2m 03.291s	104.838mph	M/MS
11	Espargaro	Art	42m 19.586s	1m 03.000s	2m 05.690s	103.937mph	S/MS
12	De Puniet	Art	42m 19.872s	1m 03.000s	2m 05.260s	103.926mph	S/MS
13	Pirro	FTR	42m 23.719s	1m 07.000s	2m 05.777s	103.768mph	M/MS
14	Ellison	Art	42m 31.211s	1m 14.000s	2m 06.678s	103.464mph	M/MS
15	Hernandez	BQR	42m 31.537s	1m 15.000s	2m 06.654s	103.450mph	M/MS
16	Edwards	Suter	42m 46.328s	1m 29.000s	2m 06.976s	102.854mph	M/MS
17	Petrucci	Ioda	42m 56.731s	1m 40.000s	2m 07.548s	102.439mph	S/MS
18	Silva	BQR	43m 08.528s	1m 52.000s	2m 07.738s	101.972mph	S/MS
19	Dovizioso	Yamaha	41m 51.265s	1 lap	2m 02.922s	99.854mph	M/MS
NF	Pasini	Art	30m 09.876s	6 laps	2m 06.594s	102.090mph	S/MS

CHAMPIONSHIP

	Rider	Team	Points
1	Lorenzo	Yamaha Factory Racing	140
2	Stoner	Repsol Honda Team	115
3	Pedrosa	Repsol Honda Team	101
4	Crutchlow	Monster Yamaha Tech 3	66
5	Dovizioso	Monster Yamaha Tech 3	60
6	Rossi	Ducati Team	58
7	Bautista	San Carlo Honda Gresini	58
8	Bradl	LCR Honda MotoGP	51
9	Hayden	Ducati Team	49
10	Barbera	Pramac Racing Team	37
11	Spies	Yamaha Factory Racing	35
12	Espargaro	Power Electronics Aspar	20
13	De Puniet	Power Electronics Aspar	11
14	Pirro	San Carlo Honda Gresini	9
15	Ellison	Paul Bird Motorsport	7
16	Pasini	Speed Master	6
17	Abraham	Cardion AB Motoracing	4
18	Edwards	NGM Mobile Forward Racing	4
19	Petrucci	Came IodaRacing Project	4
20	Hernandez	Avintia Blusens	4
21	Silva	Avintia Blusens	1

8 STEFAN BRADL Damaged the ring finger on his left hand in a crash in FP3 – it made using the clutch difficult and he had a bad start. Couldn't find his rhythm early on and made another mistake when Crutchlow came past.

9 VALENTINO ROSSI The only rider to stick with the harder tyre. Suffered from chatter mid-corner as, like the previous year, he found Silverstone difficult for his machine. Declared that the 'true Ducati today was that of Nicky'.

10 HECTOR BARBERA Good qualifying but a disappointing race. Rapid rear tyre deterioration handicapped him on corner entry and restricted his top speed.

11 ALEIX ESPARGARO Led the CRTs early on but couldn't stay with the satellite bikes on the straights. Happy to follow when de Puniet came past, until two laps from the flag when he took advantage of his team-mate's problems. A great day for the Espargaro brothers as this was his best result so far and Pol won the Moto2 race.

12 RANDY DE PUNIET Annoyed to lose out to his team-mate, having led their dice until two laps from home. Blamed this on not getting a good chassis set-up, which in turn led to grip problems with the rear tyre.

13 MICHELE PIRRO Made more progress with the bike and finished only four seconds behind Aspar's Aprilias. Getting close to his, and the team's, ambition of being top CRT bike.

14 JAMES ELLISON Made more progress with the electronics in the battle against chatter, but not helped by a heavy crash in morning warm-up. Got the better of a bit of fairing-bashing with Hernandez to take two points.

15 YONNY HERNANDEZ Had a good fight with Ellison but was beaten for the last point on the last lap.

16 COLIN EDWARDS Although faster in the race than in qualifying, problems getting the bike to turn kept Colin at the back of the CRT fight. Reported that it felt too rigid and stiff so he couldn't relax. Still a second a lap off the best CRT.

17 DANILO PETRUCCI Had an engine problem at the end of the race but as his top speed was on average 25mph (40km/h) slower than the fastest bike (Pedrosa's Honda) he was losing a second on the straights anyway. His best lap was over four seconds down on the top men.

18 IVAN SILVA Tested a new fork but reverted to the Barcelona setting in warm-up. It looked like an improvement, but lack of traction put him out of contention for a points finish.

19 ANDREA DOVIZIOSO Had just passed Pedrosa when he crashed at Copse. Pitted to sort out the throttle and rejoined the race. Had been running in fourth and felt he would have been able to challenge Stoner for second place.

IVECO TT ASSEN

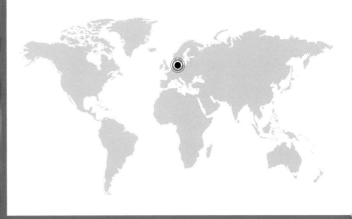

TROUBLE AND STRIFE

Stoner led a Honda one-two after Lorenzo was taken out at the first turn and Spies lost out with tyre troubles late on

Jorge Lorenzo sat on the front row at Assen with three wins in a row behind him and a comfortable 25-point lead in the championship. He said after qualifying that he found it 'really easy to make constant pace'. The two Hondas in front of him on the grid didn't bother him, because he knew he had the pace to win. Seconds after the lights went out he was in the gravel at Turn 1, contemplating a very sore ankle and the loss of a nearly new motor.

The culprit was Alvaro Bautista, who'd barrelled down the inside from the third row, gone into the corner impossibly hot and lost the front on the brakes. His Honda scooped up Lorenzo and the pair ended up in the gravel trap, with the Yamaha's throttle jammed open. The clouds of smoke and steam announced that one of Jorge's allocation of six motors for the season had just expired. It was his third engine, only brought into play the day before the race. The implications were clear. It would take some very careful management to get through the season without resorting to a seventh motor, thus incurring the penalty of starting from pit lane. Add that to the fact that Lorenzo's points advantage was wiped out by Stoner's victory and the man who'd been starting to look like an odds-on favourite for the title suddenly found himself back at square one.

Not that it had been easy for Stoner to pick up the pieces. He had a massive crash in the third free practice session, highsiding in the ultra-fast left in the run back to the final chicane. He said it was one of the biggest and certainly the most painful crashes of his career. In qualifying, though, he came out after a rain break with only a few minutes left on the clock,

'NOW WE ARE AT ZERO WITH CASEY SO WE BEGIN AGAIN'
JORGE LORENZO

having been well off the pace, and hammered in a lap that made you hold your breath. It put him half a second ahead of the rest and a lot of that was made up through the last sector. The phrase 'awe inspiring' is constantly overused, but it actually applies to this lap. And it applies in spades to that last sector. It's not a lap anyone who actually saw it is likely to forget in a hurry.

Casey merely said he was mildly surprised to have that sort of speed after all the problems. And they weren't over, because he'd managed to bang the top of his knee really badly but wouldn't take any painkillers until just before the race. He woke up aching all over on Saturday morning. It was, he said, hard to find the motivation to get out of bed; but he had a plan, and it worked.

Stoner shadowed Dani Pedrosa, making his move on lap 17 and dropping his team-mate immediately. Dani said he'd expended too much energy leading and reckoned Casey would have seen him 'getting lazy' because the bike was starting to feel heavy in the corners. The Aussie had also waited because he was on the softer tyre and didn't want to suffer in the closing stages. When Pedrosa's pace dropped fractionally there were only nine laps to go – and

THIS PAGE Lorenzo's first-corner disaster: he is scooped up by Bautista's Honda and the pair end up in the gravel trap where the Yamaha's engine revs itself to destruction

OPPOSITE It looked as if Ben Spies was at last going to have a trouble-free race and a rostrum finish, but tyre trouble relegated him to fourth

ABOVE Pirro harried the Power Electronics Aprilias and finished second CRT

OPPOSITE Dani Pedrosa played second fiddle to his team mate Stoner all weekend

BELOW Dovizioso took advantage of Spies' problem for his second rostrum of the year

Stoner knew he wouldn't suffer too much degradation in that distance so he pushed. He was suitably sporting in his post-race comments, saying: 'Nobody wants to take points over a competitor in this manner.'

Three riders did have serious tyre problems, however: Valentino Rossi, Ben Spies and Hector Barbera. Valentino suddenly dropped back from his group dice and pitted; his rear Bridgestone had shed chunks of tread rubber. Ben had a similar problem two laps from home but kept going, though in fear of imminent disaster. He lost third to Andrea Dovizioso. Barbera also dropped back suddenly on the last lap and crossed the line pointing at his rear tyre. Bridgestone

immediately said there were no obvious problems but sent the offending tyres back to their technical centre in Japan. The ensuing report found that there hadn't been a design failure; rather, the tyres had been taken to the edge of their performance envelope and overheated. It was particularly bad luck for Spies, who'd looked to have dealt with the challenge of Dovizioso and been on course for his first rostrum of the year.

Tyres weren't the only thing Rossi was upset about. His relationship with Ducati seemed to have hit another low after the post-Barcelona test. There was talk of a major row at Catalunya and Valentino had again used Italian TV to criticise the speed of the factory's response, pointing out that Honda had brought a new chassis to Assen whereas he was still making do with the one on which he'd started the season. It was not possible, said Vale, to cure the problems with settings: 'We need a plan.'

Yet again the GP Commission postponed the big decisions on future technical regulations, but there was one big surprise. Effective immediately, the bore and stroke dimensions of every manufacturers' MotoGP engines were frozen until the end of 2014. The next time the issue that has preoccupied the whole paddock would be discussed would be at Brno, after the summer break. Race Direction lost no time, though, in penalising Bautista for his first-corner indiscretion. He would be demoted to the back of the grid at the next race, a penalty the majority of the paddock thought suited the crime, although Jorge Lorenzo took a little while to come round to that point of view.

A SHOULDER TO CRY ON?

Bridgestone got their sums wrong. Post-race research suggested a combination of circumstances led to the rubber overheating. Elevated track temperature compared to last year was key. A slight change in layout led to unexpectedly faster laps, while known factors like the extra torque of the new 1,000cc bikes should have been taken into account. The allocated tyres were actually a grade softer than in 2011, a decision prompted by the riders via the Safety Commission, but the decision on what tyres to bring to each race is, of course, Bridgestone's responsibility.

To understand the failure it's necessary to know how tyres are constructed. Whatever the grade, all are built on a common carcass, which then has the tread rubber applied on top – imagine a giant thin-walled tube of rubber sliced up and applied to the carcass.

Overheating comes from working the tyre's carcass. Visualise the overlapping plies in the carcass forming hundreds of little parallelograms, and what happens to them when the tyre is 'squished' into the tarmac under power. It is the internal friction generated by this movement that heats up the body of the tyre. One counter-intuitive fact is that spinning the rear does not, on its own, lead to this sort of problem.

Bridgestone had access to the team's data afterwards and noted that Hayden was spinning the rear much more than Rossi, yet Nicky didn't run into problems. Spinning does, of course, heat up the tyre and the heat generated can and does have an effect, but only on the surface, which tends to

get left on the track in sweeping black lines. Effectively, the heat generated by spinning is easily shed whereas the deep heat generated in the carcass is not.

Bridgestone said that the new design for 2012, with a more flexible carcass for quicker warm-up, was not a contributing factor, and none of the affected tyres lost any internal pressure. Sudden deflation usually has far nastier consequences for the rider than throwing chunks of tread.

How can Bridgestone prevent this happening again? They already use a design feature called Cap & Base on tracks that generate most heat, such as Phillip Island – an extra layer of rubber on top of the carcass acts as a sink, conducting excess heat away from the tyre's edge and distributing it more evenly. Bridgestone shipped tyres with Cap & Base construction to Mugello as a way of reassuring the riders, and will almost certainly use them at Assen next year.

BRIDGESTONE
TYRE OPTIONS
FRONT SOFT (**S**) / MEDIUM (**M**)
REAR MEDIUM-SOFT (**MS**) / MEDIUM (**M**)

OFFICIAL TIMEKEEPER

RACE RESULTS

CIRCUIT LENGTH 2.822 miles
NO. OF LAPS 26
RACE DISTANCE 73.379 miles
WEATHER Dry, 23°C
TRACK TEMPERATURE 37°C
WINNER Casey Stoner
FASTEST LAP 1m 34.548s,
107.460mph, Dani Pedrosa (Record)
PREVIOUS LAP RECORD 1m 35.240s,
106.680mph, Ben Spies, 2011

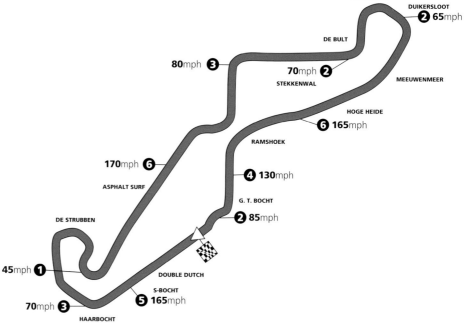

QUALIFYING

	Rider	Nationality	Team	Qualifying	Pole +	Gap
1	Stoner	AUS	Repsol Honda Team	1m 33.713s		
2	Pedrosa	SPA	Repsol Honda Team	1m 33.828s	0.115s	0.115s
3	Lorenzo	SPA	Yamaha Factory Racing	1m 34.001s	0.288s	0.173s
4	Bradl	GER	LCR Honda MotoGP	1m 34.035s	0.322s	0.034s
5	Crutchlow	GBR	Monster Yamaha Tech 3	1m 34.486s	0.773s	0.451s
6	Spies	USA	Yamaha Factory Racing	1m 34.644s	0.931s	0.158s
7	Dovizioso	ITA	Monster Yamaha Tech 3	1m 34.698s	0.985s	0.054s
8	Bautista	SPA	San Carlo Honda Gresini	1m 34.722s	1.009s	0.024s
9	Hayden	USA	Ducati Team	1m 34.751s	1.038s	0.029s
10	Rossi	ITA	Ducati Team	1m 35.057s	1.344s	0.306s
11	Barbera	SPA	Pramac Racing Team	1m 35.289s	1.576s	0.232s
12	De Puniet	FRA	Power Electronics Aspar	1m 35.830s	2.117s	0.541s
13	Espargaro	SPA	Power Electronics Aspar	1m 36.007s	2.294s	0.177s
14	Pirro	ITA	San Carlo Honda Gresini	1m 36.647s	2.934s	0.640s
15	Pasini	ITA	Speed Master	1m 36.943s	3.230s	0.296s
16	Petrucci	ITA	Came IodaRacing Project	1m 36.967s	3.254s	0.024s
17	Abraham	CZE	Cardion AB Motoracing	1m 37.110s	3.397s	0.143s
18	Hernandez	COL	Avintia Blusens	1m 37.191s	3.478s	0.081s
19	Ellison	GBR	Paul Bird Motorsport	1m 37.281s	3.568s	0.090s
20	Silva	SPA	Avintia Blusens	1m 37.554s	3.841s	0.273s
21	Edwards	USA	NGM Mobile Forward Racing	1m 38.305s	4.592s	0.751s

FINISHERS

1 CASEY STONER A superbly crafted win took Casey back to the top of the table, level on points with Lorenzo. Following is always easier than leading – after his massive qualifying crash left him bruised and battered he conserved his energy by shadowing his team-mate and pouncing when he saw Dani begin to tire.

2 DANI PEDROSA Tried everything he could, leading for 16 of the 26 laps, setting fastest lap the 15th time round, but couldn't break his team-mate. Once Casey drove past, Dani couldn't muster the stamina to fight back.

3 ANDREA DOVIZIOSO Second rostrum of the year. Diced with Spies for nearly the

whole race, making the decisive overtake on the last lap just as Ben ran into tyre trouble. Much more comfortable on this track, with the Yamaha, than he ever was on the Honda.

4 BEN SPIES Qualified well again, this time looking as if he was going to convert a good grid position into a rostrum finish. Diced for third with Dovi throughout the race but had to concede the position very late on when his rear tyre lost some tread rubber.

5 CAL CRUTCHLOW Caught up in the first-corner crash, which put him plumb last. Made it on to the back of the three Ducatis, lost the front, got back to them again and then passed them – still with a broken ankle.

6 NICKY HAYDEN Grafted away as usual to be top Ducati in qualifying and the race. Gave himself work to do by running on at the chicane on lap one but got back to the group and was the only Ducati not to hit tyre trouble.

7 HECTOR BARBERA Very happy with his race and his best finish at Assen. Ran with the factory Ducatis and Crutchlow for most of the time, but five laps from home went to pass Cal and then suffered a sudden problem with his rear tyre and dropped off the pace.

8 RANDY DE PUNIET The best result by a CRT rider so far. Reckoned he deserved the luck that had deserted him in previous races. Held off Pirro and closed right up on his team-mate in the points table.

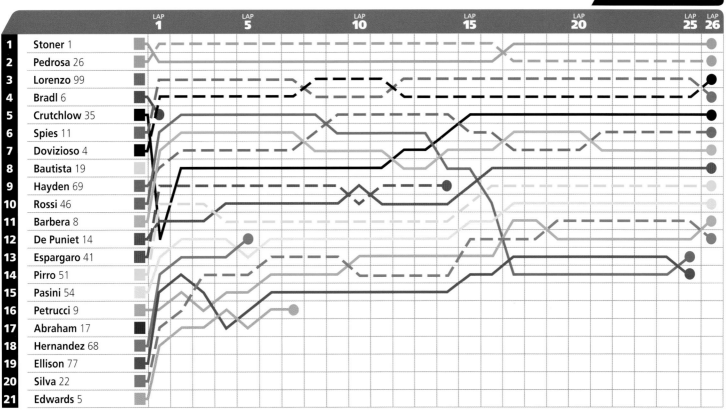

		LAP 1	LAP 5	LAP 10	LAP 15	LAP 20	LAP 25	LAP 26
1	Stoner 1							
2	Pedrosa 26							
3	Lorenzo 99							
4	Bradl 6							
5	Crutchlow 35							
6	Spies 11							
7	Dovizioso 4							
8	Bautista 19							
9	Hayden 69							
10	Rossi 46							
11	Barbera 8							
12	De Puniet 14							
13	Espargaro 41							
14	Pirro 51							
15	Pasini 54							
16	Petrucci 9							
17	Abraham 17							
18	Hernandez 68							
19	Ellison 77							
20	Silva 22							
21	Edwards 5							

RACE

	Rider	Motorcycle	Race Time	Time +	Fastest Lap	Av Speed	B
1	Stoner	Honda	41m 19.855s		1m 34.693s	106.524mph	M/MS
2	Pedrosa	Honda	41m 24.820s	4.965s	1m 34.548s	106.311mph	M/MS
3	Dovizioso	Yamaha	41m 31.849s	11.994s	1m 34.816s	106.011mph	M/M
4	Spies	Yamaha	41m 34.630s	14.775s	1m 34.828s	105.893mph	M/M
5	Crutchlow	Yamaha	41m 41.929s	22.074s	1m 34.814s	105.584mph	M/M
6	Hayden	Ducati	41m 51.515s	31.660s	1m 35.114s	105.181mph	M/M
7	Barbera	Ducati	42m 18.962s	59.107s	1m 35.575s	104.044mph	M/M
8	De Puniet	Art	42m 24.296s	1m 04.441s	1m 36.854s	103.826mph	M/MS
9	Pirro	FTR	42m 26.835s	1m 06.980s	1m 37.117s	103.722mph	M/MS
10	Pasini	Art	42m 44.942s	1m 25.087s	1m 37.246s	102.990mph	M/MS
11	Petrucci	Ioda	42m 51.958s	1m 32.103s	1m 38.025s	102.709mph	M/MS
12	Silva	BQR	42m 53.652s	1m 33.797s	1m 38.019s	102.641mph	M/MS
13	Rossi	Ducati	41m 38.492s	1 lap	1m 35.641s	101.663mph	M/M
14	Ellison	Art	41m 38.494s	1 lap	1m 38.200s	101.663mph	M/MS
NF	Espargaro	Art	22m 50.444s	12 laps	1m 36.808s	103.793mph	M/MS
NF	Edwards	Suter	12m 14.996s	19 laps	1m 39.002s	96.764mph	M/MS
NF	Hernandez	BQR	8m 13.842s	21 laps	1m 36.964s	102.868mph	M/MS
NF	Bradl	Honda	1m 40.961s	25 laps		100.660mph	M/MS
NF	Lorenzo	Yamaha					M/M
NF	Bautista	Honda					M/MS

CHAMPIONSHIP

	Rider	Team	Points
1	Lorenzo	Yamaha Factory Racing	140
2	Stoner	Repsol Honda Team	140
3	Pedrosa	Repsol Honda Team	121
4	Crutchlow	Monster Yamaha Tech 3	77
5	Dovizioso	Monster Yamaha Tech 3	76
6	Rossi	Ducati Team	61
7	Hayden	Ducati Team	59
8	Bautista	San Carlo Honda Gresini	58
9	Bradl	LCR Honda MotoGP	51
10	Spies	Yamaha Factory Racing	48
11	Barbera	Pramac Racing Team	46
12	Espargaro	Power Electronics Aspar	20
13	De Puniet	Power Electronics Aspar	19
14	Pirro	San Carlo Honda Gresini	16
15	Pasini	Speed Master	12
16	Petrucci	Came IodaRacing Project	9
17	Ellison	Paul Bird Motorsport	9
18	Silva	Avintia Blusens	5
19	Abraham	Cardion AB Motoracing	4
20	Edwards	NGM Mobile Forward Racing	4
21	Hernandez	Avintia Blusens	4

9 MICHELE PIRRO Got the ever-improving FTR Honda to within three seconds of top CRT position, provoking some satisfaction. On the other hand, being so close again annoyed him.

10 MATTIA PASINI Happy with his best result of the season so far and with the way he stayed with the fastest CRT men for the first half of the race. Had some issues when the tyres started to go off, but saw the weekend as a step forward.

11 DANILO PETRUCCI A little gem of a performance. Baulked at the first corner, got past three other CRTs and diced with Silva for the rest of the race, making the decisive pass on the last lap on the run to the final chicane.

12 IVAN SILVA Got the better of Ellison early on, then spent most of the race fighting with his team-mate and Petrucci. Lost out to the Italian on the last lap.

13 VALENTINO ROSSI Unhappy before the race for a number of reasons. Dicing with the other two Ducatis when his tyre chunked, and then had no option but to pit for new rubber.

14 JAMES ELLISON Still suffering from the effects of his big crash on Sunday morning at Silverstone. Never looked comfortable on the bike and was pipped on the line by Rossi.

NON-FINISHERS

ALEIX ESPARGARO Battling with his team-mate, as usual, for top CRT honours and feeling happier as the fuel load went down. Looking forward to another showdown with de Puniet when his engine failed on lap 14.

COLIN EDWARDS An awful weekend at the track where he has come closest to winning a MotoGP race. Nothing worked properly, with the traction control taking the blame for his retirement. When Edwards pulls in, it's clear things are bad.

YONNY HERNANDEZ Crashed out without injury on lap six while leading the dice with team-mate Silva, Pasini and Petrucci.

STEFAN BRADL Best qualifying so far, backed up by a great start on a track that he is almost alone in disliking. Blamed his crash on the brakes on overconfidence generated by the best feeling he's had so far in the opening laps.

JORGE LORENZO Knocked down at the first corner by Bautista. Lost his championship lead plus an engine, which revved itself into oblivion.

ALVARO BAUTISTA Dived up the inside off the start, completely outbraked himself, lost the front and scooped up Lorenzo. Race Direction exacted punishment by demoting him to the back of the grid at the next race.

NON-STARTERS

KAREL ABRAHAM Rode in practice and qualifying but the pain from his hand, injured at the post-Catalunya test, was too great for him to race.

eni MOTORRAD GRAND PRIX DEUTSCHLAND

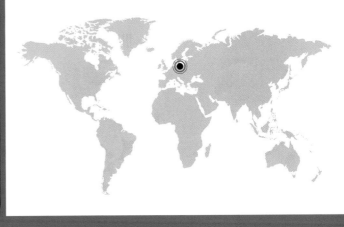

INSTANT KARMA

Casey Stoner lost the advantage he was gifted last time out when he crashed trying to pass eventual winner Dani Pedrosa

After Lorenzo had been taken out at the first corner of the Dutch TT a week earlier, Casey Stoner opined that he wouldn't wish for an advantage in that manner and that he hoped Jorge would get his own back. Well, it happened more quickly than he could have imagined. The Repsol Hondas dominated the whole weekend. Both started from the front row, split by Ben Spies, and they immediately ran away from the field, sparring for the whole race, never more than half a second apart and usually a lot closer.

Pedrosa, inevitably, got the holeshot but Stoner went past on the second lap and led for the next 17. Sachsenring is a track that suits Dani and the Honda. He won twice there on 250s and it is the only circuit on which he'd taken three victories in MotoGP, in 2007, 2010 and 2011. The great unknown on race morning was whether he'd have a set-up that would work. Yet again, practice and especially qualifying had been severely compromised by some seriously wet weather. The third free practice session was so wet that Stoner, Lorenzo and Crutchlow did not even bother going out, and Pedrosa went to the grid with dry-weather settings that were essentially untried in the new chassis that was delivered at Assen. Rather charmingly, he later talked about becoming 'familiar' with the bike.

Dani certainly looked happy. He was riding at his very best: fast, smooth and precise, as befits an ex-250 champion. The contrast with Casey's style was extreme. Stoner spent the next eleven and seven-eighths laps on average about a tenth of a second behind his team-mate's rear wheel, but where the Spaniard displayed wheels in line everywhere, or at least looked as though he did, the World Champion was his usual on-the-edge

TOP Ben Spies at last had what looked like a normal race but tyre trouble struck again and he just missed the rostrum

ABOVE Alvaro Bautista was demoted to the back of the grid for his Assen indiscretion but raced through to a strong seventh place

ABOVE The Hondas lead the Yamahas in front of another sold-out Sachsenring crowd

self. With the next man, Lorenzo, barely able to see the two Hondas in front of him, it was just a question of when and where Stoner would make his move.

Pedrosa set a fastest time on the penultimate lap of the race, but didn't gap Stoner – though neither did Casey shape to outbrake him at Turn 1, a favourite Sachsenring passing place. Would the move come at the bottom of the Waterfall? Not quite. In fact, the Aussie was planning it for the last corner, the same last-lap move he'd put on the returning Rossi two years previously, for third place. This time, however, it went wrong. Casey didn't go for the inside pass on the brakes; instead, he

stayed out on the right of the track. As he came off the brakes to drive for the inside of the final corner the front tyre cried enough, and bike and rider slid into the giant gravel trap at speed. Dani crossed the line with another fastest lap as Lorenzo noted 'an orange suit' off the track and wondered which one it was.

Stoner didn't complain about the crash, saying he was actually saving his 'win or bin it' move for the last corner, but he did voice displeasure at the marshals who refused to help him get going again. As that would have involved pushing a 1,000cc Honda uphill, uncomfortably close to the racing line, it's difficult to blame them

– although preventing Casey from trying did not seem reasonable either.

Stoner's error meant that the multi-bike dice behind Lorenzo was suddenly for the final rostrum place. As many as seven bikes had been involved, including the three other Yamahas, the Ducatis and Stefan Bradl. Alvaro Bautista, starting from the back of the grid as penance for his Assen indiscretion, joined in during the final laps. The Yamahas pulled away before being reduced to a pair when Cal Crutchlow ran on at the first corner of the 26th lap. Spies looked set to beat Dovizioso when he ran into trouble with edge grip – tyre troubles for three consecutive races

RIGHT Lorenzo finished second yet came away with a 14-point championship lead

BELOW Pedrosa and Stoner charge onto the long downhill section; Casey crashed at the next corner

– leaving Andrea to get on the podium for the second race in a row and the third time in four races.

This week, the Rossi–Ducati relationship swingometer was pointing to 'amicable'. As the takeover of the

Bologna company by Audi neared the completion of due-diligence checks, the CEO of Volkswagen Audi Group, Rupert Stadler, visited a MotoGP race for the first time. He and a small group of top brass had a lengthy

'I PLANNED TO GO FOR MY "WIN OR BIN" EFFORT IN THE LAST CORNER, NOT THAT ONE'

CASEY STONER

meeting with Valentino, after which Rossi reported that here were people he could do business with. For their part, the Germans said how impressed they were with MotoGP, but no substantive details were released.

Any pre-season hopes that the CRT bikes would be able to scare a few of the prototypes around the tight, twisty Sachsenring were dashed. Three – Silva, Petrucci and replacement rider Franco Battaini – were lapped, while the top finisher was Randy de Puniet, well over 50 seconds behind the winner and nearly 25 seconds

behind the last prototype, Nicky Hayden, who slowed badly at the end with a shot tyre. At least they'd been cheered by Michele Pirro topping the timing sheets at the end of the wet third free practice session.

As usual, the stands were packed every day despite the bad weather. The news that the Sachsenring had reached an agreement to host the German round for another four years was a great boost not just for the paddock, but also for a part of the world that genuinely loves hosting a Grand Prix.

ABOVE Stefan Bradl's fifth place kept his home fans happy

BEHIND THE WALL

Sandro Cortese's win in the Moto3 race was the first win by a German rider at the Sachsenring since 1971 when Dieter Braun, the reigning 125cc World Champion, won the 250 GP on a Yamaha. This race was, of course, before the reunification of Germany and the Sachsenring was in East Germany – the DDR – so this was the East German Grand Prix at the height of the Cold War.

It is difficult to convey to younger readers just how great was the divide between East and West and just how permanent it all seemed. Then factor in the defection of the DDR's top rider, Ernst Degner, at the end of the 1961 season when he seemed about to win a world title for the East German MZ concern. Degner went to Suzuki, who won their first world title in 1962 with the technology he brought with him. Dieter Braun also won his 125cc world title on a Suzuki.

All this would have been known to the enormous crowd, well into six figures, that used to turn up. And, of course, to the authorities. So when Braun won, around 200,000 ecstatic citizens of the communist state prepared to sing what they regarded as their national anthem. The authorities could not countenance such a demonstration. In his biography, *Fifteen*, Giacomo Agostini says armed troops emerged from under the start-line grandstands and pointed machine guns at the crowd. The PA system suffered a mysterious failure, the West German anthem wasn't played, and the East German GP only lasted one more year. The division of Germany, and Europe, however, lasted until 1989.

Those MZs that so nearly won world titles came from

Zschopau, a few kilometres from the Sachsenring, while the four companies that made up Auto Union were from other nearby towns. When the crowd applauded Sandro, they weren't just cheering a winner; they were celebrating the engineering heritage of their part of Germany.

BRIDGESTONE
TYRE OPTIONS
FRONT SOFT (S) / MEDIUM (M) /
EXTRA HARD (XH)
REAR MEDIUM (M) / HARD (H)

OFFICIAL TIMEKEEPER
TISSOT SWISS WATCHES SINCE 1853

eni MOTORRAD GRAND PRIX DEUTSCHLAND
SACHSENRING CIRCUIT

ROUND 8
July 8

RACE RESULTS

CIRCUIT LENGTH 2.281 miles
NO. OF LAPS 30
RACE DISTANCE 68.432 miles
WEATHER Dry, 26°C
TRACK TEMPERATURE 37°C
WINNER Dani Pedrosa
FASTEST LAP 1m 22.304s, 99.774mph, Dani Pedrosa
LAP RECORD 1m 21.846s, 100.351mph, Dani Pedrosa, 2011

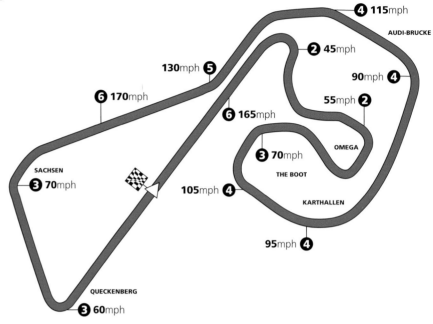

QUALIFYING

	Rider	Nationality	Team	Qualifying	Pole +	Gap
1	Stoner	AUS	Repsol Honda Team	1m 31.796s		
2	Spies	USA	Yamaha Factory Racing	1m 31.989s	0.193s	0.193s
3	Pedrosa	SPA	Repsol Honda Team	1m 32.081s	0.285s	0.092s
4	Crutchlow	GBR	Monster Yamaha Tech 3	1m 32.288s	0.492s	0.207s
5	Lorenzo	SPA	Yamaha Factory Racing	1m 32.381s	0.585s	0.093s
6	Bradl	GER	LCR Honda MotoGP	1m 32.510s	0.714s	0.129s
7	Hayden	USA	Ducati Team	1m 32.795s	0.999s	0.285s
8	Dovizioso	ITA	Monster Yamaha Tech 3	1m 33.205s	1.409s	0.410s
9	Rossi	ITA	Ducati Team	1m 33.217s	1.421s	0.012s
10	Espargaro	SPA	Power Electronics Aspar	1m 33.900s	2.104s	0.683s
11	Bautista	SPA	San Carlo Honda Gresini	1m 34.088s	2.292s	0.188s
12	Barbera	SPA	Pramac Racing Team	1m 34.542s	2.746s	0.454s
13	Edwards	USA	NGM Mobile Forward Racing	1m 34.649s	2.853s	0.107s
14	De Puniet	FRA	Power Electronics Aspar	1m 34.651s	2.855s	0.002s
15	Pasini	ITA	Speed Master	1m 34.938s	3.142s	0.287s
16	Petrucci	ITA	Came IodaRacing Project	1m 35.590s	3.794s	0.652s
17	Pirro	ITA	San Carlo Honda Gresini	1m 35.595s	3.799s	0.005s
18	Hernandez	COL	Avintia Blusens	1m 35.962s	4.166s	0.367s
19	Silva	SPA	Avintia Blusens	1m 36.183s	4.387s	0.221s
20	Ellison	GBR	Paul Bird Motorsport	1m 36.355s	4.559s	0.172s
21	Battaini	ITA	Cardion AB Motoracing	1m 36.438s	4.642s	0.083s

FINISHERS

1 DANI PEDROSA First win of the year but his third in a row at Sachsenring. Led the majority of the race with his team-mate right in his wheel tracks. Always looked the more comfortable of the two, and put in back-to-back fastest times on the final two laps. Victory also put him up to second in the championship.

2 JORGE LORENZO Advised to use the harder rear tyre for safety reasons, consigning him to a lonely race. Well ahead of the other Yamahas but never a danger to the Repsol Hondas. Would have been happy to finish third but Stoner's crash handed him a bigger championship lead.

3 ANDREA DOVIZIOSO Dovi's first podium at the Sachsenring and his second podium in consecutive races. Ran at the front of the group of three Yamahas pursuing Lorenzo, looked after his tyres and was able to fend off Spies on the run to the flag.

4 BEN SPIES Willing to take the risk on the softer tyre but had to use the harder option. Didn't have the edge grip or acceleration he needed so sat behind the two Tech 3 bikes waiting for his chance. Only missed out on third by 0.07s.

5 STEFAN BRADL Another impressive race. Followed the Yamahas until his tyre lost grip on the left side. Stayed in front of the big group thanks to some superb defensive riding in the last three laps when the Ducatis were on his tail.

6 VALENTINO ROSSI Back to the Estoril setting to conserve the rear tyre. A lot happier than usual afterwards, thanks to his best dry-weather finish so far. Realised he didn't have the pace to escape the group, so bided his time and attacked in the closing laps. The yellow flag prevented a final move on Bradl.

7 ALVARO BAUTISTA Started from the back of the grid – penalty for his Dutch misdemeanour. Took five laps to get through the CRT bikes, then rode through the big group. Actually headed Bradl and Rossi on the penultimate lap but lost the front; couldn't try again on the last lap as yellow flags were out for Stoner's crash.

8 CAL CRUTCHLOW On the tail of his team-mate and in front of Spies when he ran on at the first corner of lap 26. Disappointed

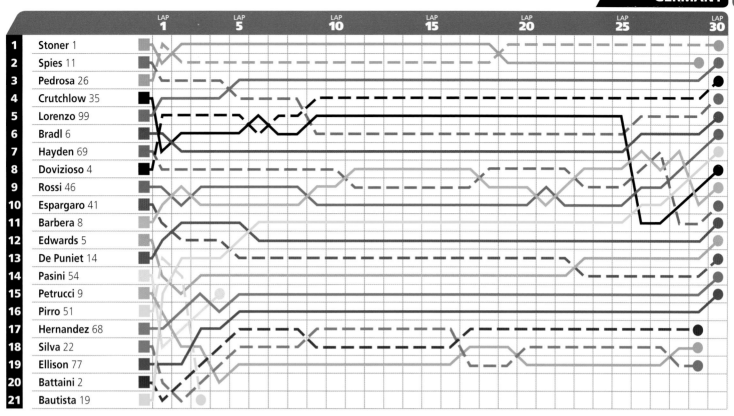

		LAP 1	LAP 5	LAP 10	LAP 15	LAP 20	LAP 25	LAP 30
1	Stoner 1							
2	Spies 11							
3	Pedrosa 26							
4	Crutchlow 35							
5	Lorenzo 99							
6	Bradl 6							
7	Hayden 69							
8	Dovizioso 4							
9	Rossi 46							
10	Espargaro 41							
11	Barbera 8							
12	Edwards 5							
13	De Puniet 14							
14	Pasini 54							
15	Petrucci 9							
16	Pirro 51							
17	Hernandez 68							
18	Silva 22							
19	Ellison 77							
20	Battaini 2							
21	Bautista 19							

RACE

	Rider	Motorcycle	Race Time	Time +	Fastest Lap	Av Speed	B
1	Pedrosa	Honda	41m 28.396s		1m 22.304s	99.001mph	XH/H
2	Lorenzo	Yamaha	41m 43.392s	14.996s	1m 23.057s	98.408mph	XH/H
3	Dovizioso	Yamaha	41m 49.065s	20.669s	1m 23.219s	98.185mph	XH/H
4	Spies	Yamaha	41m 49.136s	20.740s	1m 23.086s	98.182mph	XH/H
5	Bradl	Honda	41m 56.289s	27.893s	1m 23.416s	97.903mph	XH/H
6	Rossi	Ducati	41m 56.446s	28.050s	1m 23.293s	97.897mph	XH/H
7	Bautista	Honda	41m 56.642s	28.246s	1m 23.228s	97.890mph	XH/H
8	Crutchlow	Yamaha	41m 56.843s	28.447s	1m 23.050s	97.881mph	XH/H
9	Barbera	Ducati	41m 57.449s	29.053s	1m 23.291s	97.858mph	XH/H
10	Hayden	Ducati	41m 57.622s	29.226s	1m 23.287s	98.038mph	XH/H
11	De Puniet	Art	42m 21.572s	53.176s	1m 24.069s	96.930mph	XH/H
12	Edwards	Suter	42m 26.600s	58.204s	1m 24.238s	96.738mph	XH/M
13	Espargaro	Art	42m 33.050s	1m 04.654s	1m 24.260s	96.493mph	XH/M
14	Hernandez	BQR	42m 41.939s	1m 13.543s	1m 24.545s	96.159mph	XH/M
15	Ellison	Art	42m 58.714s	1m 30.318s	1m 24.945s	95.533mph	XH/M
16	Battaini	Ducati	41m 35.941s	1 lap	1m 25.300s	95.412mph	XH/M
17	Petrucci	Ioda	41m 43.788s	1 lap	1m 25.740s	95.113mph	M/M
18	Silva	BQR	41m 57.963s	1 lap	1m 25.339s	94.577mph	XH/M
NF	Stoner	Honda	40m 06.207s	1 lap	1m 22.510s	98.969mph	XH/H
NF	Pasini	Art	5m 44.863s	26 laps	1m 24.499s	95.247mph	XH/M
NF	Pirro	FTR	4m 39.063s	27 laps	1m 26.300s	88.279mph	XH/M

CHAMPIONSHIP

	Rider	Team	Points
1	Lorenzo	Yamaha Factory Racing	160
2	Pedrosa	Repsol Honda Team	146
3	Stoner	Repsol Honda Team	140
4	Dovizioso	Monster Yamaha Tech 3	92
5	Crutchlow	Monster Yamaha Tech 3	85
6	Rossi	Ducati Team	71
7	Bautista	San Carlo Honda Gresini	67
8	Hayden	Ducati Team	65
9	Bradl	LCR Honda MotoGP	62
10	Spies	Yamaha Factory Racing	61
11	Barbera	Pramac Racing Team	53
12	De Puniet	Power Electronics Aspar	24
13	Espargaro	Power Electronics Aspar	23
14	Pirro	San Carlo Honda Gresini	16
15	Pasini	Speed Master	12
16	Ellison	Paul Bird Motorsport	10
17	Petrucci	Came IodaRacing Project	9
18	Edwards	NGM Mobile Forward Racing	8
19	Hernandez	Avintia Blusens	6
20	Silva	Avintia Blusens	5
21	Abraham	Cardion AB Motoracing	4

that he waited so long to attack Dovizioso; thought he had the same pace as Lorenzo.

9 HECTOR BARBERA A good race after very average qualifying. Involved in the multi-bike fight for sixth and pleased to finish between the two factory Ducatis. Happier than after any other race this season.

10 NICKY HAYDEN Only a second behind fifth place in a dice where he'd been a leader until three laps from the end. The usual Ducati problem of tyre wear then really made itself felt and he started losing the rear on corner entry.

11 RANDY DE PUNIET Best CRT for the second race running and the French rider's best race of the year. Stuck with a bunch of

prototypes in the early laps, kept the pace up when they broke away and then latched on to Bautista. Took over as top CRT in the points standings.

12 COLIN EDWARDS Got a shove from Barbera in the first corner, then had a major problem with traction control settings in the early stages. Found a map he liked, hunted down Espargaro, but ran out of time to catch de Puniet.

13 ALEIX ESPARGARO Had a set-up for the wet but was lost in the dry. Lacked front-end feel and couldn't hold his line, or run with his team-mate, or fend off Edwards in the closing stages.

14 YONNY HERNANDEZ No surprise that Yonny was quick in Germany – he was

sixth in the Moto2 race in 2011 and set the fastest lap. Again, expectations of the FTR Kawasaki were exceeded.

15 JAMES ELLISON Recovered from his Silverstone warm-up crash and competitive with top CRTs – James's best lap was less than a second slower than the best CRT. In the big group early on but lost touch with Hernandez and Espargaro at half-distance.

16 FRANCO BATTAINI Ducati's test rider was drafted in to ride Karel Abraham's bike. It was Franco's first MotoGP race since he rode the ECM Blata in 2005.

17 DANILO PETRUCCI A big crash in practice left him with very sore ribs. In

the race he was able to get a good start and follow Battaini. Soon dropped back but had the resources to pass Silva on the last lap.

18 IVAN SILVA Couldn't get past Battaini's factory Ducati at the start and hit serious problems with grip later in the race, by which time the fight for the last points was too far ahead.

MATTIA PASINI Not happy in wet practice and qualifying but started the dry race well, making up a place a lap. Was then shoved off line and crashed on lap five.

MICHELE PIRRO Crashed heavily in practice but his race was ended by the chain jumping the sprockets on the fifth lap, the same problem that put him out of the Qatar GP.

NON-FINISHERS

CASEY STONER Led the first half of the race and then shadowed his team-mate for the second; planned a last-corner move for the lead but crashed out at the corner before. Not pleased with the marshals who didn't want to help him restart.

NON-STARTERS

KAREL ABRAHAM Still unfit due to hand injuries sustained at the Catalunya test. Replaced by Battaini.

GRAN PREMIO D'ITALIA TIM

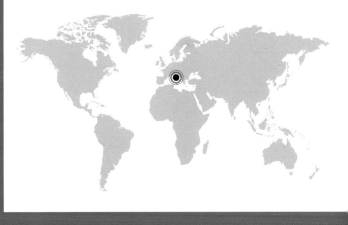

SPAIN WIN AGAIN

Lorenzo dominated as Stoner hit all kinds of trouble and Dovizioso made it three rostrums in a row

There was the usual track invasion at the end of the race, and an equally inevitable appearance on the rostrum by Valentino Rossi before the crowd would disperse. But this year it all felt a bit forced, despite the fact that the Ducatis had a much better race than usual. Hector Barbera became the first man to put a satellite Ducati on the front row, and even the most cynical observer was forced to admit that he did it without a tow from anyone. Rossi scored his best dry-weather finish, fifth, for over a year and entered his press debrief cheerily enquiring to the assembled Italian media if anyone knew where Barbera had finished – 'in front of me?'

In truth, Rossi was slightly fortunate to be first Ducati home. Nicky Hayden, fourth on the grid, caught Dovizioso and Bradl (who had spent much of the race disputing third place) in the closing stages. He put a tough pass on Bradl on the second corner of the last lap only for the young German to repay the favour at the next bend, pushing Nicky wide enough for Rossi and Crutchlow to take advantage. 'I was only thinking podium,' said a disconsolate Hayden. Valentino wasn't too thrilled with fifth place but he seemed genuinely pleased with the Ducati's performance in the race. It didn't seem the time or place to remind him that he'd qualified tenth or that we were at Ducati's test track.

Despite the fact that no-one even saw Jorge Lorenzo when the lights went out, there was plenty of hard racing through the rest of the field. It took Pedrosa a little while to sort out Dovizioso and consolidate his grip on second place, and then the crowd was treated to the sight of Bradl holding third place for eleven laps. Stefan's problems with a full tank were helped by a stiffer set-up

at the front, but he felt a little less confident in the tyre in the closing stages, which meant he couldn't hold off Dovi. It didn't stop him biting straight back at Hayden on the last lap, though. 'Nicky make a very aggressive pass and Bradl give back to him the same,' said an admiring Valentino Rossi.

Once again Dani Pedrosa was almost invisible in a strong second place. He was fastest in qualifying but you've never seen a racer less excited by the prospect of starting from pole. He knew what everyone else knew, that but for an oversight Lorenzo would have had pole, and by a distance. Jorge had looked to be comfortably on target when, inexplicably, he came down pit lane, later blaming 'a little problem in electronics'. It later emerged that he'd tried to shake off some followers by taking the short cut back to pit lane to find some track space. Unfortunately he forgot to reset the electronics. GPS is banned, contrary to popular opinion, so the system needs to have a reference point in order to know where it is on track. Jorge's short cut meant the bike didn't know its position and consequently he found himself with less and less power at every corner. He cheered up when it transpired Spaniards hadn't just monopolised the front row for the first time in Grand Prix history, they also had the pole-sitters in Moto2, Pol Espargaro, and Moto3, Maverick Viñales, as well as the fastest CRT man, the other Espargaro brother. 'We are supporting the Spanish football team,' said Dani, referring to the recent European championship final in which Spain gave Italy a lesson in that sport. Cue an outbreak of Spanish national jerseys in the press office.

'FROM THE BEGINNING I FELT GREAT ON THIS TRACK'
JORGE LORENZO

ABOVE Randy de Puniet and fiancé Lauren add a little glamour to any paddock, even Mugello

LEFT Once the Spaniards had escaped, Dovizioso, Hayden and Bradl disputed third, with the Italian making it three podiums in a row

OPPOSITE Hector Barbera became the first man to qualify a satellite Ducati on the front row – and he did it without a tow

Lorenzo duly ran away with the race, in splendid isolation, without having to use the extra-hard rear tyre that Bridgestone had brought as an insurance policy after the problems at Silverstone and, especially, Assen. After the nightmare problems getting the bike to work in Germany, he was more than happy.

He even had time to give a little wave to one of the grandstands on the last lap; the Ducati grandstand as it happens. Casey Stoner most certainly wasn't happy. He had his joint worst qualifying since he joined Honda – fifth – thanks to the perennial problem of chatter on corner exits exacerbated by difficulty in getting the bike to turn. Casey was running fifth, splitting the two Ducatis, when the RCV shook its head on the run-down from Palagio and he arrived at Correntaio pumping the lever to no effect. The off-track excursion dropped him down to tenth, ending any chance he had of achieving the third position he thought might just have been possible.

As this was MotoGP's first visit to Italy since the death of Marco Simoncelli at the 2011 Malaysian GP there were many tributes to Super Sic. The seats in the grandstand at the top of Arrabbiata spelled out his race number 58 in red and white. Honda handed over two bikes to Marco's family, one of his race bikes and a Fireblade, to be sold off to benefit the Foundation set up in his memory. There was also the welcome sight of Team Gresini's bikes reverting to their white livery after spending the first half of the year in mourning black. It was something Marco's fans had asked for, said Fausto Gresini.

The only damper on the weekend was the size of the crowd. Compared to every other year one can recall, the place was empty; even the official figure of 64,000 looked seriously optimistic. Previously punters had been buying one-day tickets on Friday and then staying all weekend, so this year the organisers made every day as expensive as a three-day pass. A Sunday-only ticket cost well over €100, which certainly didn't help matters.

HONDA ATTACKS

Mugello again showed that the new 1,000cc Yamaha M1 doesn't have any weak points; it didn't even lose out on top speed down the big front straight. The Repsol Honda riders, by contrast, had been plagued by chatter, especially Casey Stoner. The problems with the new rear Bridgestone, introduced at the start of the year, had been gradually overcome with the help of at least one new chassis. However, the new front tyre, which was the only option after the Silverstone race, brought with it a fresh set of problems, again notably for Casey.

So at the test on the Monday after the Mugello race Honda provided a completely new bike for both Repsol Honda riders which, if they liked it, would be available from Laguna Seca onwards. The chassis, said HRC vice-president Shuhei Nakamoto, was effectively the 2013 bike, while the motor was more of an evolution than a new design. He couldn't guarantee that the chatter would be eliminated on the grounds that HRC's test riders couldn't do good enough lap times to induce the sensations felt by Pedrosa and Stoner. 'If lap time same, he would be here!' Nakamoto-san pointed out. Nevertheless, the test riders had detected some changes, with Monday showing that they had been at least partly right. Dani opted to go with the new bike, Casey with the new motor for the US GP.

Honda also announced that Moto2 star Marc Marquez would join Pedrosa in the Repsol team next season, leading to the suspicion that they were throwing everything at this year's championship because they suspected that the 2013 title would be a very difficult prospect.

Ducati also had some parts to try out but their new ECU malfunctioned, causing Rossi to crash, so the test was abandoned early. All of a sudden, the optimism so apparent after the race seemed to evaporate.

OPPOSITE TOP
Crutchlow was this close to Rossi for most of the race but couldn't find a way past

OPPOSITE BOTTOM
Ivan Silva uses a bit of leg power to escape from a Mugello gravel trap

BELOW Bradl looked as if he might get his first MotoGP rostrum but fourth was still a career-best finish

BRIDGESTONE

TYRE OPTIONS
FRONT SOFT (S) / MEDIUM (M) / HARD (H)
REAR MEDIUM (M) / HARD (H) /
HARD Special construction (HS)

motoGP **TISSOT**
SWISS WATCHES SINCE 1853
OFFICIAL TIMEKEEPER

GRAN PREMIO D'ITALIA TIM
MUGELLO

ROUND 9
July 15

RACE RESULTS

CIRCUIT LENGTH 3.259 miles
NO. OF LAPS 23
RACE DISTANCE 74.959 miles
WEATHER Dry, 25°C
TRACK TEMPERATURE 45°C
WINNER Jorge Lorenzo
FASTEST LAP 1m 47.705s, 108.934mph, Dani Pedrosa (Record)
PREVIOUS LAP RECORD 1m 48.402s, 108.243mph, Jorge Lorenzo, 2011

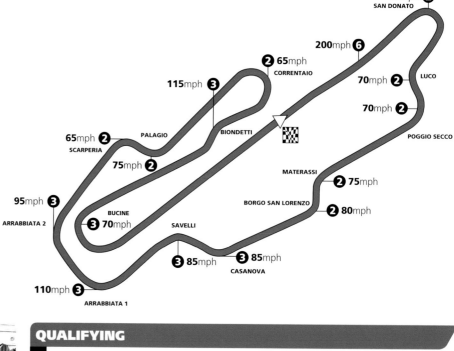

55mph SAN DONATO
200mph
65mph CORRENTAIO
115mph
70mph LUCO
70mph
PALAGIO POGGIO SECCO
65mph SCARPERIA
BIONDETTI
75mph
MATERASSI
75mph
95mph BORGO SAN LORENZO
BUCINE 80mph
ARRABBIATA 2 70mph
SAVELLI
85mph 85mph
CASANOVA
110mph
ARRABBIATA 1

QUALIFYING

	Rider	Nationality	Team	Qualifying	Pole +	Gap
1	Pedrosa	SPA	Repsol Honda Team	1m 47.284s		
2	Lorenzo	SPA	Yamaha Factory Racing	1m 47.423s	0.139s	0.139s
3	Barbera	SPA	Pramac Racing Team	1m 47.545s	0.261s	0.122s
4	Hayden	USA	Ducati Team	1m 47.671s	0.387s	0.126s
5	Stoner	AUS	Repsol Honda Team	1m 47.689s	0.405s	0.018s
6	Crutchlow	GBR	Monster Yamaha Tech 3	1m 47.749s	0.465s	0.060s
7	Dovizioso	ITA	Monster Yamaha Tech 3	1m 47.751s	0.467s	0.002s
8	Bradl	GER	LCR Honda MotoGP	1m 47.857s	0.573s	0.106s
9	Spies	USA	Yamaha Factory Racing	1m 48.149s	0.865s	0.292s
10	Rossi	ITA	Ducati Team	1m 48.502s	1.218s	0.353s
11	Bautista	SPA	San Carlo Honda Gresini	1m 48.894s	1.610s	0.392s
12	Espargaro	SPA	Power Electronics Aspar	1m 49.387s	2.103s	0.493s
13	De Puniet	FRA	Power Electronics Aspar	1m 49.450s	2.166s	0.063s
14	Pirro	ITA	San Carlo Honda Gresini	1m 50.263s	2.979s	0.813s
15	Hernandez	COL	Avintia Blusens	1m 50.610s	3.326s	0.347s
16	Ellison	GBR	Paul Bird Motorsport	1m 50.812s	3.528s	0.202s
17	Pasini	ITA	Speed Master	1m 50.953s	3.669s	0.141s
18	Silva	SPA	Avintia Blusens	1m 51.242s	3.958s	0.289s
19	Edwards	USA	NGM Mobile Forward Racing	1m 51.348s	4.064s	0.106s
20	Petrucci	ITA	Came IodaRacing Project	1m 51.473s	4.189s	0.125s

FINISHERS

1 JORGE LORENZO The only thing that stopped this being a perfect weekend was the glitch at the end of qualifying which prevented him from taking pole position. Always had stunning race pace and once he took the lead coming out of the first corner it would have taken a catastrophe to prevent Jorge making it two in a row at Mugello.

2 DANI PEDROSA Despite his pole, Dani knew that Lorenzo had superior race pace. Got the holeshot but tried too hard in Turn 1 to keep Jorge behind him, went deep and let the Yamaha through. Then Dovi pushed past, and by the time he regained second place Lorenzo was out of range.

3 ANDREA DOVIZIOSO Three third places in succession, at the track where he came a stunning second in 2011. Made up for qualifying on the third row with a great start to run in second for the first four laps. Had his hands full with Bradl for most of the race once Pedrosa had gone past. Another controlled and clinical display.

4 STEFAN BRADL Ran in third for ten laps in the middle of the race. Happier at the start thanks to a new set-up, but it cost him front-end feel in the closing stages. Couldn't hold Dovizioso back but toughed it out with Hayden for his best result so far in his best race so far.

5 VALENTINO ROSSI A much better performance, blighted only by his continued inability to make use of the softer tyre in

qualifying. Rode from tenth up to the dice for third and finished just over a second from the rostrum and 11.5s from the win. Smallest dry-race margins so far.

6 CAL CRUTCHLOW Had his fate sealed by a bad start that saw him drop to tenth on lap three; from then on he was glued to the rear wheel of Rossi's Ducati. Plus points were being only 1.4s from the podium and watching Vale's mastery of Mugello for 20 laps.

7 NICKY HAYDEN A much better weekend than it looks, with good qualifying and a competitive race that ended with a last-lap charge on Bradl and Dovi to try and take third. Got past the German rider, only to be re-passed immediately and put off line, which allowed Rossi and Crutchlow past.

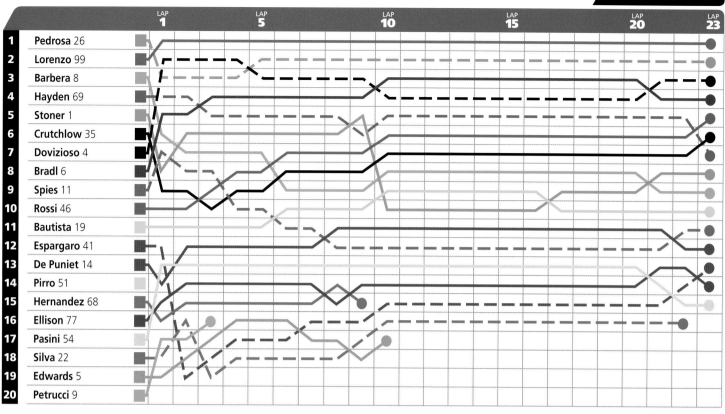

		LAP 1			LAP 5					LAP 10					LAP 15					LAP 20			LAP 23

1	Pedrosa 26
2	Lorenzo 99
3	Barbera 8
4	Hayden 69
5	Stoner 1
6	Crutchlow 35
7	Dovizioso 4
8	Bradl 6
9	Spies 11
10	Rossi 46
11	Bautista 19
12	Espargaro 41
13	De Puniet 14
14	Pirro 51
15	Hernandez 68
16	Ellison 77
17	Pasini 54
18	Silva 22
19	Edwards 5
20	Petrucci 9

RACE

	Rider	Motorcycle	Race Time	Time +	Fastest Lap	Av Speed	
1	Lorenzo	Yamaha	41m 37.477s		1m 47.795s	108.050mph	H/H
2	Pedrosa	Honda	41m 42.700s	5.000s	1m 47.705s	107.824mph	H/H
3	Dovizioso	Yamaha	41m 48.142s	10.000s	1m 48.226s	107.590mph	H/H
4	Bradl	Honda	41m 48.188s	10.000s	1m 48.121s	107.589mph	H/H
5	Rossi	Ducati	41m 49.172s	11.000s	1m 48.444s	107.546mph	H/H
6	Crutchlow	Yamaha	41m 49.537s	12.000s	1m 48.405s	107.531mph	H/H
7	Hayden	Ducati	41m 49.712s	12.000s	1m 48.179s	107.523mph	H/H
8	Stoner	Honda	42m 08.094s	30.000s	1m 48.194s	106.741mph	H/HS
9	Barbera	Ducati	42m 09.205s	31.000s	1m 48.605s	106.694mph	H/H
10	Bautista	Honda	42m 12.066s	34.000s	1m 48.652s	106.574mph	H/H
11	Spies	Yamaha	42m 35.339s	57.000s	1m 48.886s	105.603mph	H/H
12	De Puniet	Art	42m 37.440s	59.000s	1m 49.831s	105.516mph	H/M
13	Espargaro	Art	42m 48.677s	1m 11.000s	1m 50.397s	105.055mph	H/M
14	Ellison	Art	42m 48.935s	1m 11.000s	1m 50.899s	105.044mph	H/M
15	Pasini	Art	42m 49.305s	1m 11.000s	1m 50.927s	105.029mph	H/M
16	Silva	BQR	42m 02.684s	1 lap	1m 51.359s	102.319mph	H/H
NF	Edwards	Suter	19m 37.380s	13 laps	1m 52.420s	99.651mph	H/H
NF	Hernandez	BQR	16m 52.102s	14 laps	1m 50.922s	104.332mph	H/H
NF	Petrucci	Ioda	5m 44.611s	20 laps	1m 51.678s	102.139mph	H/M
EX	Pirro	FTR					H/M

CHAMPIONSHIP

	Rider	Team	Points
1	Lorenzo	Yamaha Factory Racing	185
2	Pedrosa	Repsol Honda Team	166
3	Stoner	Repsol Honda Team	148
4	Dovizioso	Monster Yamaha Tech 3	108
5	Crutchlow	Monster Yamaha Tech 3	95
6	Rossi	Ducati Team	82
7	Bradl	LCR Honda MotoGP	75
8	Hayden	Ducati Team	74
9	Bautista	San Carlo Honda Gresini	73
10	Spies	Yamaha Factory Racing	66
11	Barbera	Pramac Racing Team	60
12	De Puniet	Power Electronics Aspar	28
13	Espargaro	Power Electronics Aspar	26
14	Pirro	San Carlo Honda Gresini	16
15	Pasini	Speed Master	13
16	Ellison	Paul Bird Motorsport	12
17	Petrucci	Came IodaRacing Project	9
18	Edwards	NGM Mobile Forward Racing	8
19	Hernandez	Avintia Blusens	6
20	Silva	Avintia Blusens	5
21	Abraham	Cardion AB Motoracing	4

8 CASEY STONER Major problems with chatter in practice and qualifying. Only man to choose the super-hard tyre; made a bad start but got up to fifth. Then, just before half-distance, the Honda shook its head and knocked the brake pads back, causing him to run on at the next corner.

9 HECTOR BARBERA Started from the front row for the first time in his MotoGP career, but struggled on race day. Despite conditions being nearly identical to practice and qualifying, he found his bike sliding a lot in the many fast changes of direction.

10 ALVARO BAUTISTA Three crashes, brake problems and major grief trying to find a set-up for the harder tyre; he usually prefers the softer option. A weekend to forget – but nice to see the bike back in white.

11 BEN SPIES Qualified badly but started with aggression before feeling the effects of food poisoning. Kept out of the way of the field while feeling distinctly nauseous.

12 RANDY DE PUNIET Top CRT for the third race in a row. His only problem after the first couple of laps was keeping his concentration. Stalked by Spies, who passed him with a couple of laps to go.

13 ALEIX ESPARGARO Had his usual problem with the full tank after a good start. Ran off the track when he locked the front on the second lap. Rejoined last, then passed every other CRT rider except his team-mate.

14 JAMES ELLISON Happy with a swingarm modification, starting the weekend slowly but ending with an aggressive race. Only passed by Espargaro on the last lap.

15 MATTIA PASINI Faded badly over the last three laps, losing two positions.

16 IVAN SILVA Looking good on his first visit to Mugello and running in his team-mate's wheel tracks when his clutch cried enough going into Turn 1 at the start of lap three. Rejoined and finished the race with no clutch.

NON-FINISHERS

COLIN EDWARDS Back down to earth after the Sachsenring. The old electronics problems again made it impossible to run with the front CRTs. Not amused when Espargaro came past after having run off track.

YONNY HERNANDEZ Fell unhurt on lap nine while dicing with Pasini and Ellison.

DANILO PETRUCCI Well in the CRT fight when he lost the front at Poggio Seco on the fourth lap.

MICHELE PIRRO The same problem that put him out in Qatar and Germany, the chain jumping the sprockets, struck again

'after two gearchanges'. Cut the course to get back to the pit to change bikes, but was then black-flagged.

NON-STARTERS

KAREL ABRAHAM Still suffering from his Catalunya test injuries. Not replaced by Battaini, as had happened in Germany, because of the factory Ducati team's testing schedule the week after the GP.

RED BULL
U.S. GRAND PRIX

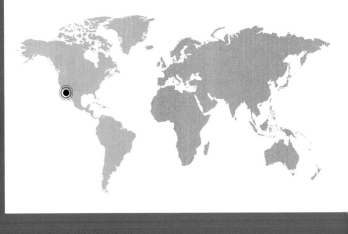

COUNTER
ATTACK

Casey Stoner got his season back on track as the silly season became very silly indeed

Anyone who thought Casey Stoner's results at the previous two GPs meant he'd lost his edge since announcing his retirement was put right in California. What's more, he had to work at it. Jorge Lorenzo looked comfortable all weekend, a little of the old swagger starting to show through, whereas Stoner was between a rock and a hard place.

Stoner and Pedrosa had both tested an all-new Honda after Mugello; Dani had elected to use the new engine and chassis, Casey stuck with the old frame but used the new engine. Any improvement was minimal, he said, but the real problem was tyre choice. There was a significant difference between the options available and all the prototype riders spent practice working on race set-up for the harder option.

Not that a lot of people took too much notice. Attention focused on the increasingly bizarre events surrounding Ben Spies. The week before the race he'd let it be known, via an email to American racing website Superbikeplanet.com, that he would be leaving Yamaha at the end of the season. Which came as a surprise to everyone, including Yamaha. There was a comment about 'a few people in Yamaha' who Ben hated to leave, implying there were a lot he wouldn't miss. American fans took solace from the announcement that Nicky Hayden had re-signed for another season with Ducati.

Colin Edwards, as usual, hijacked the Thursday press conference to slag off his Suter BMW and the CRT concept in no uncertain terms, which didn't deter two American teams from entering their own CRT bikes as wild cards.

Stoner's second place on the grid didn't do anything for his worries about tyre choice. Nevertheless, it was

RIGHT Nicky Hayden had a tough time on the track where he has won twice in the past

BELOW Turn One doesn't look like a corner until you see a MotoGP bike go through it

'CASEY WAS IN EXCELLENT FORM TODAY AND IT WASN'T POSSIBLE TO BEAT HIM'
JORGE LORENZO

a surprise, to put it mildly, when he came to the grid with the softer option rear tyre. In the last couple of races Casey hadn't got the hard one to work so this time he gambled; he was the only factory rider to use the softer tyre. He intended to use its extra grip to open up a lead that he could protect in the later part of the race. Unfortunately for him, Lorenzo had other ideas – and Pedrosa wasn't too co-operative either. The two Spaniards pushed Casey back to third off the start and it took him a couple of laps to dispose of his team-mate and get on to Lorenzo's back wheel.

Stoner now had to come up with a Plan B. Pedrosa wouldn't trouble him again: he hadn't got the all-new RCV's set-up sorted and then he had a major moment with the front which consigned him to a lonely third place. Casey, meanwhile, was giving his tyre a rest and waiting for the grip to come back to him. When Lorenzo had a similarly large front-end moment at the top of the Corkscrew Stoner snapped across the – admittedly small – gap on to the Yamaha's back wheel.

Last year, Casey had to produce one of the passes of the year, or any other year, to get past Jorge. He produced another remarkable move to do the same thing this year. Both took place at Turn 1, the ultra-fast kink over the brow after the start/finish line. In 2011 Stoner had squeezed past on the outside, a manoeuvre that made even the watching Kevin Schwantz hold his breath. This time it was different. Casey came out of the final corner, Turn 11, up on the kerb, right behind Jorge, but as they accelerated up the gearbox he somehow managed to move to the inside while the front wheel was in the air, hook up the soft rear rubber and blast

past on the inside. It was an utterly decisive move, planned and executed perfectly. In a lap the Aussie had a half-second advantage. Lorenzo's harder tyre proved to be no advantage in the closing stages and Casey rode to a victory that reminded everyone that he is still a serious contender.

Lorenzo wasn't too disappointed, and why should he be? He extended his championship lead over Pedrosa while Casey closed to within nine points of Dani. It wasn't the sort of win usually associated with Stoner. He and his crew dialled in a lot more traction control than usual to minimise spinning, and he rode conservatively until he was sure he had enough rubber left to go the distance. The move came two-thirds of the way through

ABOVE Team mates Dovizioso and Crutchlow at the top of the Corkscrew, almost inseperable

BELOW Toni Elias returned to MotoGP to deputise for the injured Hector Barbera

the race. A gamble? Yes, but a very calculated one, and it showed another side to the genius of Casey Stoner. It was his third win at Laguna; the only other man to rack up a trio of wins there is Wayne Rainey.

The other three Yamahas were squabbling among themselves, with Spies looking to have taken a decisive advantage when yet another wildly improbable incident ended his race. Coming down from the Corkscrew Ben fell, for no apparent reason. The swingarm had broken, said the team, but TV pictures suggested the rear suspension had collapsed, most probably the linkage. Thankfully, the linkage chose to fail at one of the slowest points on the circuit and Spies was lucky not to

add to the injuries he'd picked up in a massive highside in qualifying.

There was another significant crash late in the race, this time from Valentino Rossi at the top of the Corkscrew. It looked a lot like his and Nicky Hayden's crashes in practice at Silverstone, only this was on a hot, dry track. Rossi lost the front on the brakes with the bike still upright, a graphic demonstration of how the front seems to refuse to bite into the track and of how the Desmosedici's major problem hadn't changed since the start of the year. Watching Valentino trudge away and then hitch a lift back to the pits from Hayden it was hard not to believe we had just seen a man make his mind up.

ABOVE Rossi walks away from his crash going into the Corkscrew. The body language was of a man who has made a decision

OPPOSITE Aleix Espargaro, complete with Stars & Stripes numbers for the occasion, dominated the CRTs and scored his first top-ten finish

CRT BLUES

Colin Edwards did not mince his words when describing both his bike and the CRT class in the pre-event press conference. Clearly, the hope that riders like Randy de Puniet and Colin himself would be able to race with and sometimes beat the slower satellite bikes on tracks like Laguna or the Sachsenring was misplaced. The question now was how to close the gap between factory prototypes and the CRTs.

Dorna CEO Carmelo Ezpeleta was engaged in an increasingly acrimonious dialogue with the factories, whom he was accusing of writing the rules and then refusing to fill the grid. The major changes to technical rules he would like to see are a rev limit and a common ECU. As the engine control electronics are what the factories have invested most in, they're not keen and want to postpone any major changes to the 2015 season. Dorna was showing no signs of being willing to compromise.

An ECU has already been ordered from Magneti Marelli which will be offered free of charge to the whole grid for the 2013 season, although it is only likely to be used by CRT teams. The intention is to make this ECU mandatory for all in 2014. It incorporates a rev limit of 15,500rpm, which should allow the use of conventional steel valve springs. It is clear that Dorna are willing to fight the factories all the way on this, so expect some serious brinkmanship when deadlines approach.

The only major technical change to be approved so far by the Grand Prix Commission is a freezing of the bore-and-stroke dimensions used by the factory bikes; it does not apply to CRT machines.

TYRE OPTIONS
FRONT SOFT (S) / MEDIUM (M) / HARD (H)
REAR SOFT (S) / MEDIUM (M)

OFFICIAL TIMEKEEPER

RED BULL U.S. GRAND PRIX
LAGUNA SECA

ROUND 10
July 29

RACE RESULTS

CIRCUIT LENGTH 2.243 miles
NO. OF LAPS 32
RACE DISTANCE 71.781 miles
WEATHER Dry, 18°C
TRACK TEMPERATURE 24°C
WINNER Casey Stoner
FASTEST LAP 1m 21.229s, 99.414mph, Dani Pedrosa (Record)
PREVIOUS LAP RECORD 1m 21.673s, 98.860mph, Casey Stoner, 2011

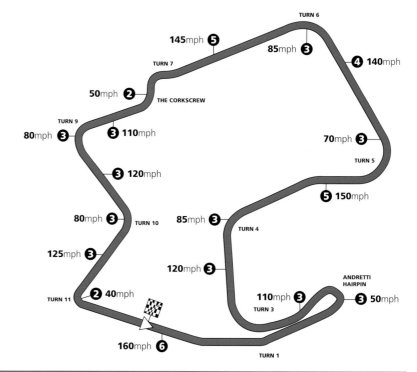

QUALIFYING

	Rider	Nationality	Team	Qualifying	Pole +	Gap
1	Lorenzo	SPA	Yamaha Factory Racing	1m 20.554s		
2	Stoner	AUS	Repsol Honda Team	1m 20.628s	0.074s	0.074s
3	Pedrosa	SPA	Repsol Honda Team	1m 20.906s	0.352s	0.278s
4	Spies	USA	Yamaha Factory Racing	1m 21.094s	0.540s	0.188s
5	Crutchlow	GBR	Monster Yamaha Tech 3	1m 21.268s	0.714s	0.174s
6	Dovizioso	ITA	Monster Yamaha Tech 3	1m 21.539s	0.985s	0.271s
7	Bautista	SPA	San Carlo Honda Gresini	1m 21.732s	1.178s	0.193s
8	Hayden	USA	Ducati Team	1m 21.734s	1.180s	0.002s
9	Bradl	GER	LCR Honda MotoGP	1m 22.753s	1.199s	0.019s
10	Rossi	ITA	Ducati Team	1m 22.544s	1.990s	0.791s
11	De Puniet	FRA	Power Electronics Aspar	1m 23.886s	2.332s	0.342s
12	Espargaro	SPA	Power Electronics Aspar	1m 23.075s	2.521s	0.189s
13	Edwards	USA	NGM Mobile Forward Racing	1m 23.699s	3.145s	0.624s
14	Abraham	CZE	Cardion AB Motoracing	1m 23.704s	3.150s	0.005s
15	Hernandez	COL	Avintia Blusens	1m 23.769s	3.215s	0.065s
16	Pirro	ITA	San Carlo Honda Gresini	1m 23.877s	3.323s	0.108s
17	Elias	SPA	Pramac Racing Team	1m 24.898s	3.344s	0.021s
18	Pasini	ITA	Speed Master	1m 24.017s	3.463s	0.119s
19	Petrucci	ITA	Came IodaRacing Project	1m 24.227s	3.673s	0.210s
20	Silva	SPA	Avintia Blusens	1m 24.560s	4.006s	0.333s
21	Ellison	GBR	Paul Bird Motorsport	1m 26.715s	4.161s	0.155s
NF	Rapp	USA	Attack Performance	1m 26.887s	6.333s	0.172s

FINISHERS

1 CASEY STONER Went with the softer tyre, a choice that dictated his race. Planned to open up a gap and control the field but it didn't work out that way, so sat behind Lorenzo, keeping it smooth, until ten laps to go. Magicked amazing traction out of the last corner and blasted past the Yamaha.

2 JORGE LORENZO Started from pole for the fourth time here but again regretted using the harder tyre. Managed to get a gap on Stoner but nearly came to grief at the top of the Corkscrew; within a lap Casey was on him and he couldn't respond. Didn't think it would have been possible to beat the Aussie on the day.

3 DANI PEDROSA Used the new engine and chassis. Lost touch with Stoner when he made a big mistake trying to retake second. Started tucking the front when he pushed on the brakes to try and close up again, so settled for third rather than ending up on the floor.

4 ANDREA DOVIZIOSO Spent the whole race keeping Crutchlow behind him and trying to catch Spies, until the American crashed out and gifted the Tech 3 teamsters fourth and fifth. It was the usual story: Cal and Dovi nose to tail, but Andrea didn't offer a chance to overtake.

5 CAL CRUTCHLOW Had to give best to his team-mate after a close fight, but a major improvement over his first visit to Laguna a year ago when he lost the front at Turn 2. Pressured Dovi all race long but couldn't induce an error.

6 NICKY HAYDEN Clashed with Bautista early on. Having crashed on cold brakes in warm-up he went cautiously for a couple of corners, worried about his brake lever. That was enough for the second group to open a gap. Got to Bradl but the bike didn't make it easy for him, though still had fourth-place pace.

7 STEFAN BRADL Had confidence in the front with a full tank but as the load went down he started experiencing chatter. Corner entry compromised, Stefan couldn't hold off Hayden.

8 ALVARO BAUTISTA Not a happy weekend. Had no confidence in the front in the race, which he thought might be down to tyre choice, and hadn't been helped by a big crash in warm-up.

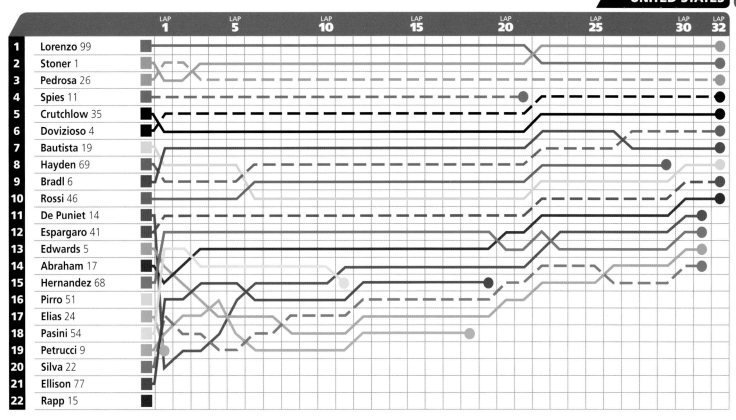

	LAP 1	LAP 5	LAP 10	LAP 15	LAP 20	LAP 25	LAP 30	LAP 32
1	Lorenzo 99							
2	Stoner 1							
3	Pedrosa 26							
4	Spies 11							
5	Crutchlow 35							
6	Dovizioso 4							
7	Bautista 19							
8	Hayden 69							
9	Bradl 6							
10	Rossi 46							
11	De Puniet 14							
12	Espargaro 41							
13	Edwards 5							
14	Abraham 17							
15	Hernandez 68							
16	Pirro 51							
17	Elias 24							
18	Pasini 54							
19	Petrucci 9							
20	Silva 22							
21	Ellison 77							
22	Rapp 15							

RACE

	Rider	Motorcycle	Race Time	Time +	Fastest Lap	Av Speed	🅱
1	Stoner	Honda	43m 45.961s		1m 21.282s	98.406mph	H/S
2	Lorenzo	Yamaha	43m 49.390s	3.000s	1m 21.255s	98.277mph	H/M
3	Pedrosa	Honda	43m 53.594s	7.000s	1m 21.229s	98.121mph	H/M
4	Dovizioso	Yamaha	44m 04.563s	18.000s	1m 21.931s	97.714mph	H/M
5	Crutchlow	Yamaha	44m 04.740s	18.000s	1m 21.914s	97.707mph	H/M
6	Hayden	Ducati	44m 12.863s	26.000s	1m 21.996s	97.408mph	H/S
7	Bradl	Honda	44m 14.354s	28.000s	1m 21.819s	97.353mph	H/S
8	Bautista	Honda	44m 36.207s	50.000s	1m 22.391s	96.559mph	M/S
9	Espargaro	Art	45m 04.954s	1m 18.000s	1m 23.514s	95.532mph	H/S
10	Abraham	Ducati	45m 08.037s	1m 22.000s	1m 23.718s	95.423mph	H/S
11	De Puniet	Art	43m 47.392s	1 lap	1m 23.640s	95.279mph	H/S
12	Hernandez	BQR	43m 55.108s	1 lap	1m 23.731s	95.000mph	H/S
13	Edwards	Suter	44m 17.426s	1 lap	1m 24.587s	94.202mph	M/M
14	Silva	BQR	44m 20.627s	1 lap	1m 24.678s	94.089mph	H/S
NF	Rossi	Ducati	40m 12.716s	3 laps	1m 22.189s	97.063mph	H/S
NF	Spies	Yamaha	28m 53.855s	11 laps	1m 21.753s	97.806mph	H/M
NF	Ellison	Art	27m 06.077s	13 laps	1m 24.555s	94.356mph	H/S
NF	Petrucci	Ioda	25m 44.849s	14 laps	1m 25.033s	94.091mph	H/S
NF	Pasini	Art	15m 39.351s	21 laps	1m 24.132s	94.563mph	H/S
NF	Elias	Ducati	1m 36.924s	31 laps		83.316mph	M/S
NF	Pirro	FTR					H/S

CHAMPIONSHIP

	Rider	Team	Points
1	Lorenzo	Yamaha Factory Racing	205
2	Pedrosa	Repsol Honda Team	182
3	Stoner	Repsol Honda Team	173
4	Dovizioso	Monster Yamaha Tech 3	121
5	Crutchlow	Monster Yamaha Tech 3	106
6	Bradl	LCR Honda MotoGP	84
7	Hayden	Ducati Team	84
8	Rossi	Ducati Team	82
9	Bautista	San Carlo Honda Gresini	81
10	Spies	Yamaha Factory Racing	66
11	Barbera	Pramac Racing Team	60
12	De Puniet	Power Electronics Aspar	33
13	Espargaro	Power Electronics Aspar	33
14	Pirro	San Carlo Honda Gresini	16
15	Pasini	Speed Master	13
16	Ellison	Paul Bird Motorsport	12
17	Edwards	NGM Mobile Forward Racing	11
18	Abraham	Cardion AB Motoracing	10
19	Hernandez	Avintia Blusens	10
20	Petrucci	Came IodaRacing Project	9
21	Silva	Avintia Blusens	7

9 ALEIX ESPARGARO Top CRT for the fifth time and inside the top ten for the first time, despite struggling for front-end feel all weekend. Followed Rossi for the first three laps to open up a decisive lead over the other CRTs.

10 KAREL ABRAHAM Back after a four-race gap but still handicapped by his injured hand. Got stuck behind Hernandez for too long, then discomfited by the gravel spread on track by Rossi's crash. Couldn't close on Espargaro so settled for his first top-ten finish of the year.

11 RANDY DE PUNIET Run off the track by Pirro's crash on the first lap. Made half a dozen passes on his way back from dead last, but couldn't avoid being lapped.

12 YONNY HERNANDEZ His usual entertaining self at the front of the CRT fight for the first half of the race. Caught by de Puniet and Abraham at the end, but was pretty impressive on his first visit to Laguna.

13 COLIN EDWARDS Went better than in recent races, but put much of that advantage down to his knowledge of Laguna; most of the other CRT riders hadn't raced there previously.

14 IVAN SILVA Followed Edwards home as final finisher. Lots of changes to the bike, plus new fork and fairing. The team were happy to have both riders score points for the first time.

VALENTINO ROSSI Dumped at the top of the Corkscrew when he lost the front on the brakes on lap 30. Like the crash he had in practice at Silverstone, he appeared to lock the front with the bike vertical. His front tyre, said Valentino, was like new.

BEN SPIES Looked to have fourth place sewn up when he suffered another unbelievable piece of bad luck. Lying in fifth, and holding off the Tech 3 Yamahas, he crashed coming down the Corkscrew. Yamaha reported a 'swingarm failure', although it looked as if the suspension linkage had failed.

JAMES ELLISON Handicapped by quickshifter problems in practice. Lapped

faster in the race but asked too much of the front on the brakes at Turn 3 while in 15th place. Ended a run of four points-scoring rides.

DANILO PETRUCCI Quickly got up to the group disputing the final points but dropped back when the front started to fold on him. Forced to retire on lap 19.

MATTIA PASINI Made up five places off the start and was looking good for a couple of points when a technical problem forced him out on lap 12.

TONI ELIAS Racing as a replacement for the injured Hector Barbera. Ran off track at the first left-hander when Pirro crashed in front of him, got back on but then crashed on the second lap.

MICHELE PIRRO Three DNFs in a row, this time after a coming-together with Randy de Puniet on the first lap.

STEVE RAPP Local veteran on a Kawasaki-powered CRT machine. Didn't qualify within the required 107% of pole-man's time and as fuel-pump trouble kept him out of warm-up he could not race.

HECTOR BARBERA Out after breaking his leg on a motocrosser. Replaced by Toni Elias.

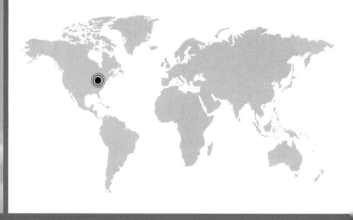

RED BULL
INDIANAPOLIS GRAND PRIX

BRICKYARD BLUES

Pedrosa took the win amid carnage of the physical – Stoner – and mechanical – Spies – kind

To be frank, the racing won't stay long in the memory, but the other events both on and off the track will. Before the MotoGP circus even pitched up at the Indianapolis Motor Speedway Valentino Rossi had made it public that he would be rejoining Yamaha for 2013, thus sending a frisson of panic through those riders who had yet to find a seat. As soon as a wheel was turned the usual complaints and fears about the patchwork track surfaced. Heavy rainfall on Thursday night didn't help grip on Friday, with lap times two seconds slower than the previous year's race. The first session saw a couple of serious crashes – first Cal Crutchlow in the left-handers before the final chicane, an area of track that would claim more victims on Saturday, and then Hector Barbera. He was trying to return less than a month after breaking his leg in a training accident but highsided at the final corner, landing squarely on top of his crash helmet.

It was a very nasty looking crash, but the way Hector was picked up and carted away was worse. When he was diagnosed with a cracked vertebra, the potential implications of his manhandling became horribly clear. Toni Elias had travelled with the Pramac team in case Barbera's leg injury prevented him racing, and he duly took over. Attention was diverted from Hector's treatment, however, by a trio of massive crashes in qualifying.

All three happened on the same stretch of tarmac, the left-handers from Turns 12 to 14. The first crash had the most serious implications: Casey Stoner suffered the biggest, most vicious highside imaginable. The bike was nearly upright when he was flicked over the bars with such violence that the Honda's rear wheel was shattered as the tyre was ripped from its rim. When Casey tried to stand it was horribly obvious that he had an injury to his

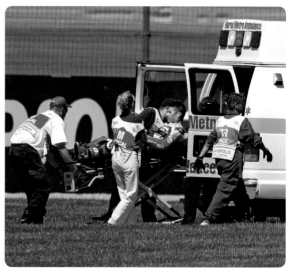

RIGHT Casey Stoner rode with serious damage to his right ankle after a massive highside in qualifying

FAR RIGHT Nicky Hayden wasn't so lucky, his highside resulted in broken bones in his right hand and concussion

right ankle. He later said it was dislocated, and went back in as he tried to move. Stoner sank to his knees and waved to the medics. It was, he said, the first crash of his entire career from which he'd been unable to walk away.

Next Ben Spies highsided at speed but did walk away, and then Nicky Hayden's Ducati spat him up the track. It was the same type of crash as Crutchlow's the previous day, leaving the local hero unconscious for worrying moments before he gave a reassuring wave. If the massive concussion hadn't put him out of the race, the two broken bones in his right hand undoubtedly would have. When the first reports on Stoner's injury came in, no-one expected him to race either. He had

torn nearly every ligament in his right ankle, as well as suffering chipped bones, small fractures and bruising to both bones in his lower leg. He didn't leave hospital until midnight. Add to that the general beating-up a rider suffers from a big highside and it's understandable the surprise he caused when he appeared in the Repsol Honda pit for Sunday morning warm-up in his leathers and with an oversize boot on his injured foot.

Just as surprisingly, Ben Spies was quickest in the warm-up. It really did look as if he was going to make a point at what he'd said would be his last MotoGP race in his home country. American media folk saw the old Spies, the man they remembered going up against Mat Mladin, and expected a serious challenge for the

RIGHT Jorge Lorenzo couldn't repeat the triumphs of previous years at the Brickyard and had to settle for second

OPPOSITE The scale of the Indianapolis Motor Speedway is breathtaking

front straight. He was able to get off the racing line, but several following riders' heart rates went sky high as they plunged into the smoke – you could smell the hot oil in the grandstands. The American was adamant that he could have run with Pedrosa and planned to attack near the end of the race, but the bike started slowing as soon as Pedrosa passed him. Just when life seemingly couldn't become any stranger for Ben, he found himself out of both American races because of mechanical failure. Not surprisingly, the garage door came down quickly and, equally unsurprisingly, Spies went berserk at Yamaha management.

All of which left Pedrosa to dominate the race, although he did try and fall late on when he found a false neutral at Turn 2. All that did was let Lorenzo take one second out of a massive lead. The only serious fight on track was for third place. Astoundingly, Stoner came through from seventh on the first lap to take third on lap ten. Andrea Dovizioso stalked him and pushed past at Turn 2 to take his fourth rostrum finish in five races and seriously worry the other riders still without a job for 2013.

It's not often that racers feel moved to say something nice about an opponent, at least while they're still competing, but Casey Stoner's ride to fourth place elicited praise from everyone. The painkillers wore off by half-distance and he had to compensate by using the left side of his body more. He finished exhausted and, ever the racer, just a little bit annoyed not to be on the rostrum. It was hard not to think that Casey's chances of leaving MotoGP as a champion had just disappeared. Dovizioso was even moved to wave a hand when he overtook Stoner, not just in apology but in admiration as well.

ABOVE James Ellison – the flag of Britain on the bike for his team, the flag of Texas on his helmet for his wife

OPPOSITE Stoner was as high as third in the race; astounding given the damage to his ankle

BELOW Joy for the Avintia Blusens team after Yonny Hernandez is top CRT

rostrum – at least. At first it looked like they might be right. Ben ripped into the lead from a second-row start, passing Dani Pedrosa at the second corner. The Honda rider had to work hard to take the lead back, powering past on the straight on the third lap. Contrary to what we've been used to seeing, Pedrosa did not immediately open up a big gap – more evidence that Yamaha have overcome their historic lack of top speed compared to the Hondas. Spies stayed in touch, pulling away from his team-mate, one of only two riders to opt for the softer rear tyre. But then, four laps later, Spies's engine expired, trailing a massive cloud of smoke down the

'IT WAS FRUSTRATING TO GIVE UP THE PODIUM POSITION'
CASEY STONER

SURFACE TENSION

It would be easy to blame Bridgestone for the rash of crashes that afflicted the MotoGP field at the IMS; easy but wrong. The problem is that the circuit used by MotoGP comprises sections of three different tracks with different surfaces. The main straight and Turn 5 are part of the world-famous two-mile oval used for the Indianapolis 500; the sections that make up Turns 1 to 4 and Turns 6 and 7 were laid for the first MotoGP race in 2008; and the rest of the infield was built for Formula 1.

Historically, the F1 circuit has always been very bumpy, and despite partial resurfacing for the 2011 race not all of the bumps were removed. It was this last section of the MotoGP circuit, the section of the Formula 1 track, that caused the vast majority of the problems, mainly because it managed to possess the seemingly mutually exclusive properties of being very abrasive and extremely slippery.

It is impossible to build a tyre that can cope with five changes of surface in one lap and act consistently. This was a very different situation from Assen, where Bridgestone simply got their sums wrong. The final sector also claimed a good number of victims in the Dunlop-shod Moto2 and Moto3 classes, with Hector Faubel proving it is possible to highside a Moto3 bike every bit as violently as a MotoGP Honda.

Conditions on race day were much the same as for qualifying, yet Dani Pedrosa lowered the race time by 13 seconds compared to Stoner's 2011 victory and he broke the

absolute lap record in qualifying as well. It is also worth noting that none of the men who finished on the rostrum fell off at any point during the race weekend.

RED BULL
INDIANAPOLIS GRAND PRIX
INDIANAPOLIS MOTOR SPEEDWAY

ROUND 11
August 19

RACE RESULTS

CIRCUIT LENGTH 2.620 miles
NO. OF LAPS 28
RACE DISTANCE 73.352 miles
WEATHER Dry, 25°C
TRACK TEMPERATURE 39°C
WINNER Dani Pedrosa
FASTEST LAP 1m 39.088s,
95.177mph, Dani Pedrosa (Record)
PREVIOUS LAP RECORD 1m 39.807s,
94.510mph, Casey Stoner, 2011

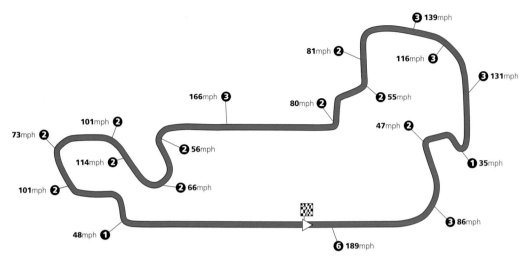

QUALIFYING

	Rider	Nationality	Team	Qualifying	Pole +	Gap
1	Pedrosa	SPA	Repsol Honda Team	1m 38.813s		
2	Lorenzo	SPA	Yamaha Factory Racing	1m 38.913s	0.100s	0.100s
3	Dovizioso	ITA	Monster Yamaha Tech 3	1m 39.235s	0.422s	0.322s
4	Spies	USA	Yamaha Factory Racing	1m 39.279s	0.466s	0.044s
5	Bradl	GER	LCR Honda MotoGP	1m 39.437s	0.624s	0.158s
6	Stoner	AUS	Repsol Honda Team	1m 39.465s	0.652s	0.028s
7	Crutchlow	GBR	Monster Yamaha Tech 3	1m 39.549s	0.736s	0.084s
8	Hayden	USA	Ducati Team	1m 39.748s	0.935s	0.199s
9	Bautista	SPA	San Carlo Honda Gresini	1m 40.072s	1.259s	0.324s
10	De Puniet	FRA	Power Electronics Aspar	1m 40.437s	1.624s	0.365s
11	Rossi	ITA	Ducati Team	1m 40.763s	1.950s	0.326s
12	Espargaro	SPA	Power Electronics Aspar	1m 40.803s	1.990s	0.040s
13	Hernandez	COL	Avintia Blusens	1m 41.197s	2.384s	0.394s
14	Abraham	CZE	Cardion AB Motoracing	1m 41.295s	2.482s	0.098s
15	Pasini	ITA	Speed Master	1m 41.370s	2.557s	0.075s
16	Pirro	ITA	San Carlo Honda Gresini	1m 41.449s	2.636s	0.079s
17	Elias	SPA	Pramac Racing Team	1m 41.866s	3.053s	0.417s
18	Ellison	GBR	Paul Bird Motorsport	1m 41.978s	3.165s	0.112s
19	Petrucci	ITA	Came IodaRacing Project	1m 42.553s	3.740s	0.575s
20	Edwards	USA	NGM Mobile Forward Racing	1m 42.599s	3.786s	0.046s
21	Silva	SPA	Avintia Blusens	1m 42.768s	3.955s	0.169s
22	Rapp	USA	Attack Performance	1m 43.673s	4.860s	0.905s
23	Yates	USA	GPTech	1m 44.312s	5.499s	0.639s

FINISHERS

1 DANI PEDROSA An impeccable weekend took him to within 18 points of the championship lead. Had to deal with a very determined Spies in the early laps, but then controlled the race, apart from one serious moment when he found a false neutral at Turn 2 that handed a second back to Lorenzo. Set a new record on lap 15.

2 JORGE LORENZO The only works rider to race with the softer rear tyre, contrary to Yamaha's recent practice of playing safe with the harder option. The hoped-for advantage in the closing stages did not materialise and he had a lonely race. Given his problems in practice, Jorge was content with the result.

3 ANDREA DOVIZIOSO A fifth rostrum in seven races and his second front-row start of the year, though he felt his performance was inconsistent. Had to fight with Stoner, who took third off him on lap ten, for the final rostrum position. Not distracted by the rumours linking him to a Ducat ride for 2013.

4 CASEY STONER Severely damaged his right ankle in a massive qualifying highside but rode with an oversize boot to protect chipped bones and torn ligaments. Still took Dovizioso some time to get past him. He was even annoyed at losing a rostrum position. An heroic ride.

5 ALVARO BAUTISTA Very happy with the whole weekend and rediscovered the feeling he had before Mugello. Only lost touch with Stoner and Dovi in the last

quarter of the race and beat the other satellite Honda handily.

6 STEFAN BRADL It's a measure of how well Stefan's season has gone that sixth was a disappointment. Couldn't push hard out of the two bottom-gear corners, especially with a full tank – a disappointment after his second-best qualification of the year.

7 VALENTINO ROSSI Couldn't match his times from earlier in the weekend, probably due to the elevated temperatures on race day. No rear grip from early on, pushing harder resulted in slower lap times and he lost the front a couple of times so settled for seventh.

8 KAREL ABRAHAM By far his best ride of the year and encouraging for his home

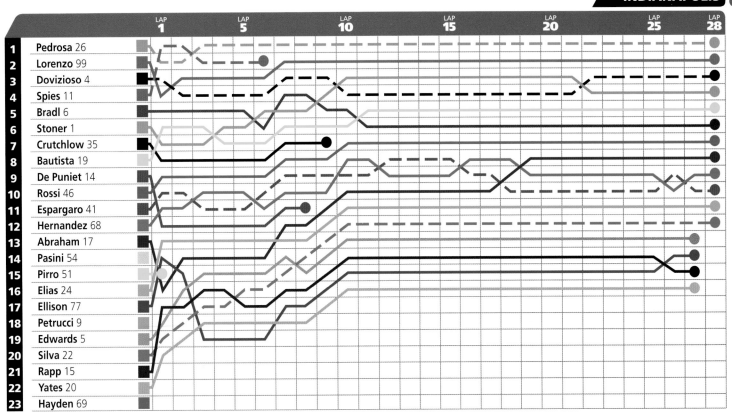

		LAP 1	LAP 5	LAP 10	LAP 15	LAP 20	LAP 25	LAP 28
1	Pedrosa 26							
2	Lorenzo 99							
3	Dovizioso 4							
4	Spies 11							
5	Bradl 6							
6	Stoner 1							
7	Crutchlow 35							
8	Bautista 19							
9	De Puniet 14							
10	Rossi 46							
11	Espargaro 41							
12	Hernandez 68							
13	Abraham 17							
14	Pasini 54							
15	Pirro 51							
16	Elias 24							
17	Ellison 77							
18	Petrucci 9							
19	Edwards 5							
20	Silva 22							
21	Rapp 15							
22	Yates 20							
23	Hayden 69							

RACE

	Rider	Motorcycle	Race Time	Time +	Fastest Lap	Av Speed	🅱
1	Pedrosa	Honda	46m 39.631s		1m 39.088s	94.322mph	XH/H
2	Lorenzo	Yamaha	46m 50.454s	10.000s	1m 39.452s	93.958mph	XH/M
3	Dovizioso	Yamaha	46m 56.941s	17.000s	1m 39.729s	93.742mph	XH/H
4	Stoner	Honda	46m 59.434s	19.000s	1m 39.785s	93.659mph	XH/H
5	Bautista	Honda	47m 02.187s	22.000s	1m 39.827s	93.567mph	XH/H
6	Bradl	Honda	47m 09.703s	30.000s	1m 40.036s	93.319mph	XH/H
7	Rossi	Ducati	47m 37.245s	57.000s	1m 40.639s	92.420mph	XH/H
8	Abraham	Ducati	47m 48.073s	1m 08.000s	1m 41.339s	92.070mph	XH/H
9	Hernandez	BQR	47m 50.737s	1m 11.000s	1m 41.311s	91.985mph	XH/M
10	Espargaro	Art	47m 53.710s	1m 14.000s	1m 41.133s	91.890mph	XH/M
11	Elias	Ducati	48m 05.936s	1m 26.000s	1m 42.273s	91.501mph	XH/M
12	Silva	BQR	48m 19.905s	1m 40.000s	1m 42.506s	91.060mph	XH/M
13	Edwards	Suter	46m 46.893s	1 lap	1m 42.725s	90.718mph	XH/H
14	Rapp	APR	47m 00.909s	1 lap	1m 43.123s	90.267mph	XH/H
15	Ellison	Art	46m 55.629s	1 lap	1m 40.831s	90.437mph	XH/M
16	Yates	BCL	47m 54.994s	1 lap	1m 45.104s	88.568mph	XH/M
NF	Crutchlow	Yamaha	15m 12.245s	19 laps	1m 39.966s	93.043mph	XH/H
NF	De Puniet	Art	13m 45.971s	20 laps	1m 41.411s	91.343mph	XH/M
NF	Spies	Yamaha	10m 04.406s	22 laps	1m 39.289s	93.621mph	XH/H
NF	Pirro	FTR	1m 51.921s	27 laps		84.264mph	XH/M
NF	Pasini	Art					XH/M
NF	Petrucci	Ioda					XH/M

CHAMPIONSHIP

	Rider	Team	Points
1	Lorenzo	Yamaha Factory Racing	225
2	Pedrosa	Repsol Honda Team	207
3	Stoner	Repsol Honda Team	186
4	Dovizioso	Monster Yamaha Tech 3	137
5	Crutchlow	Monster Yamaha Tech 3	106
6	Bradl	LCR Honda MotoGP	94
7	Bautista	San Carlo Honda Gresini	92
8	Rossi	Ducati Team	91
9	Hayden	Ducati Team	84
10	Spies	Yamaha Factory Racing	66
11	Barbera	Pramac Racing Team	60
12	Espargaro	Power Electronics Aspar	39
13	De Puniet	Power Electronics Aspar	33
14	Abraham	Cardion AB Motoracing	18
15	Hernandez	Avintia Blusens	17
16	Pirro	San Carlo Honda Gresini	16
17	Edwards	NGM Mobile Forward Racing	14
18	Pasini	Speed Master	13
19	Ellison	Paul Bird Motorsport	13
20	Silva	Avintia Blusens	11
21	Petrucci	Came IodaRacing Project	9
22	Elias	Pramac Racing Team	5
23	Rapp	Attack Performance	2

race the following week. Had a bad start and then got stuck behind Elias, before passing CRT bikes. Ran the same times as Rossi in the final laps.

9 YONNY HERNANDEZ Top CRT for the first time; also the first time for an FTR chassis. Harried Espargaro into making a mistake in the closing stages. Cited chassis modifications giving him more grip at the start of the race as a major improvement.

10 ALEIX ESPARGARO Another gearbox problem on an Aprilia: started getting false neutrals at half-distance. Under the circumstances, tenth place was a good result.

11 TONI ELIAS Replaced Hector Barbera on the Pramac Ducati for the second race in a row.

12 IVAN SILVA Nearly as happy as his team-mate, and also benefiting from chassis and suspension modifications. Satisfied with his first visit to Indy.

13 COLIN EDWARDS Points for the fourth time this season, but still a second a lap slower than the leading CRT bikes and he suffered the indignity of being lapped.

14 STEVE RAPP Wild-card entry on a Kawasaki-engined machine built by his team. Aged 40, Steve became the oldest American rider ever to take part in a Grand Prix.

15 JAMES ELLISON The gearbox problem continued to make itself felt, sending him off track three times. He fought back to cross the line in 14th,

but the Attack team protested as he'd gained 1.5s by cutting a corner on his third excursion. The protest was upheld.

16 AARON YATES His first GP at the age of 38 and a racing comeback after serious leg injuries in 2010. Was using an AMA-spec Suzuki superbike engine in his team's own chassis.

NON-FINISHERS

CAL CRUTCHLOW First DNF of the year. Lucky to walk away from a big crash on Friday (much the same as Hayden's in qualifying), then crashed at Turn 4 on Saturday. And that's the corner that got him on race day. He was on the back of the podium group when he lost the front.

RANDY DE PUNIET Sat behind his team-mate and Hernandez when he felt something break. The gearbox wouldn't downshift twice on the next lap, and a lap later the clutch failed.

BEN SPIES Another quite astounding weekend. Fast from the first practice, then was one of the three top men to suffer a massive crash in qualifying. Led from the start and was second, shadowing Pedrosa, when the engine blew up down the main straight. Not surprisingly, he was incandescent with rage.

MICHELE PIRRO A fourth consecutive retirement, again thanks to the swingarm problem. Team-owner Fausto Gresini was decidedly unamused.

MATTIA PASINI Looked like he might be

in the fight for top CRT after qualifying, but made a mistake on the first lap, touched another bike, ran off track and fell on the grass.

DANILO PETRUCCI Got away well and then his engine stopped after just a few corners.

NON-STARTERS

NICKY HAYDEN Highsided in qualifying and was knocked out, suffering a serious concussion and two broken bones in his hand.

HECTOR BARBERA Tried to come back after breaking his leg in training before Laguna, but crashed hard in the first free practice and cracked a vertebra.

bwin GRAND PRIX ČESKÉ REPUBLIKY

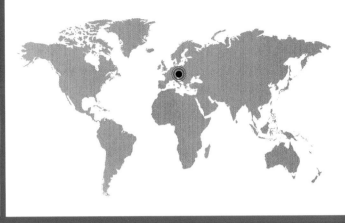

THEN THERE WERE TWO

Dani Pedrosa's win brought him within range of Jorge Lorenzo at the top of the championship table

The 2012 MotoGP World Championship came into sharp focus before a bike turned a wheel at the spectacular Czech track. Casey Stoner called a press conference on Thursday to announce that he was returning to Australia to have an operation on the ankle he'd injured at Indianapolis. His favoured surgeon, the man who diagnosed his lactose intolerance, had left Casey in no doubt about the consequences of another crash. Once Dr Lam had seen the high-resolution scans there was no doubt: the 2011 World Champion needed work on ligaments, cartilage and bones, and the injury was even more complex and unpleasant than first feared. There were no promises about a comeback, although Stoner, rather optimistically, did say that he hoped to get a couple of races in before Phillip Island. The racer showed through in a couple of remarks about how he 'could have got points back at Indy' and how the championship was now 'coming to circuits that suit me better', but there was another persona revealed as well, the young man who had never before failed to walk away from a crash and now found himself in completely unfamiliar territory. Would that alter his decision to retire? Did he need to win again? 'I'm not going to wait for a fairy-tale ending,' he said.

One of my broadcasting colleagues summed up the situation succinctly at the start of the weekend: 'Dani has to win.' He was right. The gap between Pedrosa and Lorenzo after Indy was 18 points. Reduce that tally by five and the lead looks very vulnerable; increase it by five and it's nearly a whole race's worth. Brno felt like the fulcrum on which the season would pivot. Dani knew it, Jorge knew it, and a massive crowd, claimed to be over 139,000, knew it too.

LEFT Once Casey Stoner's doctor back in Australia saw the scans of the ankle injured in Indianapolis, the rider was on the way to the airport and surgery

OPPOSITE Cal Crutchlow scored the first top-three finish by a British rider in twelve years

BELOW Danilo Petrucci survived this moment; it was his last race with the Ioda team's own bike, he swapped to Suter BMW for the next race

The race was a classic. The two Spaniards pulled away from the field, Lorenzo leading, Pedrosa taking over at mid-distance as the pair continued to demonstrate how two different motorcycles with different strengths and two riders with different styles could post near-identical lap times. Pedrosa had an advantage up the hill that ends the lap, there was nothing in it down the straights, while Lorenzo could carry more speed mid-corner – and that matters a lot here.

It was always going to come down to the last lap. There was never more than 0.45s between them, and usually a fair bit less. Each man was well aware where the other was strong, so Jorge knew he had to get past in one of the chicanes. He actually managed to pass on the inside at Turn 7, the first of a pair of second-gear left-handers at the bottom of the circuit, although it's unbelievable how he found the space. Jorge said he'd made the same move on Andrea Dovizioso to beat him in a 125cc race in 2004. Dani said he could see Jorge's fairing right next to his visor. Lorenzo held the advantage to the bottom of the hill and through the first uphill chicane – but this was where the Honda had the advantage all weekend. Pedrosa ran up the inside to take the line for the penultimate corner; Jorge did the only thing he could – he let the brake off to try and run round the outside to be on the inside for the final right. Too much corner speed; he nearly ran up pit lane. Jorge's momentum was gone, Dani was carrying speed on the racing line and held the advantage to the flag, sparking unrestrained celebrations in pit lane from his team – and even from the Japanese management.

Both men considered they had made mistakes on

the last lap. The Honda man said he'd tried too hard to counter the Yamaha's corner speed and left a gap; Lorenzo said he'd made a mistake coming up the hill, leaving Dani room to move to the inside for the final chicane. That's what decides a MotoGP race at this level for these guys: a race-deciding mistake going a foot off-line once in 45 minutes of battling at lap-record pace.

Twelve seconds behind this display of near-perfection, Cal Crutchlow became the first British rider to finish on the rostrum since Jeremy McWilliams at Donington Park in 2000. Cal denied his form had anything to do

'HE WAS VERY BRAVE'
JORGE LORENZO

with having re-signed for the Tech 3 Yamaha team that weekend, although plenty of people, including his team-manager, thought the two facts might just have been related.

Crutchlow backed up his best-ever qualifying with a perfect race, getting away from everyone but the two Spaniards and thus not involved in two first-lap incidents that created some confusion. First, Ben Spies – yes, him again – cooked his clutch getting off the line and slowed

mid-pack; then, not for the first time this season, Rossi's Ducati blew a large cloud of oil smoke out, causing consternation among those following him. Valentino's issue did resolve itself, and Spies managed to recover and cut through the pack. He was lapping fast enough to have caught Rossi when he fell.

The championship situation was now clear: it was a straight fight between Pedrosa and Lorenzo. In pit lane for the Monday test, HRC boss Shuhei Nakamoto was still grinning. 'I have new rider! Same size; looks same through visor!' Any doubts anyone ever had about Dani's ability to tough it out in a fight had been well and truly dispelled. Yes, he had to win at Brno.

ABOVE Pedrosa stalks Lorenzo in the closing stages of the best race of the year

RIGHT Cal Crutchlow remembers why you should wear sunglasses on the rostrum

OPPOSITE Stefan Bradl won the three-way fight for fifth place

REUNITED

The announcements by Yamaha and Valentino Rossi that they would be together again in 2013 sparked so much interest that Yamaha felt it necessary to hold a special press conference in Brno to reveal details of the deal. We learned that Valentino made the first move, that serious negotiations began in July, and that Jorge Lorenzo was informed at Mugello. Interestingly, Lin Jarvis, MD of Yamaha Racing, mentioned that 'five or six weeks ago' both the company's and Jorge's preference was to retain Ben Spies. That would be up until Spies made his shock announcement just before the Laguna Seca race.

There will be no wall in the pit. Yamaha expect Rossi's mechanics to come with him, including Jeremy Burgess, but not the battalion of other staff that went to Ducati. There was much interest in the story, dating back to a June interview in which it was said that 'Valentino will be on a competitive machine in 2013', and that Dorna CEO Carmelo Ezpeleta had some influence on the move. Jarvis categorically denied any such pressure: 'I have never discussed Valentino's return with him to this day.' The only touch of *Schadenfreude* that Jarvis allowed himself was observing that Yamaha 'did not have a huge budget remaining' after securing Jorge's services. There is no doubt that Yamaha had to persuade Lorenzo not to accept a very big offer from Honda by presenting him with a decent counter-offer, and that Rossi will be receiving a fraction of the salary that Ducati offered him to stay on for another year.

As for the thorny question of who will be the team number one, Jarvis emphasised that both riders will receive equal treatment in terms of machinery, but that they will regard Jorge as the rider more likely to win the title and therefore the one who will lead development.

BRIDGESTONE

TYRE OPTIONS
FRONT SOFT (S) / MEDIUM (M) / EXTRA HARD (XH)
REAR MEDIUM (M) / HARD (H)

motogp **TISSOT** Swiss watches since 1853

OFFICIAL TIMEKEEPER

bwin GRAND PRIX ČESKÉ REPUBLIKY
AUTODROM BRNO

ROUND 12
August 26

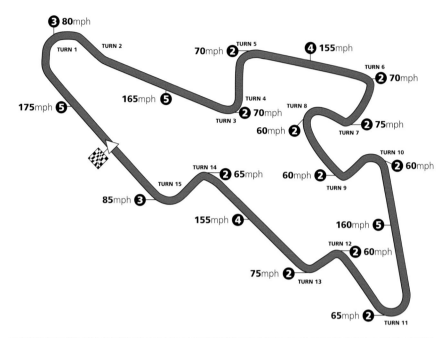

RACE RESULTS

CIRCUIT LENGTH 3.357 miles
NO. OF LAPS 22
RACE DISTANCE 73.860 miles
WEATHER Dry, 18°C
TRACK TEMPERATURE 23°C
WINNER Dani Pedrosa
FASTEST LAP 1m 56.274s, 103.945mph, Jorge Lorenzo (Record)
PREVIOUS LAP RECORD 1m 56.670s, 103.592mph, Jorge Lorenzo, 2009

QUALIFYING

	Rider	Nationality	Team	Qualifying	Pole +	Gap
1	Lorenzo	SPA	Yamaha Factory Racing	1m 55.799s		
2	Crutchlow	GBR	Monster Yamaha Tech 3	1m 55.995s	0.196s	0.196s
3	Pedrosa	SPA	Repsol Honda Team	1m 56.327s	0.528s	0.332s
4	Spies	USA	Yamaha Factory Racing	1m 56.331s	0.532s	0.004s
5	Dovizioso	ITA	Monster Yamaha Tech 3	1m 56.559s	0.760s	0.228s
6	Rossi	ITA	Ducati Team	1m 56.735s	0.936s	0.176s
7	Bradl	GER	LCR Honda MotoGP	1m 56.827s	1.028s	0.092s
8	Bautista	SPA	San Carlo Honda Gresini	1m 57.068s	1.269s	0.241s
9	Abraham	CZE	Cardion AB Motoracing	1m 57.773s	1.974s	0.705s
10	De Puniet	FRA	Power Electronics Aspar	1m 57.844s	2.045s	0.071s
11	Espargaro	SPA	Power Electronics Aspar	1m 58.153s	2.354s	0.309s
12	Hernandez	COL	Avintia Blusens	1m 59.087s	3.288s	0.934s
13	Elias	SPA	Pramac Racing Team	1m 59.120s	3.321s	0.033s
14	Pirro	ITA	San Carlo Honda Gresini	1m 59.387s	3.588s	0.267s
15	Edwards	USA	NGM Mobile Forward Racing	1m 59.863s	4.064s	0.476s
16	Pasini	ITA	Speed Master	1m 59.865s	4.066s	0.002s
17	Ellison	GBR	Paul Bird Motorsport	2m 00.316s	4.517s	0.451s
18	Silva	SPA	Avintia Blusens	2m 00.329s	4.530s	0.013s
19	Petrucci	ITA	Came IodaRacing Project	2m 00.854s	5.055s	0.525s

FINISHERS

1 DANI PEDROSA Held his nerve after fraught qualifying to go head to head with Lorenzo over race distance, at lap-record pace, taking victory after a classic confrontation at the very last corner. It was a vital win, reducing his rival's lead to just 13 points, and, as Dani said, probably his best ever.

2 JORGE LORENZO Did all he could to negate the Honda's slight advantage on the hill ending the lap by using his bike's turning ability. Made an impossible last-lap pass on the inside at Turn 7 but lost out in the final braking effort. Kept up season's record of never finishing lower than second, containing the damage to his lead.

3 CAL CRUTCHLOW First rostrum finish following his best qualifying, and the first podium for a British rider in 12 years. On his own for the whole race, managing the gap to his team-mate – 'racing my pit board' – in a triumph of concentration.

4 ANDREA DOVIZIOSO Spent most of the race trying to close down his team-mate but couldn't get within range – lost out, he said, on corner exit speed. Congratulated Cal on doing a better job on the day.

5 STEFAN BRADL Impeded by Spies's slowing Yamaha and spooked by seeing the smoke from Rossi's Ducati and getting oil from it on to his visor. Recovered to pass both Rossi and Bautista and achieve a better result than his showing in practice suggested.

6 ALVARO BAUTISTA The lower temperatures on race day caused a severe problem with front chatter. The rear was also sliding so much, he said, that it felt like he'd had the hard tyre fitted.

7 VALENTINO ROSSI Qualified on the second row for the first time this season. The bike emitted a large cloud of smoke on lap one, which also put oil on to his footrests, brake pedal and gear lever. Later in the race the rear tyre started sliding, as usual, and he had to give best to Bradl and Bautista.

8 RANDY DE PUNIET Far and away the fastest CRT. Got past several prototypes off the line, but then slightly rattled by the smoke from Rossi's Ducati. Used Spies as a reference when he came past, and when

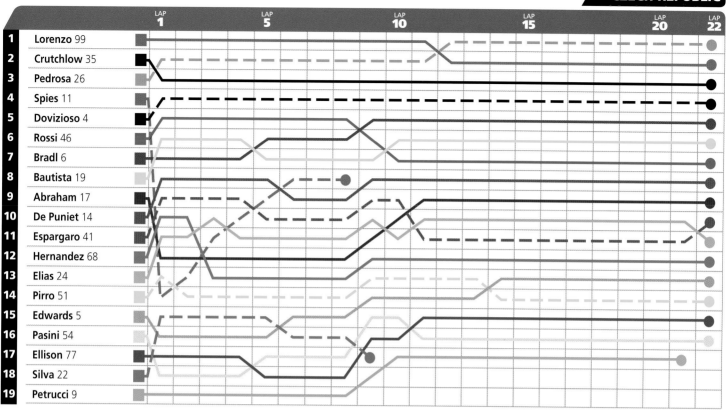

		LAP 1	LAP 5	LAP 10	LAP 15	LAP 20	LAP 22
1	Lorenzo 99						
2	Crutchlow 35						
3	Pedrosa 26						
4	Spies 11						
5	Dovizioso 4						
6	Rossi 46						
7	Bradl 6						
8	Bautista 19						
9	Abraham 17						
10	De Puniet 14						
11	Espargaro 41						
12	Hernandez 68						
13	Elias 24						
14	Pirro 51						
15	Edwards 5						
16	Pasini 54						
17	Ellison 77						
18	Silva 22						
19	Petrucci 9						

RACE

	Rider	Motorcycle	Race Time	Time +	Fastest Lap	Av Speed	
1	Pedrosa	Honda	42m 51.570s		1m 56.346s	103.398mph	XH/M
2	Lorenzo	Yamaha	42m 51.748s	0.178s	1m 56.274s	103.391mph	XH/M
3	Crutchlow	Yamaha	43m 03.913s	12.343s	1m 56.807s	102.904mph	XH/M
4	Dovizioso	Yamaha	43m 10.161s	18.591s	1m 56.883s	102.655mph	XH/M
5	Bradl	Honda	43m 17.152s	25.582s	1m 57.305s	102.380mph	XH/M
6	Bautista	Honda	43m 21.021s	29.451s	1m 57.429s	102.227mph	XH/M
7	Rossi	Ducati	43m 26.084s	34.514s	1m 57.363s	102.029mph	XH/M
8	De Puniet	Art	43m 55.855s	1m 04.285s	1m 58.781s	100.876mph	XH/M
9	Abraham	Ducati	43m 59.848s	1m 08.278s	1m 59.231s	100.724mph	XH/M
10	Espargaro	Art	44m 01.542s	1m 09.972s	1m 59.032s	100.659mph	XH/M
11	Elias	Ducati	44m 01.573s	1m 10.003s	1m 59.359s	100.658mph	XH/M
12	Hernandez	BQR	44m 15.610s	1m 24.040s	1m 59.980s	100.126mph	XH/M
13	Edwards	Suter	44m 19.468s	1m 27.898s	1m 59.633s	99.980mph	XH/M
14	Pirro	FTR	44m 27.735s	1m 36.165s	2m 00.017s	99.670mph	XH/M
15	Ellison	Art	44m 32.135s	1m 40.565s	2m 00.556s	99.506mph	XH/M
16	Pasini	Art	44m 32.796s	1m 41.226s	2m 00.624s	99.482mph	XH/M
17	Petrucci	Ioda	42m 59.186s	1 lap	2m 01.801s	98.407mph	XH/M
NF	Silva	BQR	18m 19.728s	13 laps	2m 00.583s	98.911mph	XH/M
NF	Spies	Yamaha	15m 53.910s	14 laps	1m 57.133s	101.361mph	XH/M

CHAMPIONSHIP

	Rider	Team	Points
1	Lorenzo	Yamaha Factory Racing	245
2	Pedrosa	Repsol Honda Team	232
3	Stoner	Repsol Honda Team	186
4	Dovizioso	Monster Yamaha Tech 3	150
5	Crutchlow	Monster Yamaha Tech 3	122
6	Bradl	LCR Honda MotoGP	105
7	Bautista	San Carlo Honda Gresini	102
8	Rossi	Ducati Team	100
9	Hayden	Ducati Team	84
10	Spies	Yamaha Factory Racing	66
11	Barbera	Pramac Racing Team	60
12	Espargaro	Power Electronics Aspar	45
13	De Puniet	Power Electronics Aspar	41
14	Abraham	Cardion AB Motoracing	25
15	Hernandez	Avintia Blusens	21
16	Pirro	San Carlo Honda Gresini	18
17	Edwards	NGM Mobile Forward Racing	17
18	Ellison	Paul Bird Motorsport	14
19	Pasini	Speed Master	13
20	Silva	Avintia Blusens	11
21	Elias	Pramac Racing Team	10
22	Petrucci	Came IodaRacing Project	9
23	Rapp	Attack Performance	2

Ben crashed Randy was able to keep the pace up. Beat both satellite Ducatis.

9 KAREL ABRAHAM Happy to finish his home GP for the first time in five years, but disappointed to lap a second slower than he did in qualifying.

10 ALEIX ESPARGARO Couldn't match his team-mate's pace and had problems with the bike sliding a lot in the early laps; then fighting in a group with the satellite Ducatis. Swapped places several times with Elias on the last lap and retained his position as top CRT in the points table.

11 TONI ELIAS Replaced Hector Barbera for the third race in a row, and finished in the same position as he did at Indy. Diced with Abraham and Espargaro

for much of the race, losing tenth on the last lap.

12 YONNY HERNANDEZ Another good race, considerably aided by a new rear shock and swinging arm plus the presence of Gregorio Lavilla in the pit as his race engineer.

13 COLIN EDWARDS Made serious progress through the weekend but still unimpressed with the bike, as he made plain. Rode Pasini's Aprilia at the Monday test.

14 MICHELE PIRRO Major problems with set-up, but at least finished a race for the first time in five outings. Not helped by an engine blow-up in practice, which left him with nasty burns on his leg.

15 JAMES ELLISON Made a big change to engine-braking settings after qualifying but couldn't test them because warm-up was wet. Decided to use the settings in the race but it proved too big a step, with James finding himself backing into corners way too much.

16 MATTIA PASINI Not happy to be out of the points amid rumours that his team was in severe financial trouble. Spent the whole race in close company with Ellison.

17 DANILO PETRUCCI Relegated to the back of his dice in the closing stages when gearbox problems started to make themselves felt, adding to the grip problems he suffered all race long.

NON-FINISHERS

IVAN SILVA Suffered from chatter but was put out of the race by an engine failure, the first the teams have suffered all year.

BEN SPIES Another weird weekend. Cooked the clutch off the line, despite the data showing he'd done nothing different from practice, then had to wait two laps for it to decide to work again. Charged through the field and would have caught Rossi but for pushing the front too hard and crashing while lying in eighth.

NON-STARTERS

CASEY STONER Went home to Australia before race day for an operation on the ankle he'd injured at Indianapolis.

NICKY HAYDEN Stayed home in the States to allow the two broken bones in his right hand, legacy of his Indy crash, to heal.

HECTOR BARBERA Ruled out after his crash in Indianapolis, and replaced for the third time by Toni Elias.

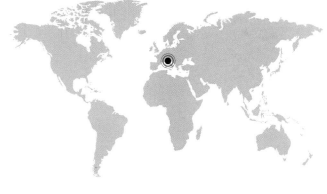

GRAN PREMIO APEROL DI SAN MARINO E DELLA RIVIERA DI RIMINI

KNOCKED OUT LOADED

Lorenzo won as Pedrosa was skittled – and Rossi returned to the rostrum

The entertainingly foul-mouthed British TV political satire 'The Thick of It' invented the now popular word 'omnishambles' for a particularly impressive collection of cock-ups. Honda in general, and Dani Pedrosa in particular, must have felt like they'd been victims of an omnishambles at Misano.

The Repsol Honda team went into the San Marino GP with Pedrosa on a roll and with every chance of closing the 13-point gap to Jorge Lorenzo at the top of the championship table. Dani should have begun the race from pole, but that's when it all went wrong because Karel Abraham stalled his Ducati on the grid and the start was abandoned. As is to be expected, riders didn't know the regulations so the sight of an orange light after the reds engendered much confusion. When the time came to get going again the tyre warmer wouldn't come off Pedrosa's front wheel; the brake had locked on. The crew couldn't rectify the situation before the one-minute board went out – after which no-one is allowed to work on a machine – so that meant Dani's bike needed to be removed from its qualifying position and start from the back of the grid. The problem was solved in pit lane and his Honda was pushed back to pole position, but that was a breach of the rules: a rider in this situation is supposed to start the warm-up lap from pit lane and then form up at the rear of the pack.

Pedrosa had more pressing worries, however, because one of his crew must inadvertently have pushed some buttons while working on the bike and Dani set off on the warm-up lap with the pit-lane speed limiter engaged. It took him half a lap to work that one out, but he was able to overtake the pace car and get to the back of the grid. He then took off with his usual speed,

RIGHT Dani Pedrosa contemplates the bizarre sequence of events that effectively ended his hopes of the championship

OPPOSITE For once, it all went right for Valentino Rossi and he put the Ducati on the rostrum at what is truly his home race

BELOW The chain of events that led to the abandoned start was set of by Karel Abraham's Ducati's clutch failing; there was nothing the rider could have done

'I COULD HAVE HAD A CHANCE TO WIN THIS RACE, EVEN STARTING FROM THE LAST PLACE ON THE GRID'
DANI PEDROSA

ripped past the CRTs before he'd reached the front row of the grid and started to work on the other prototypes. As he approached the Quercia left-hander at the end of Misano's first straight he was tailgated by Hector Barbera and ended up on the floor, along with his championship hopes. It was rather reminiscent of an event in Portugal in 2006 and also balanced out Lorenzo's first-corner wipeout at Assen this year. Unsurprisingly, Dani was not happy – not with Barbera or with anyone else; not with the restart procedure or the fact that it was first announced that the race would be shortened by two laps and then a correction was made to a one-lap reduction.

Did he have legitimate grounds for complaining about anything other than his own bad luck? The Spanish media went after Abraham and the Race Director, but blaming the Czech rider for the failure of new clutch seals supplied by Ducati Corse is clearly ridiculous, while Race Direction had done everything by the book. After the abandoned start mechanics came back on the grid in larger numbers than the regulations stipulate, and riders took their helmets off, which again they shouldn't have done. Some TV crews also returned to the grid, also contrary to regs. The rulebook stipulates only that the one-minute board should be shown. Given the chaos, crews were shocked when it went out – they were expecting to see a three-minute board first. If there's a potential criticism of Race Direction it's that they were too hasty with the restart, but it should be remembered procedure was followed. As for Pedrosa's sticking brake, that remains a mystery. Honda used the data to replicate conditions and couldn't get the brake to bind. Brembo

said there was no evidence of anything melted to the surface of either disc or pad. Stories of similar incidents surfaced later, suggesting some sort of carbon–carbon bond forming between pad and disc, or a hydraulic lock, rather than debris melting on to a hot disc.

Almost everybody else was content. Valentino Rossi's new chassis worked well enough for him to finish a clear second, running consistent lap times all through the race, thus suggesting the old problem of excessive rear-tyre wear had been cured – or at least at Misano, where the team had happened to test for a couple of days the previous week. Rossi was happy to get a rostrum for his

old friend Marco Simoncelli, at a circuit now named for him. 'I wanted to dedicate a victory to Sic but I understand this would take too long, so this second will do just as well.' Vale was also happy with the bike: his laps were all within one-third of a second, but he was well aware that these improvements would only be put into proper perspective at tracks where the team hadn't tested. The new frame and swinging arm allowed the geometry changes needed, thus improving the front-end feel and balance.

Memories of Marco were everywhere, and it was somehow fitting that his old team made it on to the rostrum, with Alvaro Bautista taking his maiden MotoGP top-three finish after a spirited last-lap fight with Andrea Dovizioso. It was a timely breakthrough. The Honda belonging to the absent Casey Stoner was being ridden by Jonathan Rea, who impressed everyone with his professional approach. The Ulsterman was Honda's favoured candidate for the Team Gresini ride in 2013, but Bautista's breakthrough and the preferences of sponsor San Carlo didn't work in his favour. Rea went back to his regular World Superbike ride in the week between the San Marino GP and the next race at Aragon.

Lorenzo's only moment came at the first corner of lap three, and it was big enough to lose him three-quarters of a second to the pursuing Rossi. 'I don't know how I stayed on,' said Jorge later. Rossi saw it and the thought that he might take the win must have crossed his mind. In the event, though, it was the only mistake Lorenzo made all weekend. Jorge, by the way, now led the championship by 38 points, but yet again no-one was talking about him.

CONTROL FREAK

Although the deafening silence over the technical regulations concerning a spec ECU and a rev limit continued – the details were supposed to be announced in May – Dorna fired another shot in their war with the factories. In the week after the San Marino GP it was announced that they had commissioned an ECU that would be available to all teams free of charge for the 2013 season. It will be supplied by Magneti Marelli, who have been told to produce a 'high-specification unit'. This is as part of a four-year contract that includes the company providing technical support at all GPs and setting up an R&D centre for the MotoGP ECU at its Bologna headquarters.

It is, of course, highly improbable that a factory team would take up the offer of using this ECU next year, but it is likely to be a useful short cut and cost-saver for CRT teams. It should be borne in mind that next year's ECU will not be a control part, merely a freebie, so in theory teams will be able to do what they want with it. However, the intention is to make this the control ECU for the whole MotoGP class in 2014 (assuming Dorna has its way).

The factories, of course, are not keen on throwing away the fruits of their labour on fuelling strategies on which they have spent so much time and effort. The question as to what this notional spec ECU will do is still open. It is no secret that the rev limit will be 15,500rpm, but what it will have in the way of, for instance, engine mapping and traction control is yet to be seen.

This doesn't sound as if much has changed since the first attempt to agree on the way forward at Catalunya. That's true, the changes have been the hardening of attitudes on both sides of the argument.

BRIDGESTONE
TYRE OPTIONS
FRONT SOFT (**S**) / MEDIUM (**M**) / HARD (**H**)
REAR MEDIUM (**M**) / HARD (**H**)

MotoGP
TISSOT
SWISS WATCHES SINCE 1853
OFFICIAL TIMEKEEPER

GRAN PREMIO APEROL DI SAN MARINO E DELLA RIVIERA DI RIMINI
MISANO WORLD CIRCUIT

ROUND **13**
September 16

RACE RESULTS

CIRCUIT LENGTH 2.626 miles
NO. OF LAPS 27
RACE DISTANCE 70.900 miles
WEATHER Dry, 23°C
TRACK TEMPERATURE 36°C
WINNER Jorge Lorenzo
FASTEST LAP 1m 34.398s, 100.143mph, Jorge Lorenzo
LAP RECORD 1m 33.906s, 100.662mph, Jorge Lorenzo, 2011

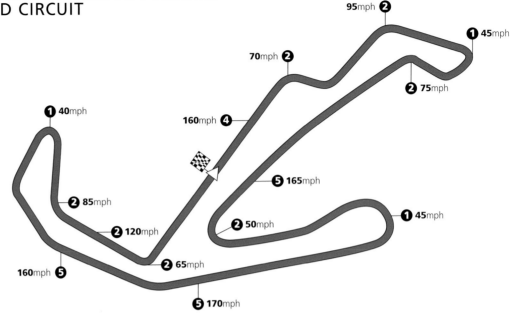

QUALIFYING

	Rider	Nationality	Team	Qualifying	Pole +	Gap
1	Pedrosa	SPA	Repsol Honda Team	1m 33.857s		
2	Lorenzo	SPA	Yamaha Factory Racing	1m 33.875s	0.018s	0.018s
3	Crutchlow	GBR	Monster Yamaha Tech 3	1m 34.001s	0.144s	0.126s
4	Bradl	GER	LCR Honda MotoGP	1m 34.221s	0.364s	0.220s
5	Bautista	SPA	San Carlo Honda Gresini	1m 34.299s	0.442s	0.078s
6	Rossi	ITA	Ducati Team	1m 34.619s	0.762s	0.320s
7	Dovizioso	ITA	Monster Yamaha Tech 3	1m 34.916s	1.059s	0.297s
8	Spies	USA	Yamaha Factory Racing	1m 34.988s	1.131s	0.072s
9	Rea	GBR	Repsol Honda Team	1m 35.358s	1.501s	0.370s
10	Hayden	USA	Ducati Team	1m 35.401s	1.544s	0.043s
11	Abraham	CZE	Cardion AB Motoracing	1m 35.648s	1.791s	0.247s
12	De Puniet	FRA	Power Electronics Aspar	1m 35.756s	1.899s	0.108s
13	Barbera	SPA	Pramac Racing Team	1m 36.048s	2.191s	0.292s
14	Espargaro	SPA	Power Electronics Aspar	1m 36.284s	2.427s	0.236s
15	Pirro	ITA	San Carlo Honda Gresini	1m 36.340s	2.483s	0.056s
16	Ellison	GBR	Paul Bird Motorsport	1m 37.124s	3.267s	0.784s
17	Pasini	ITA	Speed Master	1m 37.162s	3.305s	0.038s
18	Hernandez	COL	Avintia Blusens	1m 37.316s	3.459s	0.154s
19	Petrucci	ITA	Came IodaRacing Project	1m 37.751s	3.894s	0.435s
20	Edwards	USA	NGM Mobile Forward Racing	1m 38.068s	4.211s	0.317s
21	Salom	SPA	Avintia Blusens	1m 40.075s	6.218s	2.007s

FINISHERS

1 JORGE LORENZO An untroubled run from flag to flag: Jorge was grateful as he wasn't particularly impressed by his own race. Had one major moment early on and lost nearly a second to Rossi, but left Misano – a track where he wasn't expected to win – with a significantly extended championship lead.

2 VALENTINO ROSSI A rostrum in his final race on Italian soil as a Ducati rider. A new frame and chassis allowed the sort of adjustment the team had been asking for all year. Most impressively, the usual drop-off in lap times due to an overworked rear tyre did not happen: all his lap times were within 0.3s.

3 ALVARO BAUTISTA Made a lot of people happy by putting what would have been Marco Simoncelli's bike on the rostrum at the team's home GP, on the circuit now named after Sic. Beat Dovizioso for third in a photo finish for his first MotoGP podium.

4 ANDREA DOVIZIOSO Handicapped from the start by a problem with the front, but took nearly half a second out of Bautista on the last lap – only to run wide at the final corner and be beaten to the line by three one-thousandths of a second.

5 BEN SPIES Lost some speed mid-race with a lack of front-tyre feel but was able to catch Bradl in the final laps. Grateful for an incident-free weekend for the first time in the season.

6 STEFAN BRADL Looked like he might score his first MotoGP rostrum in his 100th GP start, but then lost ground in the closing stages with a front-end problem that affected his ability to brake. His pit crew discovered later that the front tyre had lost pressure.

7 NICKY HAYDEN Raced despite still having a problem with his right hand, broken in two places at Indianapolis. Seriously considered withdrawing and had to reduce his brake-lever effort a couple of times to let his hand recover. Kept his eye on his pit board and managed the gap to Rea.

8 JONATHAN REA Replaced Casey Stoner on the Repsol Honda and did nothing wrong in his first MotoGP race, despite scarcely turning a wheel in the first three sessions. Handily beat all the CRT bikes, but

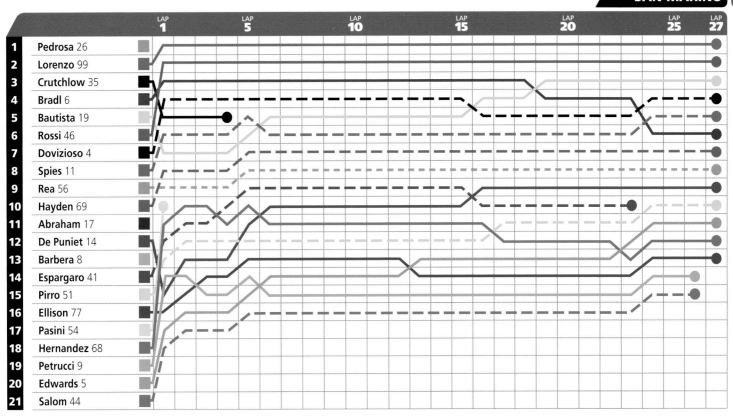

		LAP 1	LAP 5	LAP 10	LAP 15	LAP 20	LAP 25	LAP 27
1	Pedrosa 26							
2	Lorenzo 99							
3	Crutchlow 35							
4	Bradl 6							
5	Bautista 19							
6	Rossi 46							
7	Dovizioso 4							
8	Spies 11							
9	Rea 56							
10	Hayden 69							
11	Abraham 17							
12	De Puniet 14							
13	Barbera 8							
14	Espargaro 41							
15	Pirro 51							
16	Ellison 77							
17	Pasini 54							
18	Hernandez 68							
19	Petrucci 9							
20	Edwards 5							
21	Salom 44							

RACE

	Rider	Motorcycle	Race Time	Time +	Fastest Lap	Av Speed	🅱
1	Lorenzo	Yamaha	42m 49.836s		1m 34.398s	99.321mph	H/M
2	Rossi	Ducati	42m 54.234s	4.000s	1m 34.851s	99.151mph	H/M
3	Bautista	Honda	42m 55.891s	6.000s	1m 34.699s	99.088mph	H/M
4	Dovizioso	Yamaha	42m 55.894s	6.000s	1m 34.748s	99.087mph	H/M
5	Spies	Yamaha	42m 57.379s	7.000s	1m 34.719s	99.030mph	H/M
6	Bradl	Honda	43m 03.108s	13.000s	1m 34.707s	98.810mph	H/M
7	Hayden	Ducati	43m 30.743s	40.000s	1m 35.863s	97.765mph	H/M
8	Rea	Honda	43m 32.998s	43.000s	1m 36.201s	97.680mph	H/M
9	De Puniet	Art	43m 59.463s	1m 09.000s	1m 36.621s	96.701mph	H/M
10	Pirro	FTR	44m 03.441s	1m 13.000s	1m 36.931s	96.555mph	H/M
11	Edwards	Suter	44m 06.531s	1m 16.000s	1m 37.101s	96.442mph	H/M
12	Hernandez	BQR	44m 08.909s	1m 19.000s	1m 37.349s	96.356mph	H/M
13	Ellison	Art	44m 09.244s	1m 19.000s	1m 37.273s	96.344mph	H/M
14	Petrucci	Ioda-Suter	43m 22.121s	1 lap	1m 38.467s	94.455mph	H/M
15	Salom	BQR	43m 43.915s	1 lap	1m 39.023s	93.671mph	H/M
NF	Espargaro	Art	37m 26.098s	4 laps	1m 36.918s	96.801mph	H/M
NF	Crutchlow	Yamaha	6m 25.782s	23 laps	1m 34.785s	98.016mph	H/M
NF	Pasini	Art	1m 44.540s	26 laps		90.427mph	H/M
NF	Barbera	Ducati					H/M
NF	Pedrosa	Honda					H/M
NF	Abraham	Ducati					H/M

CHAMPIONSHIP

	Rider	Team	Points
1	Lorenzo	Yamaha Factory Racing	270
2	Pedrosa	Repsol Honda Team	232
3	Stoner	Repsol Honda Team	186
4	Dovizioso	Monster Yamaha Tech 3	163
5	Crutchlow	Monster Yamaha Tech 3	122
6	Rossi	Ducati Team	120
7	Bautista	San Carlo Honda Gresini	118
8	Bradl	LCR Honda MotoGP	115
9	Hayden	Ducati Team	93
10	Spies	Yamaha Factory Racing	77
11	Barbera	Pramac Racing Team	60
12	De Puniet	Power Electronics Aspar	48
13	Espargaro	Power Electronics Aspar	45
14	Abraham	Cardion AB Motoracing	25
15	Hernandez	Avintia Blusens	25
16	Pirro	San Carlo Honda Gresini	24
17	Edwards	NGM Mobile Forward Racing	22
18	Ellison	Paul Bird Motorsport	17
19	Pasini	Speed Master	13
20	Petrucci	Came IodaRacing Project	11
21	Silva	Avintia Blusens	11
22	Elias	Pramac Racing Team	10
23	Rea	Repsol Honda Team	8
24	Rapp	Attack Performance	2
25	Salom	Avintia Blusens	1

circumstances meant the satellite Ducatis weren't there for him to race against.

9 RANDY DE PUNIET Forced off track by the Barbera–Pedrosa crash, after which the bike had trouble in right-handers. Caught his team-mate and was waiting to make a move when Espargaro retired with a technical problem.

10 MICHELE PIRRO Extremely happy to finish second CRT as Team Gresini remembered their lost rider, Marco Simoncelli. Took too long to make it past Hernandez and so couldn't get up to de Puniet.

11 COLIN EDWARDS Best result of the season, despite the lack of dry track time. Took a couple of laps to figure out the new electronics, then made a few overtakes.

Described the bike as 'the best it's been all year', thanks to its new-found ability to transfer weight to the rear.

12 YONNY HERNANDEZ Started well and diced with the Aspar Aprilias but was then overhauled by Pirro and the resurgent de Puniet as the race went on, and only just held off Ellison.

13 JAMES ELLISON Had some help from Aprilia in practice to sort out the electronics, but didn't help himself when he selected the pit-lane limiter rather than launch control for the restart. Catching Hernandez when he ran out of laps.

14 DANILO PETRUCCI Rode a Suter BMW for the first time and, despite the first day-and-a-half being wet, he finished the

race. However, the quick-shifter developed a problem on lap five which in turn led to clutch problems.

15 DAVID SALOM Drafted into the Avintia team to replace Ivan Silva. Like Rea, doing double duty in the World Superbike Championship. Happy to score a point in his first Grand Prix.

NON-FINISHERS

ALEIX ESPARGARO Lost his position as lead CRT rider in the championship when his Aprilia developed an engine fault while he was running in front of his team-mate.

CAL CRUTCHLOW Made a mistake off the line and was trying to catch his team-

mate when he crashed at the first turn of lap five.

MATTIA PASINI Made a good start and was lying tenth when he crashed out on the second lap.

HECTOR BARBERA Braked too late at Quercia on the first lap, hit the back of Pedrosa's bike, and the pair crashed out.

DANI PEDROSA Sent to the back of the grid for the restart because his bike was still being worked on when the one-minute board was displayed. Tailgated by Barbera at Quercia on the very first lap.

KAREL ABRAHAM Started the chain of events that led to the abandoned start when his Ducati stalled on the grid due to a

malfunctioning clutch. Crashed on the first lap when his second bike's rear brake leaked fluid on to the tyre.

NON-STARTERS

CASEY STONER Recovering after an operation on the ankle he damaged at the Indianapolis GP.

GRAN PREMIO IVECO DE ARAGÓN

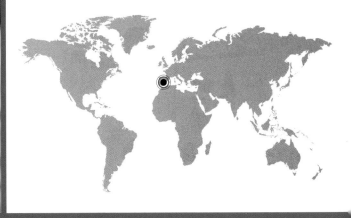

DAMAGE LIMITATION

Dani Pedrosa won but Jorge Lorenzo followed him home, retaining a very healthy championship lead

It felt a bit like a phony war. Dani Pedrosa had to win to keep his admittedly slim championship hopes alive, which he duly did. Jorge Lorenzo did what he had to do and finished second; he did have a go at escaping from the start but was stalled for half a dozen laps and then passed. Dani made a point by overtaking on the left-handed entry to the Bus Stop and not, as most were expecting, at the end of the back straight or the uphill run to the last left-hander. When Jorge pushed to try and stay with the Honda he had a massive moment and wisely decided to settle for a safe second place, not to mention a championship lead of 33 points with only four races left on the calendar.

Those are the bare facts of the race for the win but there were, of course, some nuances. Yet again the weather rendered Friday and much of Saturday useless for purposes of getting a set-up – not that it seemed to affect the Yamaha and Honda factory teams. Ducati, however, couldn't build on the advances made at the previous race without meaningful track time, so it was impossible to tell whether the new chassis was going to work at a track other than Misano.

Aragon has never been good to Valentino Rossi and he was sanguine about his race. A mistake on the back straight on the very first lap sent him off track, after he'd moved to the outside of Jonathan Rea on the brakes. Valentino rejoined last but, as at the San Marino GP, his lap times did not vary significantly. All except three were within one second, including his last four laps: more evidence that the problem of excessive rear-tyre wear was under control. Rossi was upbeat about his finishing position, saying that the best he could have done was challenge Bautista for sixth.

'I WAS CONCENTRATING SO HARD THAT I ALMOST FORGOT THAT IT WAS A RACE'

DANI PEDROSA

The same could not be said, though, for Valentino's team-mate. Nicky Hayden had a lucky escape at the end of qualifying on Saturday afternoon when he lost the front in the last corner. He saved it on his knee but ran off the track, saw a wall coming up pretty quick so hit the back brake, and then laid the bike down, fortunately without injury. On Sunday he tried to have the same crash on the second lap of the race. This time he hung on to the bike – maybe the racer's mind focuses first on the chances of getting back on track – but unfortunately Nicky now found himself fishtailing across a gravel trap with the wall coming up fast. Thinking that if he got off the bike he'd be into the wall head first, probably along with his machine, he decided to ride it for as long as he could and let go at the last moment. The Ducati hit the tyre barrier at 42mph, flicking its rider over the wall on to a service road. More by luck than judgement, Hayden escaped serious injury. However, the presence of a scooter and, ironically, an ambulance very close to where Nicky landed illustrated all too clearly what could have happened.

In his post-race tweet Ben Spies pointed out that it shouldn't be possible to hit a wall, even if you tried hard, on a new circuit built from scratch in the middle of nowhere.

Before he arrived at the next race, the first of three consecutive weekends of racing, Nicky discovered that he had, in fact, broken a bone in his forearm. His only consolation was that it could have been so much worse.

Once the two Spaniards at the front had resolved their early dispute, attention centred on an entertaining fight for third place. It looked as if Stefan Bradl might be in with a chance of his first rostrum in MotoGP. The

OPPOSITE TOP Nicky Hayden was lucky to get away with a crash that saw him flipped over a barrier and onto the track's service road. It later emerged he had a break in his forearm

ABOVE Rossi ran off-track on the first lap and had to fight his way back through the CRTs to a respectable eighth place

BELOW The pattern of the race was familiar – the two Spaniards ran away at the front

ABOVE The other Yamahas finished in line astern behind Lorenzo

BELOW Jorge Lorenzo congratulates Andrea Dovizioso on another rostrum finish, his sixth of the season

OPPOSITE Jonathan Rea impressed everybody with his two rides as replacement for Casey Stoner

German rider got in front of the Yamahas of Crutchlow, Dovizioso and Spies but lost the front on the fifth lap. It was reminiscent of the other race where he showed at the front early: Assen. That left Ben Spies in third, with what looked like a great chance for the American to take his first top-three finish of the season. He held on to third for ten laps before Andrea Dovizioso came past, and then for another three before the second Tech 3 Yamaha of Cal Crutchlow took fourth off him. The satellite bikes pulled away from the works bike, with Dovi again proving impossible to pass. Cal did have a couple of tries in the final laps, charging up the inside at the entrance to the Bus Stop, only to have an unfazed Dovizioso stay on the racing line and carve back underneath the Brit on the exit, carrying considerably more speed.

Casey Stoner's bike was raced, for the second and final time, by Jonathan Rea. The Ulsterman again impressed the whole paddock, on and off track, with his attitude and approach. As at Misano the lack of dry practice was a severe handicap, but Jonathan reduced his gap to the winner by over ten seconds. Unfortunately for MotoGP, Honda could not persuade the Gresini team that Rea should be signed for the 2013 season and he decided to continue with the Honda Ten Kate team in the World Superbike Championship. Rea was coy about whether he'd be riding at the next round if Stoner was still unfit, but he was able to take a well-deserved holiday when Casey announced that he would indeed return for the Japanese Grand Prix. The question now was what effect he would have on the title fight between the two Spaniards.

JOHN BROWN

By Nick Harris

Wednesday morning was always the highlight of the week: the day *Motorcycle News* arrived. At last a report, news and gossip from the latest Grand Prix, from locations we only dreamed about visiting. It was the beginning of a very special friendship with the man who was our messenger from exotic-sounding locations such as Monza, San Carlos and Daytona. Long before mobile phones and the internet, JB was our man on the spot – and what a man he turned out to be in real life.

Reading JB's personal accounts of what happened on and off the track at those GPs shaped my life. They inspired me to try and join him and, when I finally arrived, I was not disappointed to learn from the absolute master of his trade.

Travelling the world and living in the rarefied atmosphere of a Grand Prix paddock with JB was a complete education and just so much fun. He knew everybody, and he treated them all exactly the same. It could be Giacomo Agostini one minute and the man cleaning the truck the next – they would receive the same 'Morning, Ace' welcome. Barry Sheene had told JB when he forgot somebody's name he would always call them 'Ace', so John decided calling everybody 'Ace' was the way ahead and he stuck to it.

He taught us so much more than just reporting. The nearest supply of liquid refreshment was always high on the priority list. I remember our very first trip to Japan, staying in a tiny hotel. We spoke no Japanese and they spoke no English, but within 24 hours JB had charmed the staff into organising a supply of beer.

Accessing a telephone line to phone over your copy was a nightmare. It was only when I watched JB flirt with the telephone lady in Yugoslavia that I understood just why he never experienced the same problems as everybody else.

For almost half a century John Brown graced race paddocks throughout the world. From Mike Hailwood to Valentino Rossi he was simply JB. One thing's for certain, there will never be another. A dear friend and colleague – a true legend.

1934–2012

BRIDGESTONE
TYRE OPTIONS
FRONT SOFT (S) / MEDIUM (M) /
       EXTRA HARD (XH)
REAR   MEDIUM (M) / HARD (H)

motoGP
TISSOT
SWISS WATCHES SINCE 1853
OFFICIAL TIMEKEEPER

GRAN PREMIO IVECO DE ARAGÓN
MOTORLAND ARAGON
ROUND 14
September 30

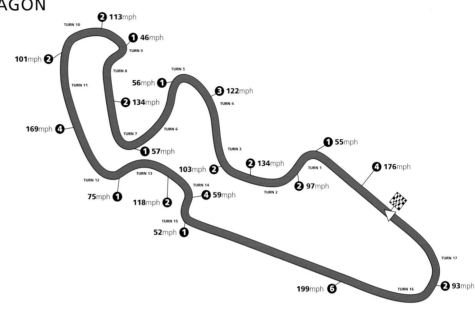

TURN 10 113mph
46mph
TURN 9
101mph
TURN 8
TURN 11
TURN 5
56mph
122mph
134mph TURN 4
TURN 7 TURN 6 TURN 3
169mph
55mph
57mph 134mph TURN 1
176mph
103mph TURN 14 97mph TURN 2
TURN 12 TURN 13
75mph 118mph 59mph
TURN 15
52mph
TURN 17
199mph TURN 16 93mph

RACE RESULTS

CIRCUIT LENGTH 3.155 miles

NO. OF LAPS 23

RACE DISTANCE 72.572 miles

WEATHER Dry, 18°C

TRACK TEMPERATURE 23°C

WINNER Dani Pedrosa

FASTEST LAP 1m 49.109s, 104.108mph, Dani Pedrosa

LAP RECORD 1m 49.046s, 104.142mph, Casey Stoner, 2011

QUALIFYING

	Rider	Nationality	Team	Qualifying	Pole +	Gap
1	Lorenzo	SPA	Yamaha Factory Racing	1m 49.404s		
2	Pedrosa	SPA	Repsol Honda Team	1m 49.492s	0.088s	0.088s
3	Crutchlow	GBR	Monster Yamaha Tech 3	1m 49.576s	0.172s	0.084s
4	Spies	USA	Yamaha Factory Racing	1m 49.748s	0.344s	0.172s
5	Bradl	GER	LCR Honda MotoGP	1m 50.034s	0.630s	0.286s
6	Dovizioso	ITA	Monster Yamaha Tech 3	1m 50.241s	0.837s	0.207s
7	Rea	GBR	Repsol Honda Team	1m 50.410s	1.006s	0.169s
8	Rossi	ITA	Ducati Team	1m 50.949s	1.545s	0.539s
9	Hayden	USA	Ducati Team	1m 51.013s	1.609s	0.064s
10	Barbera	SPA	Pramac Racing Team	1m 51.072s	1.668s	0.059s
11	Espargaro	SPA	Power Electronics Aspar	1m 51.082s	1.678s	0.010s
12	Bautista	SPA	San Carlo Honda Gresini	1m 51.155s	1.751s	0.073s
13	De Puniet	FRA	Power Electronics Aspar	1m 51.459s	2.055s	0.304s
14	Abraham	CZE	Cardion AB Motoracing	1m 51.521s	2.117s	0.062s
15	Pirro	ITA	San Carlo Honda Gresini	1m 52.606s	3.202s	1.085s
16	Pasini	ITA	Speed Master	1m 52.638s	3.234s	0.032s
17	Edwards	USA	NGM Mobile Forward Racing	1m 52.853s	3.449s	0.215s
18	Petrucci	ITA	Came IodaRacing Project	1m 53.140s	3.736s	0.287s
19	Hernandez	COL	Avintia Blusens	1m 53.233s	3.829s	0.093s
20	Ellison	GBR	Paul Bird Motorsport	1m 53.719s	4.315s	0.486s
21	Salom	SPA	Avintia Blusens	1m 55.290s	5.886s	1.571s

FINISHERS

1 DANI PEDROSA Did all he could and closed the gap at the top of the table by five points. Had to deal with post-Misano discussions with Race Direction, a big crash on Saturday (his 27th birthday) and clutch problems in the race. Followed Lorenzo from the start, put in his pass where it wasn't expected, and didn't make a mistake.

2 JORGE LORENZO Had a go at escaping from the start but was hunted down by Pedrosa. Decided, when he had a major moment soon after being passed, that second place was an acceptable bit of damage limitation.

3 ANDREA DOVIZIOSO Another excellent ride. Lacked pace in a couple of corners but managed the situation brilliantly and refused to panic under sustained attack from his team-mate. Dealt with Crutchlow's attacks on the last two laps with aplomb.

4 CAL CRUTCHLOW Another fantastic battle with his team-mate which Cal tried to win by attempting block-passes at the Bus Stop on the last two laps. Disappointed to miss the rostrum, but happy to have increased his lead over Rossi and Bautista in the championship.

5 BEN SPIES Diced for third place with the Tech 3 Yamahas for most of the race but faded towards the flag. Said his problem was with the front tyre both at the start and in the middle of the race.

6 ALVARO BAUTISTA Unable to maintain the form of Misano but rescued a respectable finishing position from very disappointing qualifying. The problem was the usual bugbear, lack of feel from the front.

7 JONATHAN REA Seriously impressive both on and off the track – again – although deciding to stay with World Superbike for 2013. Only ten seconds behind the winner despite spending the race alone and experimenting with engine-management settings.

8 VALENTINO ROSSI A mistake on the first lap sent him off the track, rejoining at the back of the field, after which he ripped through the CRTs. Not too unhappy with his pace on what has always been a difficult track for him, but thought his potential was only to fight Bautista for sixth.

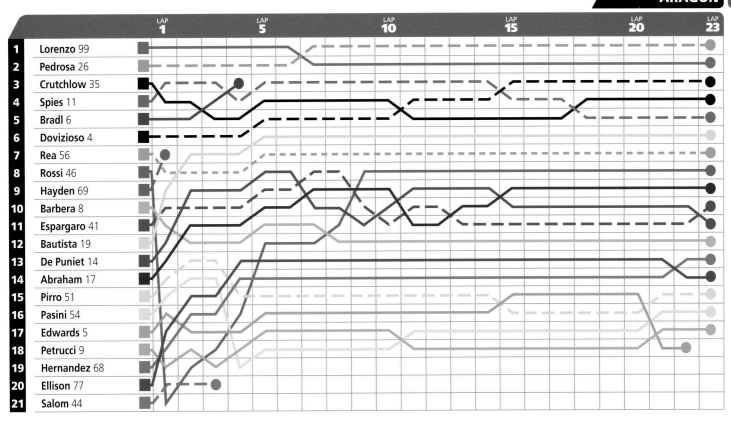

1	Lorenzo	99
2	Pedrosa	26
3	Crutchlow	35
4	Spies	11
5	Bradl	6
6	Dovizioso	4
7	Rea	56
8	Rossi	46
9	Hayden	69
10	Barbera	8
11	Espargaro	41
12	Bautista	19
13	De Puniet	14
14	Abraham	17
15	Pirro	51
16	Pasini	54
17	Edwards	5
18	Petrucci	9
19	Hernandez	68
20	Ellison	77
21	Salom	44

RACE

	Rider	Motorcycle	Race Time	Time +	Fastest Lap	Av Speed	
1	Pedrosa	Honda	42m 10.444s		1m 49.109s	103.246mph	XH/M
2	Lorenzo	Yamaha	42m 16.916s	6.472s	1m 49.134s	102.984mph	XH/M
3	Dovizioso	Yamaha	42m 21.491s	11.047s	1m 50.008s	102.798mph	XH/M
4	Crutchlow	Yamaha	42m 21.628s	11.184s	1m 49.957s	102.792mph	XH/M
5	Spies	Yamaha	42m 24.230s	13.786s	1m 49.952s	102.687mph	XH/M
6	Bautista	Honda	42m 38.610s	28.166s	1m 50.633s	102.110mph	XH/M
7	Rea	Honda	42m 42.734s	32.290s	1m 50.857s	101.946mph	XH/M
8	Rossi	Ducati	42m 54.876s	44.432s	1m 50.718s	101.465mph	XH/M
9	Abraham	Ducati	43m 07.861s	57.417s	1m 51.524s	100.956mph	XH/M
10	Espargaro	Art	43m 08.969s	58.525s	1m 51.500s	100.913mph	XH/M
11	De Puniet	Art	43m 10.307s	59.863s	1m 51.187s	100.860mph	XH/M
12	Barbera	Ducati	43m 25.005s	1m 14.561s	1m 51.856s	100.292mph	XH/M
13	Hernandez	BQR	43m 26.603s	1m 16.159s	1m 52.396s	100.230mph	XH/M
14	Ellison	Art	43m 27.024s	1m 16.580s	1m 52.243s	100.214mph	M/M
15	Pirro	FTR	43m 36.259s	1m 25.815s	1m 52.832s	99.860mph	XH/M
16	Pasini	Art	43m 42.245s	1m 31.801s	1m 52.611s	99.632mph	M/M
17	Petrucci	Ioda-Suter	43m 52.744s	1m 42.300s	1m 53.660s	99.235mph	M/M
18	Edwards	Suter	42m 52.997s	1 lap	1m 52.688s	97.125mph	XH/M
NF	Bradl	Honda	7m 23.595s	19 laps	1m 49.936s	102.428mph	XH/M
NF	Salom	BQR	6m 04.349s	20 laps	1m 56.953s	93.529mph	XH/M
NF	Hayden	Ducati	1m 55.246s	22 laps		98.564mph	XH/M

CHAMPIONSHIP

	Rider	Team	Points
1	Lorenzo	Yamaha Factory Racing	290
2	Pedrosa	Repsol Honda Team	257
3	Stoner	Repsol Honda Team	186
4	Dovizioso	Monster Yamaha Tech 3	179
5	Crutchlow	Monster Yamaha Tech 3	135
6	Rossi	Ducati Team	128
7	Bautista	San Carlo Honda Gresini	128
8	Bradl	LCR Honda MotoGP	115
9	Hayden	Ducati Team	93
10	Spies	Yamaha Factory Racing	88
11	Barbera	Pramac Racing Team	64
12	De Puniet	Power Electronics Aspar	53
13	Espargaro	Power Electronics Aspar	51
14	Abraham	Cardion AB Motoracing	32
15	Hernandez	Avintia Blusens	28
16	Pirro	San Carlo Honda Gresini	25
17	Edwards	NGM Mobile Forward Racing	22
18	Ellison	Paul Bird Motorsport	19
19	Rea	Repsol Honda Team	17
20	Pasini	Speed Master	13
21	Petrucci	Came IodaRacing Project	11
22	Silva	Avintia Blusens	11
23	Elias	Pramac Racing Team	10
24	Rapp	Attack Performance	2
25	Salom	Avintia Blusens	1

9 KAREL ABRAHAM More like his old self – a good result from 14th on the grid, with consistent lap times. Passed the Aspar bikes and Barbera, ran off track while trying to catch Rossi, then had to re-pass Espargaro and de Puniet.

10 ALEIX ESPARGARO Top CRT after what he called the 'hardest race of the season so far'. Took advantage of de Puniet's mistakes but couldn't stop Abraham escaping from the three-way fight. Passed his team-mate on the last lap at the mini-Corkscrew.

11 RANDY DE PUNIET Two mistakes cost the French rider the chance to finish as top CRT. Had opened up a good gap over his pursuers when he made a mistake on lap seven and lost two seconds, dropping from eighth to tenth. On the last lap he ran wide when trying to retake his team-mate.

12 HECTOR BARBERA More an exercise in regaining confidence than a race. Ran with the other satellite Ducati and the Aspar CRT bikes but had no feel at all and spent most of the race in his final position.

13 YONNY HERNANDEZ Followed Ellison for most of the race, but was able to pass him a lap from home and hold on for the extra point.

14 JAMES ELLISON Used a new-spec Aprilia motor which he said was an improvement. Practice did not go well but the race was considerably better, although unable to hold off Hernandez, who went past on the penultimate lap.

15 MICHELE PIRRO Team Gresini's CRT side of the pit also failed to back up the promise of Misano, but at least Michele managed to take the final point, despite problems that appeared early in the race, due to the lack of dry testing time.

16 MATTIA PASINI A better race than the result suggests: well in the points when he ran off track at the last corner of the fourth lap. Rejoined in last place, but lapped at a good consistent pace and was happy with the way the bike worked.

17 DANILO PETRUCCI Had to guess at settings for the dry race after wet practice and then missing warm-up thanks to a problem with the front-wheel sensor of the traction-control system. In a points-scoring position early on, but the lack of data for a bike he was riding for only the second time told.

18 COLIN EDWARDS Used the hard tyre, which he hadn't tried in practice, and went faster than he did in qualifying. Got past Pirro but couldn't close the gap to the group in front – and then the gear lever broke. Finished the last lap rather than pulling in, just in case there was a point to be had.

NON-FINISHERS

STEFAN BRADL It was a repeat of Assen: moved into a rostrum position early on, then lost the front and slid out of the race at Turn 3 on the fifth lap. He'd just overtaken Spies and thought he might have been riding a little too aggressively.

DAVID SALOM Retired from the race in the early stages and was promptly fired by the team, who reinstated Ivan Silva for the rest of the year.

NICKY HAYDEN Victim of a very scary incident: ran off at the final corner, hit a wall and was flung over it on to a service road. Thankfully he seemed relatively unscathed, although it could easily have been much worse.

NON-STARTERS

CASEY STONER Back home in Australia, recovering from an operation on the ankle he damaged in qualifying for the Indianapolis GP, but threatening to return at the next race.

AIRASIA GRAND PRIX OF JAPAN

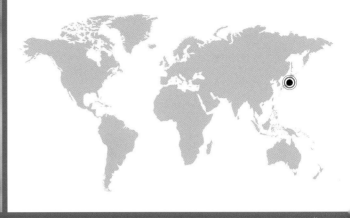

THIRSTY WORK

Pedrosa beat Lorenzo again, as the rest of the field suffered from overheating brakes and heavy fuel consumption

On the face of it, this was Aragon revisited. Jorge Lorenzo gave it his all but was reeled in by Dani Pedrosa, who, once he'd found a way past, instantly pulled out a lead. In the previous race Lorenzo appeared to settle equably for 20 points and limited damage to his championship lead. Now he didn't seem so calm. Jorge set pole and led the race, attempting again to break away from his rival. This time it took half the race for Pedrosa to find a way past, but when he did he instantly opened up a gap and Lorenzo had no reply.

However, there was a good deal of difference in Lorenzo's reaction to the two defeats. At home in Spain he'd seemed content with second place and was calm in his post-race pronouncements. Jorge was not so philosophical this time around. He bemoaned his Yamaha's lack of power compared to the Honda and exhibited a few signs that the pressure might be getting to him just a little. Mathematically, of course, his lead should still be unassailable, but giving away ten points in two races is enough to put the frighteners on anybody, even Jorge Lorenzo. As in their previous clash, the pass did not come at the usual place, and Dani commented that Jorge had 'settled for second'. Some mild mind games going on there, perhaps?

In another echo of Aragon, the best fight of the race was for third, on this occasion between Cal Crutchlow and Alvaro Bautista. The Englishman improved his lap times astonishingly over the weekend, following a very lacklustre Friday, qualifying on the front row for the seventh time this season after looking like he might get his first pole. True to form, he went faster again in the race, but that was his undoing. Motegi is the heaviest track of the year for fuel consumption; the multiple

slow corners followed by heavy acceleration with wide-open throttles made the crews' calculations difficult – especially in the first year of the new 1,000cc formula. Yamaha were expected to suffer more than the other makers, and that was indeed the case.

Ben Spies's crew would have been pleasantly surprised if he'd finished the race, but he was a victim of the other technical issue of the day – brakes on the first corner of the second lap. No-one gets on the throttle harder than the American, or grabs the brakes with more initial force. He managed to get his brakes way above the temperature range in which they work efficiently in just one lap. He flew across the – very large – gravel trap and still had enough speed left to hit the air fence hard enough to ensure the bike couldn't rejoin the race.

Cal Crutchlow's crew were also worrying about whether 21 litres would be enough fuel to get him home. Unfortunately, it wasn't. Alvaro Bautista followed Cal for most of the race and attacked him in the last five laps. The Spaniard had tried to keep his brakes cool but Crutchlow was able to fight back and, after a succession of passes and re-passes, it was obvious that the final rostrum place would be decided on the last lap. It was – but not in the way most people expected. Three corners into the final lap Crutchlow's M1 coasted to a halt, the rider slumped over his tank. He hadn't had the benefit of a slipstream all race long so it is doubtful he could have done anything about his fuel consumption in any event. The other Tech 3 rider, Andrea Dovizioso, had a quiet weekend by his standards in both qualifying – brake problems – and the race – finishing a distant

'I WAS COMPLETELY AT THE MAXIMUM TRYING TO STAY WITH DANI'
JORGE LORENZO

ABOVE It was Lorenzo versus Pedrosa – again – with the rest out of sight

OPPOSITE Impressive wild card Nakasuga (Yamaha) shadows Nicky Hayden

LEFT Cal Crutchlow was out of luck, he ran out of gas on the last lap while fighting for third

fourth after Crutchlow's retirement. He also ran out of fuel, but this time on the slow-down lap.

Valentino Rossi wasn't too happy either. He and his crew worked well, he said, but the phrase he used back in the bad old days was rolled out yet again to describe his seventh place, 26 seconds behind the winner: 'This

was our potential.' It was one thing, he explained, to finish sixth or seventh when they couldn't get the bike right; it was quite another to finish there when they'd got the bike as right as it could be and he himself had ridden 'at the maximum for the whole race'. That's what Valentino said, in English, but again he saved his most

ABOVE Alvaro Bautista took his second rostrum-finish of the year

RIGHT Ben Spies was a victim of overheated brakes at the first corner of the second lap

HOT STUFF

For the second time in three races, the subject of carbon brakes was at the top of the agenda. Nearly every rider reported problems with their brakes fading or failing completely. Andrea Dovizioso had to change his front discs during qualifying, and Ben Spies wore his out in just one lap of racing. Yet since they first appeared, and won, on Wayne Rainey's Yamaha at Donington Park in 1988, carbon brakes have been notable for their reliability. What has happened is that the new-for-2012 1,000cc bikes are 4kg heavier than the 800s and travelling a few miles per hour faster at the end of straights. Using them at Motegi, the circuit with the heaviest aggregate braking of the year, meant that brake temperatures were pushed above their safe operating range.

Carbon brakes should properly be called carbon-carbon brakes. They are made from short lengths of carbon fibre held in a matrix of carbon. The binder can start out as graphite, but the assembly is baked for a considerable time to produce the material used. It is light in weight, highly resistant to thermal shock, and doesn't expand or deform over a very large temperature range. The type of carbon-carbon used for motorcycle brakes will happily work without any problem at over 700° Centigrade. At Motegi, teams reported temperatures of over 1,000°.

When carbon-carbon is heated that far above its comfort zone, it chars. That is, the matrix material starts to break down. All of a sudden, the rider starts to experience the same symptoms as occur with overheating steel brakes: excessive lever movement, lack of feel and, of course, a

distinct lack of retardation. The brakes also wear at an amazing rate as the charred carbon matrix material loses its structural integrity and crumbles.

The cure? Bigger brakes or a different specification for the composition of the carbon-carbon used. Both solutions will, of course, cost more money.

telling comments for the Italian media, to whom he was more direct. Rossi described both the Honda and the Yamaha as 'almost perfect', while the Ducati needed to find another half-second per lap to be truly competitive. There was also a sideswipe at the factory for their tendency to try to find someone who could ride the bike rather than fixing the bike. Just like old times...

Casey Stoner returned, as he'd hoped, two races before his home round, but he found the recently repaired ankle too much of a handicap. The doctors had told him what to expect but, typically, he had assumed he'd be able to ride around any problems. He discovered

he couldn't push himself forward off the footrests to get his weight over the front to stop the bike doing wheelies out of corners, as it frequently does at Motegi.

The only riders who didn't report some sort of trouble (a little chatter excepted) were the top two. Yes, Dani did complain of a little chatter late in the race and Jorge would have liked a little more horsepower, but the two were again so much faster than anyone else it's almost impossible to envisage another winner, unless Stoner suddenly recovers. And both championship contenders managed to ride at this level without overheating their brakes or running out of fuel. That is one clever trick.

BELOW Lots of attention focused on the returning champion

BRIDGESTONE

TYRE OPTIONS
FRONT SOFT (S) / MEDIUM (M) / HARD (H)
REAR SOFT (S) / MEDIUM (M)

OFFICIAL TIMEKEEPER

AIRASIA GRAND PRIX OF JAPAN
TWIN-RING MOTEGI

ROUND 15
October 14

RACE RESULTS

CIRCUIT LENGTH 2.983 miles

NO. OF LAPS 24

RACE DISTANCE 71.597 miles

WEATHER Dry, 20°C

TRACK TEMPERATURE 23°C

WINNER Dani Pedrosa

FASTEST LAP 1m 45.589s, 62.768mph, Dani Pedrosa (Record)

PREVIOUS LAP RECORD 1m 46.090s, 101.221mph, Dani Pedrosa, 2011

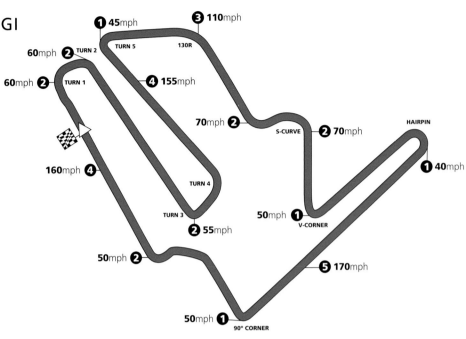

QUALIFYING

	Rider	Nationality	Team	Qualifying	Pole +	Gap
1	Lorenzo	SPA	Yamaha Factory Racing	1m 44.969s		
2	Pedrosa	SPA	Repsol Honda Team	1m 45.215s	0.246s	0.246s
3	Crutchlow	GBR	Monster Yamaha Tech 3	1m 45.257s	0.288s	0.042s
4	Spies	USA	Yamaha Factory Racing	1m 45.336s	0.367s	0.079s
5	Bautista	SPA	San Carlo Honda Gresini	1m 45.481s	0.512s	0.145s
6	Dovizioso	ITA	Monster Yamaha Tech 3	1m 45.612s	0.643s	0.131s
7	Stoner	AUS	Repsol Honda Team	1m 45.745s	0.776s	0.133s
8	Bradl	GER	LCR Honda MotoGP	1m 45.848s	0.879s	0.103s
9	Rossi	ITA	Ducati Team	1m 45.976s	1.007s	0.128s
10	Hayden	USA	Ducati Team	1m 46.461s	1.492s	0.485s
11	Nakasuga	JPN	Yamaha YSP Racing Team	1m 46.780s	1.811s	0.319s
12	Barbera	SPA	Pramac Racing Team	1m 46.881s	1.912s	0.101s
13	Espargaro	SPA	Power Electronics Aspar	1m 47.383s	2.414s	0.502s
14	De Puniet	FRA	Power Electronics Aspar	1m 47.581s	2.612s	0.198s
15	Abraham	CZE	Cardion AB Motoracing	1m 47.791s	2.822s	0.210s
16	Edwards	USA	NGM Mobile Forward Racing	1m 48.125s	3.156s	0.334s
17	Hernandez	COL	Avintia Blusens	1m 48.513s	3.544s	0.388s
18	Pirro	ITA	San Carlo Honda Gresini	1m 48.653s	3.684s	0.140s
19	Petrucci	ITA	Came IodaRacing Project	1m 48.831s	3.862s	0.178s
20	Ellison	GBR	Paul Bird Motorsport	1m 49.023s	4.054s	0.192s
21	Rolfo	ITA	Speed Master	1m 49.183s	4.214s	0.160s
22	Silva	SPA	Avintia Blusens	1m 49.831s	4.862s	0.648s

FINISHERS

1 DANI PEDROSA A replay of Aragon: front-row start, stalked Lorenzo for half the race, found a way past, then pulled out a significant lead, reducing the gap between them at the top of the championship table to 28 points. His only problem was chatter towards the end.

2 JORGE LORENZO Again laid it on the line with a heroic pole position and an attempt to pull ahead at the start, but there was nothing Jorge could do. Once Pedrosa got well away he settled for second place, but not happy with the gap in straight-line performance between his Yamaha and the Honda.

3 ALVARO BAUTISTA Celebrated signing for Team Gresini for 2013 with his second MotoGP rostrum. Didn't start well but moved into fourth behind Crutchlow on the third lap, following him until the last five laps when he started to press. The best fight of the race ended on the last lap when Cal ran out of fuel.

4 ANDREA DOVIZIOSO A quiet weekend by his standards. Big problems with overheating brakes in qualifying meant he only qualified sixth. There were also difficulties with the brakes at the start of the race, and he never challenged the leaders.

5 CASEY STONER Back racing eight weeks after injuring his ankle badly at Indianapolis. His major problem was the inability to push himself forward to counter

the bike's tendency to wheelie out of corners. The Honda also rediscovered chatter. Typically, Casey was disappointed with fifth.

6 STEFAN BRADL Looked to be easily matching the pace of Stoner and Dovizioso until he started suffering badly from arm pump around lap ten. The problem with his braking hand meant he had to slow down.

7 VALENTINO ROSSI After the optimism engendered by the new frame, this felt like a return to the bad old days. Although the lap times didn't drop off, Vale was back to repeating his well-worn mantra of 'this is our potential'; also felt the need to have a dig at Ducati in the Italian media.

8 NICKY HAYDEN Rode with a fracture in his right forearm, a legacy of the scary

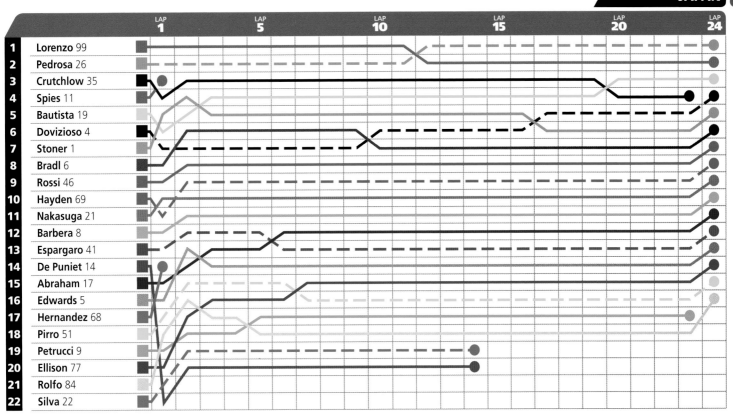

			LAP 1	LAP 5	LAP 10	LAP 15	LAP 20	LAP 24
1	Lorenzo	99						
2	Pedrosa	26						
3	Crutchlow	35						
4	Spies	11						
5	Bautista	19						
6	Dovizioso	4						
7	Stoner	1						
8	Bradl	6						
9	Rossi	46						
10	Hayden	69						
11	Nakasuga	21						
12	Barbera	8						
13	Espargaro	41						
14	De Puniet	14						
15	Abraham	17						
16	Edwards	5						
17	Hernandez	68						
18	Pirro	51						
19	Petrucci	9						
20	Ellison	77						
21	Rolfo	84						
22	Silva	22						

RACE

	Rider	Motorcycle	Race Time	Time +	Fastest Lap	Av Speed	
1	Pedrosa	Honda	42m 31.569s		1m 45.589s	101.016mph	H/S
2	Lorenzo	Yamaha	42m 35.844s	4.000s	1m 45.727s	100.847mph	H/S
3	Bautista	Honda	42m 38.321s	6.000s	1m 46.033s	100.749mph	H/S
4	Dovizioso	Yamaha	42m 47.966s	16.000s	1m 46.196s	100.371mph	H/S
5	Stoner	Honda	42m 52.135s	20.000s	1m 46.240s	100.208mph	H/S
6	Bradl	Honda	42m 56.136s	24.000s	1m 46.223s	100.052mph	H/S
7	Rossi	Ducati	42m 57.641s	26.000s	1m 46.739s	99.994mph	H/S
8	Hayden	Ducati	43m 08.293s	36.000s	1m 47.071s	99.582mph	H/S
9	Nakasuga	Yamaha	43m 08.363s	36.000s	1m 47.220s	99.580mph	H/S
10	Barbera	Ducati	43m 42.298s	1m 10.000s	1m 47.771s	98.291mph	H/S
11	Abraham	Ducati	43m 47.227s	1m 15.000s	1m 48.560s	98.106mph	H/S
12	Espargaro	Art	43m 54.338s	1m 22.000s	1m 48.842s	97.842mph	H/S
13	Edwards	Suter	43m 56.537s	1m 24.000s	1m 48.820s	97.760mph	H/S
14	Ellison	Art	44m 00.957s	1m 29.000s	1m 49.158s	97.596mph	H/S
15	Pirro	FTR	44m 06.181s	1m 34.000s	1m 49.344s	97.404mph	H/S
16	Rolfo	Art	44m 22.422s	1m 50.000s	1m 50.023s	96.810mph	H/S
NF	Crutchlow	Yamaha	40m 52.384s	1 lap	1m 45.907s	100.722mph	H/S
NF	Petrucci	Ioda-Suter	42m 23.577s	1 lap	1m 49.635s	97.110mph	H/S
NF	Silva	BQR	25m 59.326s	10 laps	1m 49.636s	96.422mph	H/S
NF	De Puniet	Art	26m 18.639s	10 laps	1m 49.642s	95.242mph	H/S
NF	Spies	Yamaha	1m 53.106s	23 laps		94.950mph	H/S
NF	Hernandez	BQR	1m 57.956s	23 laps		91.046mph	H/S

CHAMPIONSHIP

	Rider	Team	Points
1	Lorenzo	Yamaha Factory Racing	310
2	Pedrosa	Repsol Honda Team	282
3	Stoner	Repsol Honda Team	197
4	Dovizioso	Monster Yamaha Tech 3	192
5	Bautista	San Carlo Honda Gresini	144
6	Rossi	Ducati Team	137
7	Crutchlow	Monster Yamaha Tech 3	135
8	Bradl	LCR Honda MotoGP	125
9	Hayden	Ducati Team	101
10	Spies	Yamaha Factory Racing	88
11	Barbera	Pramac Racing Team	70
12	Espargaro	Power Electronics Aspar	55
13	De Puniet	Power Electronics Aspar	53
14	Abraham	Cardion AB Motoracing	37
15	Hernandez	Avintia Blusens	28
16	Pirro	San Carlo Honda Gresini	26
17	Edwards	NGM Mobile Forward Racing	25
18	Ellison	Paul Bird Motorsport	21
19	Rea	Repsol Honda Team	17
20	Pasini	Speed Master	13
21	Petrucci	Came IodaRacing Project	11
22	Silva	Avintia Blusens	11
23	Elias	Pramac Racing Team	10
24	Nakasuga	Yamaha YSP Racing Team	7
25	Rapp	Attack Performance	2
26	Salom	Avintia Blusens	1

crash at the Aragon GP. Never achieved a set-up, couldn't even rely on the usual Ducati strength of stability under braking, and couldn't make the bike turn in the early laps.

9 KATSUYUKI NAKASUGA More a test rider than a wild-card entry, presumably to try out some aspects of the 2013 Yamaha M1, Nakasuga followed Hayden for the whole race, attempting to slipstream past out of the very last corner only to fall short by 0.07s.

10 HECTOR BARBERA Got away with Hayden and Nakasuga but couldn't run their pace. After that, it was a matter of concentrating to the flag and keeping an eye on the gap to the pursuers. Admitted he was lucky to have a top-ten finish after a lacklustre weekend.

11 KAREL ABRAHAM Two crashes in practice and severe problems with the brakes in the first four laps consigned the Czech rider to a lonely race. Once the brakes had started to respond in the usual way he held station and made sure the CRTs didn't catch him.

12 ALEIX ESPARGARO Used an old engine in the race after noticing a problem with a fresh one in warm-up. Nevertheless, finished top CRT and regained the advantage over his team-mate in the points table.

13 COLIN EDWARDS Another good race for the Texan. Only a couple of seconds behind the first CRT, despite ripping his right kneeslider off on the fourth lap which compromised his riding style. Reported a few problems with the electronics, but overall a small improvement.

14 JAMES ELLISON Severely hampered by a couple of first-lap moves from Petrucci, which let the group escape, but finished third CRT, only seven seconds behind top man Espargaro.

15 MICHELE PIRRO Struggled with chatter but impressed his team-owner with the determination he showed. Partially, at least, achieved the target of closing on the top three CRT bikes in the championship.

16 ROBERTO ROLFO Recruited to the Speed Master team as a replacement for Mattia Pasini. Rode the bike for the first time on Friday so, not surprisingly, couldn't run with the other CRT bikes for very long.

CAL CRUTCHLOW Fighting for the final rostrum position when he ran out of fuel on the last lap. Much faster than in qualifying and, especially, free practice. Knew fuel would be critical but wasn't able to take advantage of anyone's slipstream. Lost valuable points in the fight for fifth place in the championship.

DANILO PETRUCCI Ran out of fuel on the last lap while lying in 16th place.

IVAN SILVA Back in favour with the Avintia team after being replaced for two races. Caught up in the first-lap crashes and never got back on terms before retiring.

RANDY DE PUNIET Three crashes during the weekend, including a fiery spill in warm-up which hurt both his ankles. Crashed in the same place in the race and remounted, only to retire later. Reported both crashes felt like they were down to the brakes binding on.

BEN SPIES Ran on at speed at the first corner of the second lap. Blamed the brakes, although his crew later said that the fuel consumption rate meant he might not have finished the race anyway.

YONNY HERNANDEZ Running second of the CRT bikes when he crashed on lap two, suffering a dislocated collarbone and contusions to his left foot.

MALAYSIAN MOTORCYCLE GRAND PRIX

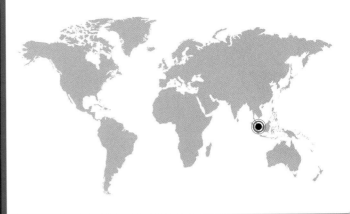

RIDERS ON THE STORM

Stoner returned to the rostrum, Pedrosa won again but Lorenzo limited the damage

Dani Pedrosa was pretty happy in *parc fermé*, as was Lorenzo, although Jorge's overwhelming emotion was probably relief. The other man there was Casey Stoner, who you'd have expected to be delighted with a top-three finish in his second race after a comprehensive repair to his ankle, but life is never that simple where Casey is concerned.

Pedrosa was happy for several reasons. First, like every other man on the track, he was immensely relieved when the red flag came out to stop the race. It had started in wet conditions but they were perfectly raceable. However, the monsoon season had arrived a month early in Malaysia and at about half-distance the rain turned from an ordinary downpour, of the kind recognisable to a European, into a genuine tropical storm. The red flag came out a couple of laps later and the field assumed that would be the end of it, especially as enough laps had been completed to allow full points to be awarded. However, there was lengthy a pause before Race Direction gave in to the obvious. The rulebook specifies that the race be restarted if possible, and if the weather had allowed it there would have been a seven-lap dash with the thirteen laps that had already been run used to form the grid. Once Race Direction had admitted there could be no new race the only dashing done was to the airport.

Not one rider criticised the decision to stop the race. There had been a spate of crashes at Turn 7 and at the final corner, both probably due to standing water, and several riders reported aquaplaning. It was the only possible decision in the circumstances, although Stoner couldn't help but speculate on what might have happened if he'd run a few more laps. Casey had seriously considered not racing due to the increased likelihood

of crashing and thus doing permanent damage to his ankle. He started the race steadily but couldn't resist pressing when the rain got really heavy, conditions in which he has always excelled, and was closing down second-placed Lorenzo hand over fist when the red flag was shown. He'd even had thoughts of victory.

Stoner's team-mate Dani Pedrosa could probably have coped with another couple of laps too, especially if it meant Lorenzo losing second place. As it was, Dani had to be content with reducing Jorge's championship lead by another five points in exactly the same way he'd done in the previous two races. First he followed Jorge, then he found a way past, pulling away immediately to ensure there was no chance of a counter-attack. There were other reasons for Dani to smile. It was the first time in his MotoGP career of 114 races that he had won three in a row. Amazingly, it was also the first time he had won a race in the wet.

Somewhat surprisingly, Lorenzo also looked happy. When he was beaten in almost identical fashion a week earlier he'd not hidden his feelings – it seemed as if the pressure was starting to get to him. Why so happy this week? Mainly because he was feeling lucky that the flag had come out when it did. He'd gone with the softer rear tyre, which had worn rapidly in the centre during the drier early stages and left him with precious little grip when the water got deep. His speed dropped dramatically and Stoner was closing in rapidly. Jorge was the first rider to raise his arm to indicate to Race Direction that the race should be stopped, although it's worth repeating that nobody argued with the decision or its timing.

There were some questions, though. The first was

'IT'S THE FIRST TIME I'VE WON IN THE WET IN MY LIFE'
DANI PEDROSA

over the scheduling of the races. The MotoGP race started at 4pm local time, two hours later than normal, to suit European TV viewers. In the tropics the rains always come later in the day, so was this change worth the risk? Valentino Rossi, among others, queried the decision. The second issue was chatter, reported by

nearly everyone except Andrea Dovizioso. This time Valentino's opinion was that it could be down to the track surface, which is exceedingly worn.

On past form one would have expected the Ducatis to be nearer the front but Rossi, despite starting well, ran on at Turn 7; Hayden got knocked about on the

LEFT For once, wet conditions didn't improve the Ducatis' chances

OPPOSITE Roby Rolfo, an ace in the rain in his 250 days, didn't enjoy the conditions any more than the rest of the grid

BELOW Wet or dry, the second half of the season was about Pedrosa and Lorenzo

first lap but recovered for his best finish of the year. Valentino would probably have beaten his team-mate if he'd had a mistake-free race, but he conceded that he wouldn't have beaten Stoner.

The spate of crashes sorted out a few issues. De Puniet's crash might well have handed the top CRT spot for the year to his team-mate Aleix Espargaro, while Cal Crutchlow's put him at a serious disadvantage in the fight for fifth overall. It didn't look as if any of the fallers had been hurt, until further investigation after the race showed an injury to Ben Spies. The American had fully expected to be racing in Australia the following weekend and then some Monday morning investigation showed up a dislocated collarbone, a bruised lung and a cracked rib. Surgery back home in the USA revealed even worse damage than expected; Ben wouldn't ride the last two races of the year and, worse still, would be unable to take part in the post-Valencia test for his new Ducati team. Thus ended the most singular, strange and downright bizarre individual season anyone can recall.

When details of engine use were released after the race another reason for Jorge's relief became apparent. After his Assen disaster, which had seen a nearly new motor grenade itself, one of his allocation of six motors for the year was going to have to run four races instead of the planned three. What better time to take that calculated risk than in the wet, when the stress on the motor would be reduced and, with any luck, the race would be shortened? Lorenzo's season so far had been a perfect model of consistency, but at Sepang he managed to get away with a couple of calculated gambles.

ABOVE Casey Stoner nearly didn't ride but was fastest when the weather was really bad

BELOW Nicky Hayden and Ben Spies got close on the first lap

OPPOSITE The weather let the CRTs get in among the satellite factory bikes; here James Ellison leads Karel Abraham

LOCAL HEROES

The 2012 Malaysian Grand Prix attracted a record crowd of nearly 80,000 to see a little bit of history in the Moto3 race and a new star born in Moto2. These facts are, of course, related. In Moto3 Zulfamhi Khairuddin took pole on his 21st birthday and came within a corner of winning the race; both pole and a rostrum finish were firsts for a Malaysian rider. In Moto2, wild card Hafizh Syahrin both led the race and set the fastest lap on his way to fourth place.

Both riders – and there are others on the way – are products of astute investment by the Malaysian Federation, sponsor Petronas and the Sepang circuit itself, which has set much store by its Wild Card Development Programme over the years. The country's GP pioneer Shahrol Yuzy, a useful 250 rider ten years ago, is also involved. In the early days of the Malaysian GP the objective was simply to reward good local talent with a ride at their home GP, but nowadays the programme is more ambitious.

With the help of Air Asia, Khairuddin was sent to Europe in 2010 to become a full-time GP rider, having first appeared as a wild card at Sepang in 2009. Syahrin was spotted by a local team-manager when he was racing pocket bikes to such effect that he was known as the 'King of Pocket Bike'. This year he has been racing Moto2 in the Spanish Championship, and it was the mixed Spanish/Malaysian team that ran him in the GP. He has also raced Formula Extreme in Australia.

Watch out, too, for Azlan Shah who has won the Suzuka 4 Hours for the last two years. The 4 Hours is the curtain raiser for the 8 Hours and is run with 600cc bikes. Shah also rode for Honda Team Asia in the main race, alongside veterans Makoto Tamada and Chosun Kameya, who are instructors for the Asia Dream Cup class in the Asian Road Racing Championship where Shah is teamed with Ryuichi Kiyonari. Team Asia have an entry in the 2013 Moto2 championship.

BELOW Eighteen-year-old wild card Hafizh Syahrin ran at the front of the Moto2 race

TYRE OPTIONS
FRONT WET SOFT (**WS**) / WET HARD (**WH**)
REAR WET SOFT (**WS**) / WET HARD (**WH**)

OFFICIAL TIMEKEEPER

MALAYSIAN MOTORCYCLE GRAND PRIX
SEPANG INTERNATIONAL CIRCUIT
ROUND **16**
October 21

RACE RESULTS

CIRCUIT LENGTH 3.447 miles
NO. OF LAPS 13
RACE DISTANCE 44.812 miles
WEATHER Wet, 25°C
TRACK TEMPERATURE 31°C
WINNER Dani Pedrosa
FASTEST LAP 2m 14.670s, 92.155mph, Dani Pedrosa
LAP RECORD 2m 02.108s, 101.635mph, Casey Stoner, 2007

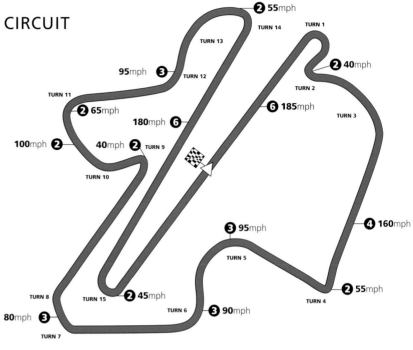

QUALIFYING

	Rider	Nationality	Team	Qualifying	Pole +	Gap
1	Lorenzo	SPA	Yamaha Factory Racing	2m 00.334s		
2	Pedrosa	SPA	Repsol Honda Team	2m 00.528s	0.194s	0.194s
3	Dovizioso	ITA	Monster Yamaha Tech 3	2m 00.567s	0.233s	0.039s
4	Stoner	AUS	Repsol Honda Team	2m 00.811s	0.477s	0.244s
5	Crutchlow	GBR	Monster Yamaha Tech 3	2m 01.178s	0.844s	0.367s
6	Spies	USA	Yamaha Factory Racing	2m 01.185s	0.851s	0.007s
7	Barbera	SPA	Pramac Racing Team	2m 01.294s	0.960s	0.109s
8	Bradl	GER	LCR Honda MotoGP	2m 01.491s	1.157s	0.197s
9	Hayden	USA	Ducati Team	2m 01.526s	1.192s	0.035s
10	Bautista	SPA	San Carlo Honda Gresini	2m 01.640s	1.306s	0.114s
11	Rossi	ITA	Ducati Team	2m 01.783s	1.449s	0.143s
12	Espargaro	SPA	Power Electronics Aspar	2m 02.842s	2.508s	1.059s
13	De Puniet	FRA	Power Electronics Aspar	2m 03.389s	3.055s	0.547s
14	Abraham	CZE	Cardion AB Motoracing	2m 03.774s	3.440s	0.385s
15	Pirro	ITA	San Carlo Honda Gresini	2m 04.152s	3.818s	0.378s
16	Ellison	GBR	Paul Bird Motorsport	2m 04.515s	4.181s	0.363s
17	Petrucci	ITA	Came IodaRacing Project	2m 04.726s	4.392s	0.211s
18	Edwards	USA	NGM Mobile Forward Racing	2m 04.941s	4.607s	0.215s
19	Rolfo	ITA	Speed Master	2m 05.100s	4.766s	0.159s
20	Silva	SPA	Avintia Blusens	2m 05.921s	5.587s	0.821s
NF	Hernandez	COL	Avintia Blusens			

FINISHERS

1 DANI PEDROSA Repeated what he'd done in Japan the week before, stalking Lorenzo until half-distance, then passing him and pulling away. Pleased not just to reduce the deficit at the top of the championship to 23 points but also to take his first victory ever in wet conditions.

2 JORGE LORENZO Went with the softer rear tyre, unlike both Repsol Hondas, and used more of the centre of the tread in the drier conditions early on, so when the rain came down harder he was in trouble. Made one astonishing save late on and was grateful to see the red flag as Stoner was closing fast.

3 CASEY STONER Nearly didn't race because of the increased danger of crashing and further damaging his ankle in the tricky conditions. Closing fast on Lorenzo and even thinking he might win when the red flag went out.

4 NICKY HAYDEN His best result of the year so far, but disappointed not to give the team a rostrum finish. Cautious at the start, had to avoid Dovizioso going sideways and got barged by Spies, but found a good rhythm in the closing stages.

5 VALENTINO ROSSI Looked like he might be able to exploit the Ducati's strength in the wet when he got a great start and was up with Stoner and Dovizioso, but then had problems with his visor fogging up. Ran on at Turn 7, scene of

several crashes, which ended his chances of taking fourth place.

6 ALVARO BAUTISTA Problems on the brakes and over the bumps, but happy to have improved the feel of the bike in the wet. Not so happy with the chatter problems that persisted in the dry.

7 HECTOR BARBERA Pleasantly surprised to equal his best result of the year so far and in a wet race. Had a few problems with engine-management electronics but a good start helped him build confidence and stay upright when many others fell.

8 ALEIX ESPARGARO Top CRT in the race with the best finish so far by a CRT bike. Followed his team-mate early on, passed him and then trailed Barbera. Settled for a steady

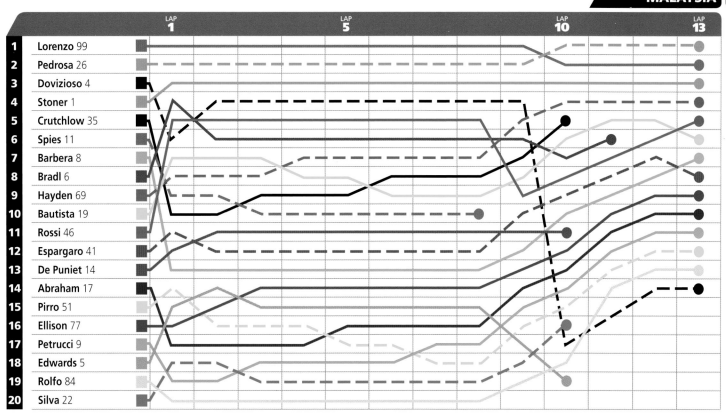

			LAP 1		LAP 5		LAP 10		LAP 13
1	Lorenzo 99								
2	Pedrosa 26								
3	Dovizioso 4								
4	Stoner 1								
5	Crutchlow 35								
6	Spies 11								
7	Barbera 8								
8	Bradl 6								
9	Hayden 69								
10	Bautista 19								
11	Rossi 46								
12	Espargaro 41								
13	De Puniet 14								
14	Abraham 17								
15	Pirro 51								
16	Ellison 77								
17	Petrucci 9								
18	Edwards 5								
19	Rolfo 84								
20	Silva 22								

RACE

	Rider	Motorcycle	Race Time	Time +	Fastest Lap	Av Speed	B
1	Pedrosa	Honda	29m 29.049s		2m 14.670s	91.199mph	WH/WH
2	Lorenzo	Yamaha	29m 32.823s	3.000s	2m 14.703s	91.005mph	WH/WS
3	Stoner	Honda	29m 36.193s	7.000s	2m 14.954s	90.833mph	WH/WH
4	Hayden	Ducati	29m 39.567s	10.000s	2m 15.324s	90.661mph	WH/WH
5	Rossi	Ducati	29m 45.808s	16.000s	2m 15.181s	90.344mph	WH/WH
6	Bautista	Honda	29m 46.325s	17.000s	2m 15.221s	90.317mph	WH/WH
7	Barbera	Ducati	30m 19.331s	50.000s	2m 17.466s	88.679mph	WH/WS
8	Espargaro	Art	30m 20.634s	51.000s	2m 17.649s	88.616mph	WH/WH
9	Ellison	Art	30m 25.725s	56.000s	2m 18.687s	88.368mph	WH/WH
10	Abraham	Ducati	30m 26.671s	57.000s	2m 18.006s	88.322mph	WH/WS
11	Petrucci	Ioda-Suter	30m 31.854s	1m 02.000s	2m 18.391s	88.073mph	WH/WS
12	Pirro	FTR	30m 31.940s	1m 02.000s	2m 19.125s	88.069mph	WH/WH
13	Dovizioso	Yamaha	30m 58.038s	1m 28.000s	2m 14.997s	86.832mph	WH/WH
NF	Bradl	Honda	25m 10.154s	2 laps	2m 15.076s	90.398mph	WH/WH
NF	Crutchlow	Yamaha	22m 51.268s	3 laps	2m 15.097s	90.504mph	WH/WH
NF	De Puniet	Art	23m 20.028s	3 laps	2m 17.736s	88.645mph	WH/WH
NF	Silva	BQR	23m 38.031s	3 laps	2m 19.740s	87.519mph	WH/WH
NF	Edwards	Suter	24m 12.202s	3 laps	2m 18.652s	85.460mph	WH/WH
NF	Spies	Yamaha	18m 23.381s	5 laps	2m 14.893s	89.981mph	WH/WS
EX	Rolfo	Art			2m 20.561s		WH/WS

CHAMPIONSHIP

	Rider	Team	Points
1	Lorenzo	Yamaha Factory Racing	330
2	Pedrosa	Repsol Honda Team	307
3	Stoner	Repsol Honda Team	213
4	Dovizioso	Monster Yamaha Tech 3	195
5	Bautista	San Carlo Honda Gresini	154
6	Rossi	Ducati Team	148
7	Crutchlow	Monster Yamaha Tech 3	135
8	Bradl	LCR Honda MotoGP	125
9	Hayden	Ducati Team	114
10	Spies	Yamaha Factory Racing	88
11	Barbera	Pramac Racing Team	79
12	Espargaro	Power Electronics Aspar	63
13	De Puniet	Power Electronics Aspar	53
14	Abraham	Cardion AB Motoracing	43
15	Pirro	San Carlo Honda Gresini	30
16	Ellison	Paul Bird Motorsport	28
17	Hernandez	Avintia Blusens	28
18	Edwards	NGM Mobile Forward Racing	25
19	Rea	Repsol Honda Team	17
20	Petrucci	Came IodaRacing Project	16
21	Pasini	Speed Master	13
22	Silva	Avintia Blusens	11
23	Elias	Pramac Racing Team	10
24	Nakasuga	Yamaha YSP Racing Team	7
25	Rapp	Attack Performance	2
26	Salom	Avintia Blusens	1

finish when he saw de Puniet on the floor.

9 JAMES ELLISON Best result of the season so far, including his top CRT finish at Le Mans. Passed several other Aprilias and was closing on Espargaro when the race was stopped, but he had no argument with the decision.

10 KAREL ABRAHAM Upset with his performance, especially in the early laps when, said his crew chief, Karel 'hardly raced at all'. Probably should have caught Ellison but, as he said, that was hardly the issue given his performance.

11 DANILO PETRUCCI Equalled his best result of the year, at Assen. Happy with the progress of the Suter BMW even though he had to switch off the traction control because

it was too intrusive. Caught Abraham's Ducati and was running behind him when the race was stopped.

12 MICHELE PIRRO The only CRT rider to start with the harder rear so was also the only one who wasn't too happy when the flag came out. Had wanted a better result to dedicate to Marco Simoncelli.

13 ANDREA DOVIZIOSO Made up for a bad start and was lying in fourth, following Stoner, when he lost the front on lap ten, crashing on full lean without touching the brakes. Remounted to claim what may well be three valuable points in the fight for fifth in the championship.

NON-FINISHERS

ROBERTO ROLFO One of the many victims of Turn 7. Fell while lying in 13th place, just before the decision to stop the race.

STEFAN BRADL Crashed two laps before the flag came out while in sixth. Hit trouble when he changed the engine map because of too much engine braking, only to find the bike was now pushing him on into corners. Switched back to the standard map and slowed, only to lose the rear. Unconvinced the crash was all his fault.

CAL CRUTCHLOW Like his team-mate, he was making time on the brakes to compensate for lack of grip out of corners. Lost the front on the brakes at the final

corner, with the bike upright, just as the rain became really heavy; probably caught out by standing water.

RANDY DE PUNIET Faster than his team-mate at the start but not when the heavens opened; crashed at the final corner, probably due to standing water. Said afterwards that the incident had probably decided who would be top CRT at the end of the year – he now had a ten-point deficit on team-mate Espargaro.

IVAN SILVA Enjoyed being the fastest man in second free practice but fell out of the race thanks to the rear moving round on him when he came off the throttle.

COLIN EDWARDS No idea of what settings to use in the wet so utilised his

Aragon ones, but had no drive out of corners. Sat behind a trio of Aprilias, waiting for a mistake, only for an electrical problem to force him to retire while in 15th place.

BEN SPIES The unluckiest season in living memory ended with a crash on lap nine. At first the damage was thought to be minimal but further investigation revealed a dislocated collarbone and ligament damage that needed surgery, forcing him to return home to the USA.

NON-STARTERS

YONNY HERNANDEZ Rode in first free practice but the injuries from his second-lap crash at Motegi proved too painful for him to contemplate racing.

AIRASIA AUSTRALIAN GRAND PRIX

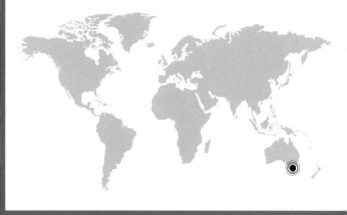

HOME SWEET HOME

Jorge Lorenzo wrapped up his second world title as Casey Stoner showed just why MotoGP will miss him

Professional sportsmen do not heap praise on the heads of their opponents. The mindset of a rider competing at world championship level simply wouldn't allow it – it's tantamount to an admission of defeat. Yet before the Australian GP, world champions were happy to predict that they'd be beaten on Sunday, such was the certainty that Casey Stoner's farewell to his home fans would be crowned with a victory. Casey duly won the race, and in the manner everybody expected. If there is one statistic that shows just what he has done over the past six years at Phillip Island it is that he has led all but two of the 162 laps completed. Put another way, of the 447.7 miles (720.5km) raced since 2007 Casey has led 442.2 (711.6km) of them.

It seems a little strange to start a report on a race where the world title was decided by talking about the guy who finished third in the championship, but the whole weekend was about Casey Stoner, not Jorge Lorenzo. Even before he flew home from Indianapolis for surgery on his ankle Stoner was saying he hoped to get back on a bike a couple of races before Phillip Island. The message was clear. Casey was focusing his attention on winning his home race for the sixth year in a row. And he didn't just take the victory, he dominated the whole weekend in a manner of which the watching Mick Doohan would have thoroughly approved. Casey was fastest in every session by 0.905s, 0.885s and 1.019s in the free practice sessions, by 0.517s in rain-curtailed qualifying, by a mere 0.447s in warm-up and his fastest lap of the race was 0.512s faster than the next best. So, on a short lap that lasts only 1m 30s, he was on average 0.714s faster than the rest. Ignore warm-up and the average goes up to over three-quarters of

LEFT Crutchclow was not a well boy, but third made up for the disappointments of the previous two races

OPPOSITE The Stoner family, Casey, Adrianna and little Alessandra, with the plaque presented by the circuit to mark the renaming of Turn 3 as Stoner Corner

BELOW Pedrosa did what he had to and gambled everything on going for the win

a second. Ben Spies, watching from his hospital bed, tweeted that even other Grand Prix racers sometimes found it impossible to comprehend what Casey did on a motorcycle.

Perhaps the most awe-inspiring five minutes of the year came on Saturday morning when Casey put together three consecutive 1m 29s laps. Bear in mind that no other rider put in anything below a 1m 30s lap all weekend. Fittingly, the corner at Phillip Island that

Casey likes above all others was named in his honour on the Thursday before practice started. Turn 3 is one of the fastest corners on the calendar; it is taken in fifth gear with plenty of throttle and lots of lean angle. Stoner says he has something special there. Valentino Rossi thinks he knows what it is: Casey gets on the throttle 20 yards earlier than anyone else. Slow-motion TV pictures show graphically how he slams the bike to maximum lean on entry, compressing the suspension

'I DID WHAT I HAD TO DO AND
I HAVE NO REGRETS'
DANI PEDROSA

RIGHT Jorge Lorenzo did what he had to do: second place and the title

OPPOSITE Casey Stoner doing what only he can do

BELOW Casey seemed relaxed (not a word normally used about him) after his final Australian GP; Cal Crutchlow just looks happy with his second MotoGP rostrum

at both ends, and then leaves black lines on the tarmac as he powers through the long left-hander. In Saturday morning's free practice Casey was gaining over 0.4s in the second sector of the track, the one that consists mainly of what is now called Stoner Corner.

At times it was difficult to remember that the world title was still at stake. Lorenzo's 23-point lead meant that if he finished ahead of Pedrosa, assuming they were

both on the rostrum, then he would be champion. Dani Pedrosa had no option but to go for broke. He had to try to do the impossible – beat Stoner and hope that Lorenzo came third or worse. Given Jorge had not yet finished a race lower than second it was always going to be a long shot. Nevertheless, Dani went for it. He took the lead off Lorenzo at Honda Hairpin on the first lap but fell at the same corner second time round, having gone in a little too hot and run a fraction wide on to some very worn tarmac. The front tucked and those faint chances of the title were gone.

So Casey progressed to an unchallenged victory, to the delight of the record home crowd. It was noticeable that he made a point of doing a slow in-lap after every session and waving to the crowd all the way round. Not his usual style. On Sunday the whole family were waiting for him at *parc fermé* where Casey looked more relaxed than at any time this season, and maybe any other one as well. Job done, said the body language; don't think you'll see me again.

Jorge Lorenzo duly followed him home and secured his second world title in the top class with a race to spare. Here was proof that consistency wins titles. He never finished lower than second and his long runs at race pace in practice sessions are a model of how to go about the job. The influence and input of his race engineer Ramon Forcada should not be underestimated. In third place was Cal Crutchlow, scoring his second top-three finish of the year, handily outpacing his team-mate and the dice by the satellite Hondas, and joking about not challenging Jorge because he didn't want to be sacked. It was a happy rostrum: the fastest man, the new champion and the most improved rider of the year.

However, there is only one image that will stay in the memory from Phillip Island 2012: Casey Stoner, Turn 3, on the gas in fifth gear, 50 degrees of lean, suspension compressed, front tyre skimming the bumps, rear tyre leaving a black line as it spins. It took a long time for the members of the MotoGP paddock to understand the extent of Stoner's talent, but it may take even longer for them to get over losing him.

BIG NUMBERS

It's one of sport's clichés that to win a championship what you need above all else is consistency. Jorge Lorenzo's second MotoGP World Championship title demonstrates the truth of that.

In 17 races he never finished lower than second place, and his only non-finish was down to Alvaro Bautista's ram raid at the first corner of the Dutch TT. Jorge's second place at the Australian GP was therefore his 16th top-two finish of the year, a new record for a single season in the premier class. It also equalled the record for the number of podium finishes achieved in a single season, held by Jorge himself (2010), Casey Stoner (2011) and Valentino Rossi (2003, '05 and '08).

As well as becoming the first Spaniard to win the top title twice, Jorge joins a very select group who have won more than once in both the intermediate and top classes of Grand Prix motorcycle racing – the only other riders to have achieved this are Mike Hailwood and Phil Read. Australia was Jorge's 98th podium across all classes, which took him level with six-time World Champion Jim Redman.

This was Jorge's 60th podium from his 85 starts in MotoGP, a strike rate of 70.6% – the highest of any rider in the MotoGP era. His 44 victories across all classes put him ninth in the all-time winners list. Twenty-three of those wins have come in the top class, one fewer than Wayne Rainey achieved.

Perhaps the most astonishing statistic is that since the start of the 2009 season, Jorge has only once finished a race outside the top four. That was Assen in 2011 when he was knocked off and remounted to finish sixth. This season, the only riders who beat him to the flag were Dani Pedrosa and Casey Stoner. That's another first for the MotoGP era – the first time a rider has been beaten by only two competitors all season long. There's the secret of Jorge's consistency – he never has a bad weekend.

AIRASIA AUSTRALIAN GRAND PRIX
PHILLIP ISLAND
ROUND 17
October 28

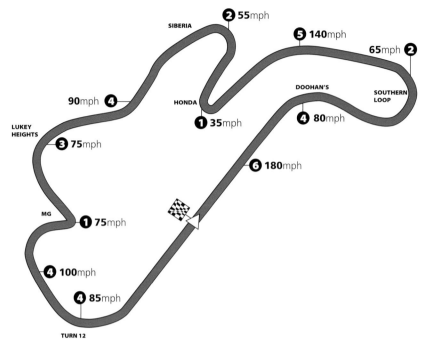

RACE RESULTS

CIRCUIT LENGTH 2.764 miles
NO. OF LAPS 27
RACE DISTANCE 74.624 miles
WEATHER Dry, 15°C
TRACK TEMPERATURE 26°C
WINNER Casey Stoner
FASTEST LAP 1m 30.191s, 110.320mph, Casey Stoner
LAP RECORD 1m 30.059s, 110.482mph, Nicky Hayden, 2008

AIRASIA AUSTRALIAN GRAND PRIX
Phillip Island 201...

QUALIFYING

	Rider	Nationality	Team	Qualifying	Pole +	Gap
1	Stoner	AUS	Repsol Honda Team	1m 29.623s		
2	Lorenzo	SPA	Yamaha Factory Racing	1m 30.140s	0.517s	0.517s
3	Pedrosa	SPA	Repsol Honda Team	1m 30.575s	0.952s	0.435s
4	Crutchlow	GBR	Monster Yamaha Tech 3	1m 30.763s	1.140s	0.188s
5	Bradl	GER	LCR Honda MotoGP	1m 30.798s	1.175s	0.035s
6	Dovizioso	ITA	Monster Yamaha Tech 3	1m 31.200s	1.577s	0.402s
7	Bautista	SPA	San Carlo Honda Gresini	1m 31.490s	1.867s	0.290s
8	Rossi	ITA	Ducati Team	1m 31.661s	2.038s	0.171s
9	De Puniet	FRA	Power Electronics Aspar	1m 31.667s	2.044s	0.006s
10	Hayden	USA	Ducati Team	1m 31.681s	2.058s	0.014s
11	Abraham	CZE	Cardion AB Motoracing	1m 31.910s	2.287s	0.229s
12	Espargaro	SPA	Power Electronics Aspar	1m 31.990s	2.367s	0.080s
13	Barbera	SPA	Pramac Racing Team	1m 32.231s	2.608s	0.241s
14	Pirro	ITA	San Carlo Honda Gresini	1m 33.050s	3.427s	0.819s
15	Petrucci	ITA	Came IodaRacing Project	1m 33.069s	3.446s	0.019s
16	Edwards	USA	NGM Mobile Forward Racing	1m 33.450s	3.827s	0.381s
17	Ellison	GBR	Paul Bird Motorsport	1m 33.489s	3.866s	0.039s
18	Rolfo	ITA	Speed Master	1m 34.577s	3.954s	0.088s
19	Silva	SPA	Avintia Blusens	1m 35.156s	3.533s	0.579s
NQ	McLaren	AUS	Avintia Blusens	1m 36.324s	6.701s	2.168s

FINISHERS

1 CASEY STONER Said goodbye to his fans in the way he would have wanted – quickest in every session, fastest race lap and the victory, to make it six in a row at Phillip Island. Just as importantly, he proved that he could win again after serious injury.

2 JORGE LORENZO Did exactly what he had to do and kept up his record of finishing no lower than second to become the first Spaniard to win the 500cc/MotoGP title twice. Saw Pedrosa crash and knew all he needed was to hold the gap to Crutchlow.

3 CAL CRUTCHLOW Second MotoGP podium despite suffering from bronchitis and a high temperature. Pulled away from his team-mate early in the race, but knew he couldn't – or shouldn't – catch Lorenzo. A great way to bounce back from the disappointments of the previous two races.

4 ANDREA DOVIZIOSO Knew he did not have the pace of his team-mate so when he couldn't get in front at the start he enjoyed the fight with the satellite Hondas. Cal and Dovi's third and fourth secured third in the team championship for Monster Yamaha Tech 3.

5 ALVARO BAUTISTA Useful points in his fight to finish fifth in the championship. His Honda didn't have the speed of Dovizioso's Yamaha down the straight, and despite many changes of place in the fight with Dovi and Bradl he was passed there by the Italian on the penultimate lap.

6 STEFAN BRADL A much better race than he expected after qualifying, but disappointed to lose out in the fight for fourth. Thought using hard tyres might give him the advantage but lost momentum on the last lap when Baustista blocked him and Dovizioso went past.

7 VALENTINO ROSSI A grim weekend at a track where he and his team-mate have fought for the win, not helped by a crash in warm-up. Never able to shake Hayden off, and repeated the sad mantra that seventh was the best he could do. Felt moved to comment that towards the end of his two years with Ducati the problems hadn't changed.

8 NICKY HAYDEN The only good thing about the race was that his 2008 lap record

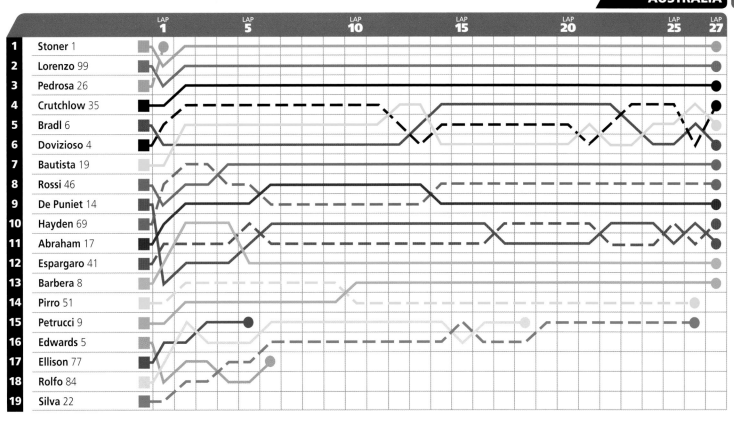

		LAP 1	LAP 5	LAP 10	LAP 15	LAP 20	LAP 25	LAP 27
1	Stoner 1							
2	Lorenzo 99							
3	Pedrosa 26							
4	Crutchlow 35							
5	Bradl 6							
6	Dovizioso 4							
7	Bautista 19							
8	Rossi 46							
9	De Puniet 14							
10	Hayden 69							
11	Abraham 17							
12	Espargaro 41							
13	Barbera 8							
14	Pirro 51							
15	Petrucci 9							
16	Edwards 5							
17	Ellison 77							
18	Rolfo 84							
19	Silva 22							

RACE

	Rider	Motorcycle	Race Time	Time +	Fastest Lap	Av Speed	
1	Stoner	Honda	41m 01.324s		1m 30.191s	109.147mph	S/M
2	Lorenzo	Yamaha	41m 10.547s	9.223s	1m 30.703s	108.739mph	S/M
3	Crutchlow	Yamaha	41m 15.894s	14.570s	1m 30.947s	108.505mph	S/M
4	Dovizioso	Yamaha	41m 24.627s	23.303s	1m 31.214s	108.124mph	S/M
5	Bautista	Honda	41m 24.756s	23.432s	1m 30.986s	108.118mph	S/M
6	Bradl	Honda	41m 24.791s	23.467s	1m 30.976s	108.116mph	S/H
7	Rossi	Ducati	41m 38.437s	37.113s	1m 31.662s	107.526mph	S/M
8	Hayden	Ducati	41m 39.711s	38.387s	1m 31.713s	107.471mph	S/M
9	Abraham	Ducati	41m 53.937s	52.613s	1m 31.646s	106.863mph	S/M
10	Espargaro	Art	42m 01.623s	1m 00.299s	1m 32.305s	106.537mph	S/M
11	De Puniet	Art	42m 01.666s	1m 00.342s	1m 32.379s	106.535mph	S/M
12	Barbera	Ducati	42m 23.275s	1m 21.951s	1m 32.355s	105.630mph	S/M
13	Petrucci	Ioda-Suter	42m 29.181s	1m 27.857s	1m 33.096s	105.385mph	S/M
14	Pirro	FTR	41m 13.539s	1 lap	1m 33.013s	104.585mph	S/M
15	Silva	BQR	41m 35.733s	1 lap	1m 33.892s	103.655mph	S/M
NF	Rolfo	Art	28m 33.372s	9 laps	1m 33.867s	104.530mph	S/M
NF	Edwards	Suter	9m 46.759s	21 laps	1m 34.131s	101.744mph	S/M
NF	Ellison	Art	7m 58.865s	22 laps	1m 33.590s	103.890mph	S/M
NF	Pedrosa	Honda	1m 37.097s	26 laps	1m 00.000s	102.473mph	S/M

CHAMPIONSHIP

	Rider	Team	Points
1	Lorenzo	Yamaha Factory Racing	350
2	Pedrosa	Repsol Honda Team	307
3	Stoner	Repsol Honda Team	238
4	Dovizioso	Monster Yamaha Tech 3	208
5	Bautista	San Carlo Honda Gresini	165
6	Rossi	Ducati Team	157
7	Crutchlow	Monster Yamaha Tech 3	151
8	Bradl	LCR Honda MotoGP	135
9	Hayden	Ducati Team	122
10	Spies	Yamaha Factory Racing	88
11	Barbera	Pramac Racing Team	83
12	Espargaro	Power Electronics Aspar	69
13	De Puniet	Power Electronics Aspar	58
14	Abraham	Cardion AB Motoracing	50
15	Pirro	San Carlo Honda Gresini	32
16	Ellison	Paul Bird Motorsport	28
17	Hernandez	Avintia Blusens	28
18	Edwards	NGM Mobile Forward Racing	25
19	Petrucci	Came IodaRacing Project	19
20	Rea	Repsol Honda Team	17
21	Pasini	Speed Master	13
22	Silva	Avintia Blusens	12
23	Elias	Pramac Racing Team	10
24	Nakasuga	Yamaha YSP Racing Team	7
25	Rapp	Attack Performance	2
26	Salom	Avintia Blusens	1

wasn't beaten. Tried everything but couldn't improve from Friday morning. Got closer to his team-mate once the tyres were worn but then suffered from too much front-tyre wear. Thought about attacking Rossi but ran wide on the final left and lost touch.

9 KAREL ABRAHAM Happy for the first time all year, in total contrast to Sepang. Seventh-best fastest lap and split the factory Ducatis for much of the race. Lost out to Hayden when the rear started sliding after 12 laps, but a little perplexed afterwards to see that the tyre looked perfect.

10 ALEIX ESPARGARO Top CRT again, after passing his team-mate on the last lap. Now had an 11-point lead over de Puniet, making Aleix favourite to finish the season as top man in the class.

11 RANDY DE PUNIET Superb in qualifying but his engine bogged as he changed from second to third off the line, losing positions and denying him the chance to race with the factory Ducatis. Really upset afterwards because his lap times showed he could have been up with them.

12 HECTOR BARBERA Not happy all weekend, then afflicted by severe chatter in the race, something he hadn't previously experienced during the season.

13 DANILO PETRUCCI A problem-free race after losing a few places off the start. Halved the gap to Barbera's Ducati in the second half of the race. Both rider and team were happy.

14 MICHELE PIRRO The objective was to be third CRT, but a problem with the fairing towards the end of the race meant he couldn't attack Petrucci.

15 IVAN SILVA The lone Avintia team rider picked up the last point after dicing with Rolfo at the back of the field.

NON-FINISHERS

ROBERTO ROLFO Stopped by a mechanical problem, but never on the pace all weekend.

COLIN EDWARDS Couldn't change down at the end of the main straight, after which he could hear a metal-on-metal noise. May have been due to a missed gear during warm-up.

JAMES ELLISON Ended a run of six points-scoring finishes when he crashed on lap five. Didn't like the feedback from the front during warm-up but thought it might be down to track temperature. Slow to get away, but was up to 15th when he crashed.

DANI PEDROSA Fell at the Honda corner on the second lap as he gambled everything on trying to win the race and keep his title hopes alive. Made no apologies and said he was proud of his championship challenge.

NON-STARTERS

BEN SPIES Out for the rest of the season following an operation on the shoulder he hurt in Sepang.

YONNY HERNANDEZ Had not yet recovered from the shoulder injury sustained in Motegi. Replaced by Kris McLaren.

KRIS MCLAREN Replaced Hernandez but failed to get within the requisite 107% of the pole-sitter's time in any session so not allowed to race.

ROUND 18

BRIDGESTONE
HONDA
REPSOL
NOLAN
HRC
alpinestars
Satu HATI.
REPSOL

GRAN PREMIO GENERALI DE LA COMUNITAT VALENCIANA

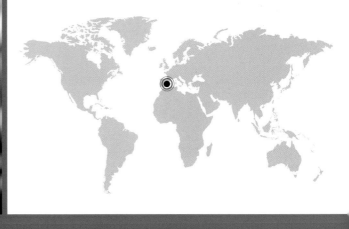

WEIRD SCENES

Everything you thought you'd never see, in one race…

The winner started from pit lane, a replacement rider finished second and the man who came third went into the pits mid-race to change his bike. The new World Champion crashed out, spoiling his almost-perfect record and missing the chance to set a new mark for podium finishes in a season, and a CRT bike led a MotoGP race for the first time. It was as if the powers that be had rolled a dice, having decided that MotoGP had been too predictable for too long. Mind you, there were still three factory bikes in *parc fermé*, two of them Repsol Hondas and the other a factory Yamaha, but the ways in which they arrived there were so different as to be mind-boggling.

From the margin of victory one would be forgiven for thinking that Dani Pedrosa had cruised to an easy win, especially if you'd witnessed his pole-position lap. Nothing could be further from the truth, however. He left the pits on treaded wet-weather tyres, then realised almost immediately that he'd made the wrong decision. The plan was to open up a lead on the slick-shod machine before pitting, but at the end of the warm-up lap instinct took over and Dani dived into the pits to swap bikes, meaning he would have to start the race from the end of pit lane. He was followed by Crutchlow, Bautista and Hayden. All left pit lane after the field had gone by, but in Dani's case only after the rear slick had spun so violently that the bike nearly spat him off.

To the surprise of many, both factory Yamahas started the race on slicks, as did Stefan Bradl. It was a brave choice and would require total precision on a very narrow dry line – just what everyone expects from Lorenzo. After the initial skirmish, led by the

ever-exuberant Aleix Espargaro, Jorge took the lead
wheeled out their Inmotec on lap four only to see on his pit board, two laps
chassis – part aluminium, part later, that Pedrosa was through to second place. The
carbon, and unseen since the pair pulled away as usual, and it began to look like a
start of the year – for wild normal race. Casey Stoner, in his last outing, was a little
card Claudio Corti subdued. He admitted, as he'd said in Malaysia, that he
couldn't summon up the motivation to push hard in wet
BELOW It was not a happy conditions due to his damaged ankle. This risk aversion
race for anyone in the works meant he started the race on wet tyres and was one of
Ducati pit no fewer than 11 riders to change to a slick-shod bike
during the race, at the cost of around 30 seconds.

Lorenzo's gamble didn't pay off. Pedrosa was on
him, but then Dani suddenly lost over three seconds
thanks to a run-on when he found a false neutral.
Jorge now sought to take advantage, knowing that
Pedrosa had the pace to close the gap again. This
was when Lorenzo came up behind James Ellison,
who was running in 12th, third CRT on track. Anxious
to pass rather than wait for the straight and hand
Pedrosa a second or two, Jorge got off the dry line
and promptly highsided. The crash prevented him

from setting a new record for the number of podium finishes in the top class in a season.

Yamaha's gamble wasn't over, though. Katsuyuki Nakasuga, replacing Ben Spies, had also started on slicks; he worked his way steadily to the front and was looking settled in third. Ahead of him, Cal Crutchlow seemed to be heading for a career-best second place when he crashed going down the hill to the final corner. Cal didn't think he was pushing, but his partial times from the start of the lap said otherwise. That left

'I COULDN'T PUT THE BIKE WHERE I WANTED'
VALENTINO ROSSI

ABOVE Aleix Espargaro leads the first lap on treaded tyres; first man on slicks is Jorge Lorenzo in seventh

Nakasuga in a safe second and Bautista wondering whether to try and fight Stoner for third. The Gresini crew, with an eye on the championship, signalled Alvaro that fourth was fine by them. Thanks to Crutchlow's crash and a horrible day for Valentino Rossi, Bautista was able to take fifth in the final standings.

In fact, it wasn't just a bad day for Rossi, it was a pretty horrible weekend for the whole Ducati team. A rumour that Ducati Corse boss and the man who designed the Desmosedici, Filippo Preziosi, was about to be replaced was neither confirmed nor denied by stony-faced riders. Both Hayden and Rossi flattered to deceive earlier in the weekend, especially when the track was wet. Come the race, Valentino was as high as third in the early laps but ended up being lapped.

TOP Michele Pirro on his way to fifth, his fairing covered in messages from fans in memory of Marco Simoncelli

ABOVE Danilo Petrucci, who started on slicks, is caught mid-race by Stoner, who had to change bikes

RIGHT Several riders crashed after changing to slicks, including Hector Barbera

Jorge Lorenzo even said that Rossi was the only slower rider who moved over for him… it felt like a metaphor for the whole unhappy two-year marriage between the two Italian national icons.

The slicks gamble also paid off in the CRT race. Michele Pirro started on slicks and worked his way steadily up from 15th on the grid to fifth before half-distance. He held on to it, as well, for his first finish as top CRT and by far the best result of the season for a CRT rider. It was also, of course, the best result of Nakasuga's career – he's done three MotoGP races and finished sixth, ninth and second – and was enough to reduce the Yamaha M1 project leader Tsuji-san to tears in *parc fermé*. That may also have had something to do with the fact that Katsuyuki's second son had been born the night before. Valencia 2012 is not a weekend he will forget in a hurry.

Neither will Dani Pedrosa. His pole-position time, an absolute lap record, removed the last of the 990cc marks, set on Michelin qualifying tyres, from the record books. The win was his seventh of the season, making Dani the most prolific winner of the year – Jorge won six, Casey five. In the end, Lorenzo's winning margin at the top of the table was reduced to a mere 18 points.

BELOW Nakasuga's second place meant Japan didn't lose its record of having a rider on the rostrum at a Grand Prix every year since 1985

AT LAST

Finally, smoke issued from the chimney. Dorna and the MSMA reached a compromise on the technical regulations for 2014. Essentially, the idea is that there will be two classes of bike, both of which will utilise the ECU and data-logger supplied by Dorna. The prototypes built by MSMA members will use the control hardware and have freedom on software but they will be limited to 20 litres of fuel, one litre less than now. As at present, each factory will be limited to four of these bikes. Engine allocation will drop from six to five, except for members who are new to MotoGP; they will be allowed nine. Interestingly, there is no mention of a rev limit, a concession that will please the factories, although the reduction in fuel may act as a *de facto* restriction.

Teams who run the spec ECU and spec software will get the same 24-litre fuel allowance and 12 engines for the season currently enjoyed by CRT bikes. The factories are happy with these rules, and with a freeze on bore-and-stroke dimensions for three years from the start of next season.

There is some small print to take into account, however. This agreement is subject to further negotiations between Dorna and the MSMA over the supply of bikes and engines to private teams. Presumably these are the V4 Hondas that HRC have said could be built and sold at affordable prices, plus some engines that Yamaha may be willing to supply for teams to build their own bikes around.

Following the weighing of all Moto2 riders in full race kit at Phillip Island, the class will have a minimum combined bike and rider weight limit from next season of 215kg. Under these regulations Marc Marquez would only have had to carry about 3kg of ballast this year, which wouldn't have made much of a difference to anything.

TYRE OPTIONS
FRONT: SOFT (**S**) / MEDIUM (**M**) / WET SOFT (**WS**) / WET HARD (**WH**)
REAR: MEDIUM (**M**) / HARD (**H**) / WET SOFT (**WS**) / WET HARD (**WH**)

OFFICIAL TIMEKEEPER

GRAN PREMIO GENERALI DE LA COMUNITAT VALENCIANA
CIRCUITO RICARDO TORMO

ROUND **18**
November 11

RACE RESULTS

CIRCUIT LENGTH 2.489 miles
NO. OF LAPS 30
RACE DISTANCE 74.658 miles
WEATHER Wet, 13°C
TRACK TEMPERATURE 15°C
WINNER Dani Pedrosa
FASTEST LAP 1m 33.119s, 96.209mph, Dani Pedrosa
LAP RECORD 1m 32.582s, 96.767mph, Casey Stoner, 2008

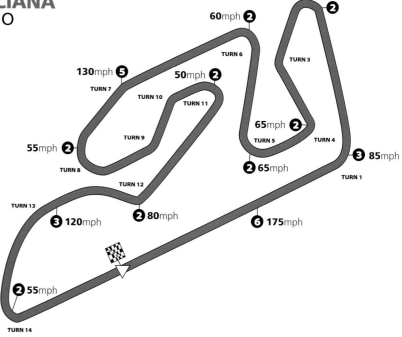

QUALIFYING

	Rider	Nationality	Team	Qualifying	Pole +	Gap
1	Pedrosa	SPA	Repsol Honda Team	1m 30.844s		
2	Lorenzo	SPA	Yamaha Factory Racing	1m 31.195s	0.351s	0.351s
3	Stoner	AUS	Repsol Honda Team	1m 31.428s	0.584s	0.233s
4	Crutchlow	GBR	Monster Yamaha Tech 3	1m 31.512s	0.668s	0.084s
5	Bradl	GER	LCR Honda MotoGP	1m 31.757s	0.913s	0.245s
6	Dovizioso	ITA	Monster Yamaha Tech 3	1m 31.795s	0.951s	0.038s
7	Hayden	USA	Ducati Team	1m 32.503s	1.659s	0.708s
8	Bautista	SPA	San Carlo Honda Gresini	1m 32.585s	1.741s	0.082s
9	Barbera	SPA	Pramac Racing Team	1m 32.605s	1.761s	0.020s
10	Espargaro	SPA	Power Electronics Aspar	1m 32.834s	1.990s	0.229s
11	Rossi	ITA	Ducati Team	1m 32.877s	2.033s	0.043s
12	De Puniet	FRA	Power Electronics Aspar	1m 33.346s	2.502s	0.469s
13	Abraham	CZE	Cardion AB Motoracing	1m 33.442s	2.598s	0.096s
14	Edwards	USA	NGM Mobile Forward Racing	1m 33.453s	2.609s	0.011s
15	Pirro	ITA	San Carlo Honda Gresini	1m 33.971s	3.127s	0.518s
16	Nakasuga	JPN	Yamaha Factory Racing	1m 33.979s	3.135s	0.008s
17	Petrucci	ITA	Came IodaRacing Project	1m 33.980s	3.136s	0.001s
18	Silva	SPA	Avintia Blusens	1m 34.407s	3.563s	0.427s
19	Rolfo	ITA	Speed Master	1m 34.866s	4.022s	0.459s
20	Ellison	GBR	Paul Bird Motorsport	1m 34.918s	4.074s	0.052s
21	Aoyama	JPN	Avintia Blusens	1m 35.363s	4.519s	0.445s
22	Corti	ITA	Avintia Blusens	1m 36.531s	5.687s	1.168s

FINISHERS

1 DANI PEDROSA Pole position, fastest lap and race win despite starting from pit lane. Swapped to the dry bike at the end of the warm-up lap, then survived a big moment when he missed a gear while right behind Lorenzo. The win was his seventh of the season, more than any other rider.

2 KATSUYUKI NAKASUGA A rostrum in only his third MotoGP race for the factory tester and All-Japan Superbike Champion, replacing Ben Spies in the works Yamaha team. Like his team-mate, started on slicks but rode steadily with no mistakes.

3 CASEY STONER Bowed out of bike racing with a rostrum, his 89th from 176 starts in all classes. Took no risks with his injured ankle, starting on wets and carefully climbing to a rostrum finish. Caught Bautista three laps from home.

4 ALVARO BAUTISTA Achieved his primary objective of securing fifth place in the championship table, despite a tough weekend. Again complained of no feedback from the front tyre. Benefited from his decision to follow Pedrosa's example and pit at the end of the warm-up lap.

5 MICHELE PIRRO The best result from a CRT rider all season. Started on slicks and 'felt the hand of Marco on his shoulder', as he had a year ago when winning the Moto2 race here for Team Gresini.

6 ANDREA DOVIZIOSO Started on wets and led on lap three yet managed to be lapped and then unlap himself. Made the wrong decision at the start and waited too long before coming in to change bikes; stalling the dry bike didn't help either. A sad way to say goodbye to Tech 3.

7 KAREL ABRAHAM Top Ducati rider and his best result of the year. Started on wets but, like Dovi, waited too long to change bikes, and was then lapped and unlapped. Last rider to finish the race on the same lap as the winner.

8 DANILO PETRUCCI His best result of the year and his third consecutive CRT 'podium'. Spent most of the race with Pirro, who also started on slicks, before the prototypes of Stoner, Abraham and Dovizioso split them up.

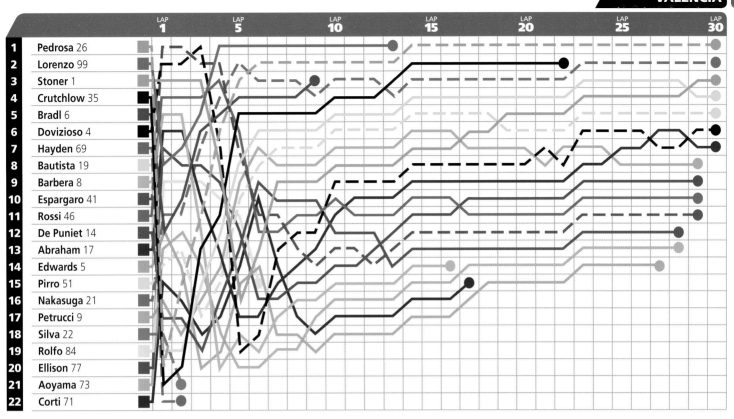

		LAP 1		LAP 5		LAP 10		LAP 15		LAP 20		LAP 25		LAP 30
1	Pedrosa 26													
2	Lorenzo 99													
3	Stoner 1													
4	Crutchlow 35													
5	Bradl 6													
6	Dovizioso 4													
7	Hayden 69													
8	Bautista 19													
9	Barbera 8													
10	Espargaro 41													
11	Rossi 46													
12	De Puniet 14													
13	Abraham 17													
14	Edwards 5													
15	Pirro 51													
16	Nakasuga 21													
17	Petrucci 9													
18	Silva 22													
19	Rolfo 84													
20	Ellison 77													
21	Aoyama 73													
22	Corti 71													

RACE

	Rider	Motorcycle	Race Time	Time +	Fastest Lap	Av Speed	
1	Pedrosa	Honda	48m 23.819s		1m 33.119s	92.556mph	S/M
2	Nakasuga	Yamaha	49m 01.480s	37.661s	1m 35.529s	91.371mph	S/M
3	Stoner	Honda	49m 24.452s	1m 00.633s	1m 33.836s	90.663mph	WH/WS
4	Bautista	Honda	49m 26.630s	1m 02.811s	1m 35.338s	90.597mph	S/M
5	Pirro	FTR	49m 50.427s	1m 26.608s	1m 36.597s	89.876mph	S/M
6	Dovizioso	Yamaha	49m 54.242s	1m 30.423s	1m 33.909s	89.461mph	WH/WH
7	Abraham	Ducati	49m 55.608s	1m 31.789s	1m 35.000s	89.720mph	WH/WH
8	Petrucci	Ioda-Suter	49m 32.847s	1 lap	1m 37.789s	89.194mph	S/M
9	Ellison	Art	48m 41.030s	1 lap	1m 35.555s	88.944mph	WS/WS
10	Rossi	Ducati	48m 45.740s	1 lap	1m 35.996s	88.801mph	WH/WH
11	Espargaro	Art	49m 23.359s	1 lap	1m 36.339s	87.674mph	WS/WS
12	De Puniet	Art	48m 38.162s	2 laps	1m 39.482s	85.961mph	S/M
13	Aoyama	BQR	49m 13.795s	2 laps	1m 39.603s	84.924mph	WH/WH
14	Edwards	Suter	48m 55.662s	3 laps	1m 39.964s	82.397mph	WS/WS
NF	Crutchlow	Yamaha	36m 01.838s	8 laps	1m 34.704s	91.171mph	S/M
NF	Corti	Inmotec	31m 25.346s	13 laps	1m 42.579s	80.781mph	WS/WS
NF	Barbera	Ducati	28m 34.853s	14 laps	1m 41.339s	83.589mph	WH/WH
NF	Lorenzo	Yamaha	21m 18.139s	17 laps	1m 33.296s	91.122mph	S/M
NF	Bradl	Honda	15m 15.012s	21 laps	1m 36.089s	88.119mph	S/M
NF	Rolfo	Art	11m 14.135s	24 laps	1m 44.398s	79.737mph	WS/WS
NF	Silva	BQR	3m 47.152s	28 laps	1m 48.774s	78.880mph	S/M
NF	Hayden	Ducati	3m 47.173s	28 laps	1m 46.510s	78.873mph	S/M

CHAMPIONSHIP

	Rider	Team	Points
1	Lorenzo	Yamaha Factory Racing	350
2	Pedrosa	Repsol Honda Team	332
3	Stoner	Repsol Honda Team	254
4	Dovizioso	Monster Yamaha Tech 3	218
5	Bautista	San Carlo Honda Gresini	178
6	Rossi	Ducati Team	163
7	Crutchlow	Monster Yamaha Tech 3	151
8	Bradl	LCR Honda MotoGP	135
9	Hayden	Ducati Team	122
10	Spies	Yamaha Factory Racing	88
11	Barbera	Pramac Racing Team	83
12	Espargaro	Power Electronics Aspar	74
13	De Puniet	Power Electronics Aspar	62
14	Abraham	Cardion AB Motoracing	59
15	Pirro	San Carlo Honda Gresini	43
16	Ellison	Paul Bird Motorsport	35
17	Hernandez	Avintia Blusens	28
18	Nakasuga	Yamaha YSP Racing Team	27
19	Petrucci	Came IodaRacing Project	27
20	Edwards	NGM Mobile Forward Racing	27
21	Rea	Repsol Honda Team	17
22	Pasini	Speed Master	13
23	Silva	Avintia Blusens	12
24	Elias	Pramac Racing Team	10
25	Aoyama	Avintia Blusens	3
26	Rapp	Attack Performance	2
27	Salom	Avintia Blusens	1

9 JAMES ELLISON The first CRT home to change bikes. Equalled his career-best finish and was as high as seventh in the first couple of laps after a great start. Did nothing wrong when Lorenzo came up behind him.

10 VALENTINO ROSSI A horrible race and a horrible way to leave Ducati. Went well on the wet tyres but when he got on the dry bike he couldn't persuade the front to work or stay on the narrow dry line. In the end, it was simply a matter of getting to the flag.

11 ALEIX ESPARGARO Led the first couple of laps, the first time a CRT bike has headed a race, and gleefully diced with Lorenzo when he was trying to get by. Pressed hard until the tyres went off, then concentrated on catching his team-mate, after which he just enjoyed finishing the season as top CRT rider.

12 RANDY DE PUNIET Started on slicks, unlike his team-mate, which was the right decision and should have produced a good result. Instead, he didn't have any confidence in the front and ran wide on a number of occasions. Annoyed that he couldn't take advantage of the correct tyre choice.

13 HIROSHI AOYAMA Racing for the Blusens team as a replacement for the injured Hernandez. Rode the bike for the first time on Friday and just concentrated on finishing the race. Will be back with the team full time in 2013.

14 COLIN EDWARDS The wet bike wouldn't accelerate and the dry bike wouldn't change down, so it was merely a case of keeping going and collecting some points.

NON-FINISHERS

CAL CRUTCHLOW In a safe second place when he fell coming down to the last corner. The data seem to show the front locked for a few inches, probably on a wet patch of track, while the bike was only leaned over 20 degrees.

CLAUDIO CORTI Raced as a wild card on the Avintia team's carbon/aluminium Inmotec chassis with a Kawasaki engine. Crashed soon after changing to the dry set-up.

HECTOR BARBERA Another late crasher: not a nice way to say farewell to the Blusens team. Qualified as second Ducati at his home track and was quick early on but, despite changing bikes early, was lapped before his accident.

JORGE LORENZO The new World Champion ended the season on the floor after a big highside. Got off-line looking for a way past Ellison, hit the wet part of the track and went down. He was leading at the time, and pressing to try and maintain the gap to Pedrosa.

STEFAN BRADL Maintained his unenviable record at Valencia: he has now failed to finish the six races he has started there. Began on slicks and was running third when he crashed, but still ended the season as Rookie of the Year.

ROBERTO ROLFO Another rider who went well on wets early on but crashed soon after changing to his dry bike. Thought he must have got slightly off-line and on to a wet section of track.

IVAN SILVA Crashed on the third lap when his gamble on using slicks went wrong. Got off-line and was flicked off unceremoniously.

NICKY HAYDEN One of the quartet who changed bikes after the warm-up lap. Was looking to get past Petrucci on the third lap when he put slick tyres down on wet tarmac.

NON-STARTERS

YONNY HERNANDEZ Recovering from a dislocated collarbone due to his Motegi crash. Replaced by Aoyama.

BEN SPIES Recuperating from the shoulder operation needed to repair the damage from his Sepang crash. Replaced by Nakasuga.

WORLD CHAMPIONSHIP CLASSIFICATION

MotoGP

	Rider	Nation	Motorcycle	QAT	SPA	POR	FRA	CAT	GBR	NED	GER	ITA	USA	INP	CZE	RSM	ARA	JPN	MAL	AUS	VAL	Points
1	Lorenzo	SPA	Yamaha	25	20	20	25	25	25	–	20	25	20	20	20	25	20	20	20	20	–	350
2	Pedrosa	SPA	Honda	20	16	16	13	20	16	20	25	20	16	25	25	–	25	25	25	–	25	332
3	Stoner	AUS	Honda	16	25	25	16	13	20	25	–	8	25	13	–	–	–	11	16	25	16	254
4	Dovizioso	ITA	Yamaha	11	11	13	9	16	–	16	16	16	13	16	13	13	16	13	3	13	10	218
5	Bautista	SPA	Honda	9	10	10	6	10	13	–	9	6	8	11	10	16	10	16	10	11	13	178
6	Rossi	ITA	Ducati	6	7	9	20	9	7	3	10	11	–	9	9	20	8	9	11	9	6	163
7	Crutchlow	GBR	Yamaha	13	13	11	8	11	10	11	8	10	11	–	16	–	13	–	–	16	–	151
8	Bradl	GER	Honda	8	9	7	11	8	8	–	11	13	9	10	11	10	–	10	–	10	–	135
9	Hayden	USA	Ducati	10	8	5	10	7	9	10	6	9	10	–	–	9	–	8	13	8	–	122
10	Spies	USA	Yamaha	5	5	8	–	6	11	13	13	5	–	–	–	11	11	–	–	–	–	88
11	Barbera	SPA	Ducati	7	6	6	7	5	6	9	7	7	–	–	–	–	–	4	6	9	4	83
12	Espargaro	SPA	ART	1	4	4	3	3	5	–	3	3	7	6	6	–	6	4	8	6	5	74
13	De Puniet	FRA	ART	3	–	3	–	1	4	8	5	4	5	–	8	7	5	–	–	5	4	62
14	Abraham	CZE	Ducati	–	–	–	–	4	–	–	–	–	6	8	7	–	7	5	6	7	9	59
15	Pirro	ITA	FTR	–	–	2	2	2	3	7	–	–	–	2	6	1	1	4	2	–	11	43
16	Ellison	GBR	ART	–	–	–	5	–	2	2	1	2	–	1	1	3	2	7	–	–	7	35
17	Hernandez	COL	BQR	2	–	–	1	–	1	–	2	–	4	7	4	4	3	–	–	–	–	28
18	Nakasuga	JPN	Yamaha	–	–	–	–	–	–	–	–	–	–	–	–	–	–	7	–	–	20	27
19	Petrucci	ITA	Ioda-Suter	–	3	1	–	–	–	5	–	–	–	–	–	2	–	–	5	3	8	27
20	Edwards	USA	Suter	4	–	–	–	–	–	–	4	–	3	3	3	5	–	3	–	–	2	27
21	Rea	GBR	Honda	–	–	–	–	–	–	–	–	–	–	8	9	–	–	–	–	–	–	17
22	Pasini	ITA	ART	–	2	–	4	–	–	–	6	–	1	–	–	–	–	–	–	–	–	13
23	Silva	SPA	BQR	–	1	–	–	–	–	4	–	4	–	–	2	–	–	–	–	1	–	12
24	Elias	SPA	Ducati	–	–	–	–	–	–	–	–	–	5	5	–	–	–	–	–	–	–	10
25	Aoyama	JPN	BQR	–	–	–	–	–	–	–	–	–	–	–	–	–	–	–	–	3	–	3
26	Rapp	USA	APR	–	–	–	–	–	–	–	–	–	–	2	–	–	–	–	–	–	–	2
27	Salom	SPA	BQR	–	–	–	–	–	–	–	–	–	–	–	–	–	1	–	–	–	–	1

CONSTRUCTOR

	Motorcycle	QAT	SPA	POR	FRA	CAT	GBR	NED	GER	ITA	USA	INP	CZE	RSM	ARA	JPN	MAL	AUS	VAL	Points
1	Honda	20	25	25	16	20	20	25	25	20	25	25	25	16	25	25	25	25	25	412
2	Yamaha	25	20	20	25	25	25	16	20	25	20	20	20	25	20	20	20	20	20	386
3	Ducati	10	8	9	20	9	9	10	10	11	10	9	9	20	8	9	13	9	7	192
4	ART	3	4	4	5	3	5	8	5	4	7	6	8	7	6	4	8	6	7	100
5	FTR	–	–	2	2	2	3	7	–	–	–	2	6	1	1	4	2	–	11	43
6	BQR	–	1	–	1	–	1	4	2	–	4	7	4	4	3	–	–	1	3	35
7	Suter	4	–	–	–	–	–	–	4	–	3	3	3	5	–	3	–	–	2	27
8	Ioda-Suter	–	–	–	–	–	–	–	–	–	–	–	–	2	–	–	5	3	8	18
9	Ioda	–	3	1	–	–	–	5	–	–	–	–	–	–	–	–	–	–	–	9
10	APR	–	–	–	–	–	–	–	–	–	–	2	–	–	–	–	–	–	–	2
11	BQR-FTR	2	–	–	–	–	–	–	–	–	–	–	–	–	–	–	–	–	–	2

TEAM

	Motorcycle	QAT	SPA	POR	FRA	CAT	GBR	NED	GER	ITA	USA	INP	CZE	RSM	ARA	JPN	MAL	AUS	VAL	Points
1	Repsol Honda Team	36	41	41	29	33	36	45	25	28	41	38	25	8	34	36	41	25	41	603
2	Yamaha Factory Racing	30	25	28	25	31	36	13	33	30	20	20	20	36	31	20	20	20	20	458
3	Monster Yamaha Tech 3	24	24	24	17	27	10	27	24	26	24	16	29	13	29	13	3	29	10	369
4	Ducati Team	16	15	14	30	16	16	13	16	20	10	9	9	29	8	17	24	17	6	285
5	San Carlo Honda Gresini	9	10	12	8	12	16	7	9	6	8	11	12	22	11	17	14	13	24	221
6	Power Electronics Aspar	4	4	7	3	4	9	8	8	7	12	6	14	7	11	4	8	11	9	136
7	LCR Honda MotoGP	8	9	7	11	8	8	–	11	13	9	10	11	10	–	10	–	10	–	135
8	Pramac Racing Team	7	6	6	7	5	6	9	7	7	–	5	5	–	4	6	9	4	–	93
9	Cardion AB Motoracing	–	–	–	–	4	–	–	–	–	6	8	7	–	7	5	6	7	9	59
10	Avintia Blusens	2	1	–	1	–	1	4	2	–	6	11	4	5	3	–	–	1	3	44
11	Paul Bird Motorsport	–	–	–	5	–	2	2	1	2	–	1	1	3	2	2	7	–	7	35
12	Came IodaRacing Project	–	3	1	–	–	–	5	–	–	–	–	–	2	–	–	5	3	8	27
13	NGM Mobile Forward Racing	4	–	–	–	–	–	–	4	–	3	3	3	5	–	3	–	–	2	27
14	Speed Master	–	2	–	–	4	–	–	6	–	–	–	–	–	–	–	–	–	–	13

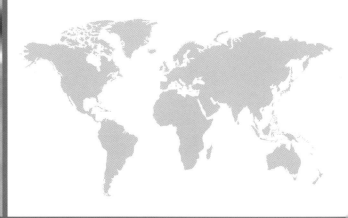

MARQUEZ THE MERCILESS

The third season of Moto2 gave us more thrilling racing, a new champion, and a few questions

This year there was no doubt about it. Marc Marquez made up for last year's disappointment by winning the title with a race to spare; he now moves up to MotoGP with the Repsol Honda team with 125cc and Moto2 titles to his name.

It will be fascinating to see how his ultra-aggressive style and win-at-all-costs approach transfers to the big class. This season Marc had to deal with a rider nearly as fast and aggressive as himself in the shape of Pol Espargaro, with only occasional interruptions from Tom Luthi, Scott Redding and Andrea Iannone. The rest of the field were hard put to find a rostrum between them.

As for machinery, the third year of the championship brought things into focus. As you'd expect from such a tightly controlled championship in terms of engine, electronics, tyres and fuel, a preferred solution started to emerge.

Only Marquez and Luthi made the Suter work whereas a raft of riders were quick on the Kalex. Iannone used a new Speed Up chassis, as did Ant West later in the season. His QMMF team's change plus Team Gresini's move to Suter saw the last Moriwakis leave the grid. The manufacturer that won the first Moto2 championship was gone, and the bike that looked like the one to have at the end of last season, the FTR, also had a tough year and didn't get a bike on the rostrum until Alex de Angelis, whose Forward Racing team dumped Suter to go to FTR, was third in Germany. The man seen as FTR's lead rider, Simone Corsi, didn't shine, especially when the weather turned nasty, which it did all too often, usually condemning him to a start from deep on the grid.

Nevertheless, there was still a great deal of close

LEFT AND BELOW Scott Redding's best finish was second at Silverstone, one of his four rostrum finishes of the season

racing, last-lap sort-outs and controversy – usually over Marquez's riding. He courted controversy at the very first round by chopping across Tom Luthi at the end of the long straight, had a coming-together with Espargaro in Barcelona, another with Kallio in Japan, and finally got penalised for knocking Corsi off in practice at Valencia. All of which tends to obscure the fact that his riding was more often than not brilliant – which we knew.

Espargaro's form was the revelation of the year. Pol was fast enough often enough to attract serious attention from Yamaha. He started slow, getting to know the Kalex, and finished the season fast. Marquez had to deal with an over-stiff Suter at the start of the year, but once he got the revised chassis he looked even more confident and aggressive.

The other man looking more comfortable on a Kalex

1 – QATARI GP

Moto2 may be the closest, most chaotic class in GP racing, but there's always a sense of inevitability when Marc Marquez is about. As usual the Spanish teenager – racing for the first time since suffering eye damage in a huge crash at the 2011 Malaysian GP – played his part in a race-long skirmish, this time with Andrea Iannone, Thomas Luthi and Pol Espargaro and Esteve Rabat.

Marquez did make a couple of mistakes, once slipping to sixth at the rear of the lead group, but he fought back. In the final laps it was Luthi just ahead of Marquez and Iannone. Into the last lap Marquez used his top-speed advantage (he's not a big man) to sneak past Luthi towards Turn 1, pushing the Swiss wide, on to the kerb. Depending on one's viewpoint, Marquez's move was either tough or dangerous.

From there it was a straight duel: Marquez v. Iannone. The Italian got ahead a few corners from the end, but Marquez pulled past Iannone on the run to the flag. Luthi ended up fifth behind Espargaro and Rabat.

2 – SPANISH GP

Marc Marquez may seem unstoppable, but there's one thing that can halt the Spanish genius – an act of the gods. At Jerez the he was involved in a typically entertaining Moto2 skirmish with Pol Espargaro, Thomas Luthi, Scott Redding and Mika Kallio – then the rain started to fall.

Luthi and Redding dominated the opening laps, then Espargaro moved into the lead before Marquez thrust ahead as the red flags came out. But the results were taken from the previous lap, giving Espargaro his first Moto2 win, just ahead of Marquez and Luthi. By then Redding had dropped back some way, the British rider finishing fourth, just ahead of the closing pair of Takaami Nakagami and Claudio Corti.

'The race was so difficult,' said the younger of the Espargaro brothers, a former 125 GP winner. 'The track wasn't completely dry at the start, so it was very difficult to find the fast line without touching the wet, and then the rain came down and it got even more difficult!'

3 – PORTUGUESE GP

Marc Marquez is well known for his merciless riding tactics, so it made a change to see him on the receiving end of a full-on assault.

Marquez and Jerez winner Pol Espargaro dominated this race after dispensing with early leader Thomas Luthi. Marquez appeared to have the upper hand but that didn't stop Espargaro from launching an incredible last-lap attack, hurling himself past on several occasions and ramming his rival once. It's a credit to Marquez that, after the race, he didn't complain about Espargaro's riding.

One of Marquez's greatest talents is his race strategy and, once again, he was cleverer than everyone else. 'Early in the race I was trying to save the rear tyre,' he said. 'I waited and then when I got into the lead I tried to push really hard and make a gap.'

Although he wasn't able to get away from his compatriot he did end up crossing the finish line almost two seconds ahead, after Espargaro nearly crashed at the chicane. Luthi was third and rookie Johann Zarco an impressive fourth.

4 – FRENCH GP

Thomas Luthi put himself back in the Moto2 title fight with a dominant win on a soaking track. The Swiss struggled with rear grip in the early stages and had to bide his time, only moving forward once his tyre got up to temperature. He took the lead from Pol Espargaro just before half-distance and then quickly built a three-second advantage. The only man who looked like pressuring him was local Johann Zarco, but the Frenchman tried too hard and slid off.

Zarco's demise promoted Claudio Corti into second place, the Italian taking his first GP podium ahead of Scott Redding.

Marc Marquez was one of the fallers, crashing out just before half-distance while lying in fourth place. His tumble moved sixth-place finisher Espargaro into the championship lead.

5 – CATALAN GP

Andrea Iannone won a controversial and thrilling Moto2 battle, getting the better of Thomas Luthi just four corners from the chequered flag. The contest for the lead was a frantic three-way affair, with Iannone and Marc Marquez swapping places while Luthi watched and waited.

With three laps to go Luthi began his advance to the front, diving inside Marquez at Turn 10. The Spaniard then nearly fell and when he came back on line he collided with Pol Espargaro, who tumbled out. Marquez crossed the line third but was given a one-minute penalty, which put him out of the points. Later he was reinstated.

In the final two laps Iannone and Luthi swapped the lead several times, Luthi's final push going awry at Turn 10 on the final lap when he went inside the Italian, only to run wide. Espargaro's team-mate Esteve Rabat crossed the line in fourth, 11 seconds behind Marquez.

was Scott Redding. He had a centimetre or two more clearance to fit his lanky frame, but the tallest and heaviest rider in the class still suffered on acceleration and tyre wear. The introduction of a combined minimum bike-and-rider weight limit for 2013 will level the playing field significantly for him. However, it's worth noting that the new regulation would have required Marquez to carry only three extra kilos this season – and no-one thinks that would have made any difference.

After all, in his last Moto2 race Marquez showed that starting from the back of the grid couldn't stop him winning. It was a race that will live long in the memory of all who saw it as he risked everything for the win despite having already wrapped up the championship. His performance at Valencia left you wondering what he has in store for his new rivals in MotoGP.

ABOVE Bradley Smith couldn't force the Mistral onto the podium, with fourth place his best result

RIGHT Andrea Iannone won twice, including at home in Italy with a Fire Service tribute colour scheme to thank the rescue services for their work after the Italian earthquake

6 – BRITISH GP

Pol Espargaro ruled this Moto2 race, finding enough pace to make the break in a class where races are usually won by a few tenths.

The Spaniard took the lead just before half-distance, motoring past lanky Briton Scott Redding on the Hangar straight. As Espargaro made good his escape, Redding came under pressure from Andrea Iannone and Marc Marquez. In the final few laps it was Redding and Marquez going for second, the local hero winning the battle at the final chicane.

'I knew it would be elbows at the finish, because we are both hard riders,' said Redding. 'It was very intense!'

Marquez's third place returned him to the championship lead, ahead of Espargaro and Thomas Luthi, who had a poor weekend, finishing eighth.

7 – DUTCH TT

Marc Marquez scored his first victory since May's Portuguese GP, coming from way behind to defeat runaway leader Andrea Iannone on the final lap. But it wasn't only Marquez's third win of the year that made this a turning point in the 2012 Moto2 championship; his biggest title rivals both crashed out in the early stages. Luthi was the innocent victim of a first-lap pile-up, while Espargaro crashed out of the lead on the very next lap.

Iannone took the lead from Dominique Aegerter on lap four and quickly set about building what looked to be an unbeatable gap. At two-thirds distance he was three seconds ahead of Marquez, who had only just broken clear of the group battling for second. From then on the Spaniard's progress was relentless and as Iannone ran out of rubber – having pushed too hard, too soon – Marquez reeled him in. The pair swapped places several times during the last two laps but there seemed little doubt which one would win.

Scott Redding took third, beating Esteve Rabat on the final

8 – GERMAN GP

Marc Marquez strengthened his grip on the Moto2 championship with his fourth win of the year. The Spanish teenager won by two seconds, with Mika Kallio just getting the better of Alex de Angelis for second place.

Marquez's biggest rival, Andrea Iannone, slid off just after one-third distance, remounting but finishing a distant 16th. 'The tyres felt better when the grip dropped, but then I started to have problems with the rear chattering,' said Marquez after extending his lead over Pol Espargaro to 43 points.

Espargaro rode a hero's race to fourth, having started way down the field after struggling in the rain-lashed qualifying session. He finished just ahead of Thomas Luthi.

9 – ITALIAN GP

Andrea Iannone won a dazzling Moto2 race, throwing his all into beating Pol Espargaro on the last lap. Espargaro had a lead of 1.3 seconds at one point but Iannone hauled him in, chased hard by Thomas Luthi who made a last-lap mistake that nearly lost him third place to Bradley Smith.

For once, series leader Marc Marquez wasn't in the fight for the win. He decided to cool it after nearly crashing while in the lead group at three-quarters distance. He finished fifth but still led the championship by 34 points from Espargaro.

10 – INDIANAPOLIS GP

Marc Marquez took his fifth victory of the year by a margin of over five seconds. He didn't qualify on pole or start quickly on the slippery track, but he overhauled early leaders Dominique Aegerter and Andrea Iannone to win easily. Marquez's victory extended his championship lead to 39 points.

Pol Espargaro, who was on pole by over a quarter of a second, was never in the hunt for the win. Despite starting well, he dropped back and didn't pass Julian Simon until late in the race. This was Simon's first rostrum of the season, after only one other top-ten finish from the season's previous races.

Fourth place went to Mika Kallio after a good fight with Tom Luthi and the other Marc VDS rider, Scott Redding.

11 – CZECH REPUBLIC GP

Marc Marquez won a thrilling four-way battle with Thomas Luthi, Pol Espargaro and Andrea Iannone to take his sixth victory and extend his championship lead to 48 points. The leading quartet was covered by just half a second at the finish line.

As always, Marquez played his hand perfectly, spending nearly all the race in second place, finally sweeping past Luthi with three laps to go. 'It was a different tactic to normal but this track is difficult for me and I wanted to keep something in reserve,' he said.

Luthi did everything in his power to retake the lead but couldn't quite make it. Espargaro set the fastest lap to finish third, a fraction in front of Iannone, last year's Brno winner.

12 – SAN MARINO GP

Once again Marc Marquez proved his genius, taking his seventh win and first hat-trick of 2012. The Spaniard nearly crashed in the early stages and slipped to fourth before making a perfect comeback, grabbing the lead from title rival Pol Espargaro on the final lap. The lead changed a further four times, Marquez crossing the line just three-tenths ahead.

'I liked winning like that, above all because of how I planned the race,' said the Repsol Suter rider after stretching his series lead to 53 points. But Espargaro wasn't happy with Marquez's last lap. 'He is very aggressive, maybe too aggressive,' said the runner-up. Third place went to early leader Andrea Iannone.

13 – ARAGON GP

Aragon has to be one of the best modern MotoGP tracks, with a layout that flows up and then downhill. The Moto2 men made the most of it, serving up a breathtaking battle that had the first six men crossing the finish line just 2.9 seconds apart.

Pol Espargaro took his first win since Silverstone, making the break in the final few laps while his pursuers got in each other's way as they argued over second place. Championship leader Marc Marquez might have been able to chase his compatriot if he hadn't come under incessant attack from Andrea Iannone. The pair were bouncing off each other over the mountain during the final two laps, Scott Redding taking advantage to dive inside Iannone as they came down the hill for the last time.

That was the finishing order: Espargaro, Marquez, Redding and Iannone, with Bradley Smith and Johann Zarco right behind in fifth and sixth.

14 – JAPANESE GP

Marc Marquez has won some impressive victories, but his eighth Moto2 win of 2012 was something remarkable. It began with a potentially lethal problem – his CBR600 didn't engage first gear properly at the start – and most of the grid came rocketing past him as he struggled to get going.

The series leader was 29th into the first corner, but by the time he got to Turn 5 he was tenth. Has there ever been such a furious first few corners? By lap five Marquez was with the leading group of Scott Redding and the Pons HP Kalex duo Esteve Rabat and Pol Espargaro. He led for the first time just before half-distance, then spent the final part of the race fighting with Espargaro. It was a thrilling encounter, Marquez crossing the line 0.4 seconds ahead.

Rabat was nine seconds down in third and fractionally ahead of Redding, who just beat Thomas Luthi for fourth. Revitalised former champ Toni Elias had been with them until he fell.

15 – MALAYSIAN GP

The race started late and on a streaming wet track, but turned into a brilliant four-way battle for the lead between a local wild card, two wet-weather specialists and a former Moto2 winner.

Wild card Hafizh Syahrin and Alex de Angelis were the strongest of the group, Syahrin charging through in the early laps, having qualified 27th in the dry. The 18-year-old rider, who usually races in the Spanish Moto2 series, grabbed the lead at half-distance, his FTR fishtailing wildly as he braked for Turn 9.

Rain-men Ant West and Gino Rea were the others in the battle at the front, Rea grabbing the lead on lap 16 as the rain intensified, just before the race was red-flagged. The results were taken back a lap, leaving de Angelis the winner, marginally ahead of West and Rea, with Syahrin fourth.

TOP Marc Marquez celebrates victory at Motegi, one of his nine wins

ABOVE Gino Rea turned out to be as fast as anyone in the wet

OPPOSITE Typical action from Marc Marquez – always on the edge

ABOVE RIGHT Marquez in *parc fermé* at Phillip Island after clinching the title

CHAMPIONSHIP STANDINGS

	Rider	Nat	Team	Motorcycle	Points
1	Marc Marquez	SPA	Team Catalunya Caixa Repsol	Suter	324
2	Pol Espargaro	SPA	Tuenti Movil HP 40	Kalex	268
3	Andrea Iannone	ITA	Speed Master	Speed Up	193
4	Thomas Luthi	SWI	Interwetten-Paddock	Suter	190
5	Scott Redding	GBR	Marc VDS Racing Team	Kalex	161
6	Mika Kallio	FIN	Marc VDS Racing Team	Kalex	128
7	Esteve Rabat	SPA	Tuenti Movil HP 40	Kalex	114
8	Dominique Aegerter	SWI	Technomag-CIP	Suter	110
9	Bradley Smith	GBR	Tech 3 Racing	Tech 3	109
10	Johann Zarco	FRA	JIR Moto2	Motobi	94
11	Simone Corsi	ITA	Came IodaRacing Project	FTR	87
12	Alex de Angelis	RSM	NGM Mobile Forward Racing	FTR	86
13	Julian Simon	SPA	Blusens Avintia	Suter	79
14	Claudio Corti	ITA	Italtrans Racing Team	Kalex	74
15	Takaaki Nakagami	JPN	Italtrans Racing Team	Kalex	56
16	Anthony West	AUS	QMMF Racing Team	Speed Up	52
17	Toni Elias	SPA	Mapfre Aspar Team Moto2	Suter	48
18	Nicolas Terol	SPA	Mapfre Aspar Team Moto2	Suter	36
19	Randy Krummenacher	SWI	GP Team Switzerland	Kalex	31
20	Jordi Torres	SPA	Mapfre Aspar Team Moto2	Suter	29
21	Gino Rea	GBR	Federal Oil Gresini Moto2	Suter	21
22	Xavier Simeon	BEL	Tech 3 Racing	Tech 3	21
23	Mike di Meglio	FRA	Kiefer Racing	Kalex	14
24	Hafizh Syahrin	MAL	Petronas Raceline Malaysia	FTR	13
25	Axel Pons	SPA	Tuenti Movil HP 40	Kalex	10
26	Max Neukirchner	GER	Kiefer Racing	Kalex	9
27	Ratthapark Wilairot	THA	Thai Honda PTT Gresini Moto2	Suter	9
28	Ricard Cardus	SPA	Arguiñano Racing Team	AJR	8
29	Dani Rivas	SPA	TSR Galicia School	Kalex	3
30	Yuki Takahashi	JPN	NGM Mobile Forward Racing	FTR	2
31	Roberto Rolfo	ITA	Technomag-CIP	Suter	1

16 – AUSTRALIAN GP

Pol Espargaro's world title hopes ended at Phillip Island, but the Spaniard compensated as best he could, winning the race by 16.8 seconds, a record in Moto2.

While Espargaro impressed with his speed, the fans' focus was on a thrilling battle for the last two podium places between Marc Marquez, Scott Redding and Ant West. Redding held the leading position for most of the race, with Marquez right behind. Then West broke from the pack and gained on the pair, passing both in the final stages for his second consecutive podium. At the last corner Marquez went inside Redding to claim third place and secure the World Championship.

'I love this circuit and had a really good feeling with the bike,' said Espargaro after his fourth win of the year.

Former 125 champ Marquez was just delighted to claim his second world title, following his crash at Sepang the previous weekend. 'I had many troubles with my eye injury last winter, so to win the title is like a dream come true,' he said.

17 – VALENCIAN GP

Marc Marquez's final Moto2 victory was almost certainly the greatest of his already brilliant career. Sent to the back of the grid for a Friday misdemeanour, Marquez danced around the damp track, making his rivals look like old men. At two-thirds distance Julian Simon was five seconds ahead and must have been counting his bonus money, but he hadn't reckoned on Marquez, who hunted him down relentlessly.

The last man Marquez passed before Simon was 2011 125 champ Nico Terol, scoring his first Moto2 podium in third. Marquez dispensed of Terol mercilessly, cutting inside him at the very same turn where he had dispatched Simone Corsi two days earlier.

'When I saw Julian and Nico so far ahead I didn't expect to beat them,' said Marquez. 'But I rode on the limit every corner: okay, if I crash, I crash…'

Moto2
CHAMPIONSHIP-WINNING BIKE

Eskil Suter's bikes always tend to look very similar: pointy tail, arrow-like bodywork and very small in stature. They suit small, hard and very fast riders, and in Moto2 Champion Marc Marquez that's exactly what they have.

The bike started the year looking quite menacing, with the front of the main beams not the usual polished alloy but matt black, having been sheathed in carbon fibre. The coating was there to stiffen the bike under braking and to do so without it affecting the bike's stiffness while leaned over. The whole idea was to make up for a perceived softness in Dunlop's front tyre construction.

The bike was fast and Marquez could win on it, but in fact Suter had made the structure too stiff – so by the middle of the year the carbon coating was gone. The chassis now is very similar in stiffness to the original 2009 version…

Over the years the engine position has changed and the swingarm construction has moved from the original 'braced over the top' design to a 'braced underneath' configuration. This allows Suter to maintain torsional rigidity while allowing greater lateral flexibility.

Three years after Shoya Tomizawa won the first Moto2 race on a Suter, they have finally won the championship. And at the final race in Valencia they proved that they are very, very good – in wet conditions at least – by taking the top six places.

FAR LEFT The Suter at the start of the year – note the carbon cladding on chassis

LEFT The late-season version of the Suter, without the carbon stiffening structure

THE CIRCUIT OF WALES

A visionary development that responds to the demands and anticipates the needs of the modern motorsport industry.

A transformational investment programme in a unique partnership between industry, government and the financial community to create a world class motorsport destination and deliver :

• The most spectacular purpose built facilities for international and national motorsports

Moto3
CHAMPIONSHIP

ALL THE YOUNG DUDES

The rule makers got it right: the first year of Moto3 was a spectacular success

MotoGP's newest class had a big job to do: Moto3 had to convince everyone that it was a worthy succesor to the 125s, the last class left from the original championship categories. That's a lot of history to fight. The inevitable move to four-strokes happened because only one factory, Aprilia, was willing to build competitive 125cc bikes and only the recipients of their top equipment, usually two teams, could hope to win the title. That gave other teams very little to try and sell to a sponsor.

Moto3 was the answer. With the benefit of a couple of years' experience with Moto2, the rule book was a little more relaxed. The main objective was still to keep costs down, although that might have been difficult to believe for some impecunious privateer teams. Overall, bringing in four-strokes has put costs up but even the most expensive Moto3 bike will cost a fraction of what it cost to lease a factory Aprilia 125. It is to be hoped that the after-market and the appearance of secondhand equipment will lower average costs.

Whatever the costs, Moto3 started life with grids full of quality teams with some experienced names like Sandro Cortese and Hector Faubel up against new stars such as Romano Fenati and Alex Rins. The Austrian KTM factory fielded four bikes, and four more riders used their engines in Kalex chassis. Honda's over-the-counter NSF250 was the basis for most of the rest of the field's machinery, with FTR or Suter providing the chassis. Some teams saw no point in changing chassis (or couldn't afford it) and ran very stock-looking NSFs.

Giampiero Sacchi's Ioda team built both their own engine and frame, while Mahindra used Oral's motor in their own chassis. Both projects were short

on development time and the giant Indian Mahindra concern tried to ensure future competitiveness by joining forces with Suter Engineering for 2013.

In broad terms, the KTM riders found they had a slight advantage on top end while those using Honda power had a more flexible motor that punched out of the corners better. By season's end, KTM appeared to have the upper hand.

The last race won by a Honda-powered bike was Mugello, which was also the last race won by the hot pre-season favourite Maverick Viñales. The teenage Spaniard was regarded at home as a nailed-on favourite, so the early-season form of GP debutant Fenati came as a surprise to everyone. The Italian was on the rostrum at the first race of the year and won the

second to go top of the table, only to crash in the next two races and not get in the top three again until his home race at Mugello.

By then Cortese had got into his stride on the factory KTM. He won the third race of the year from pole with the fastest lap and went top of the table. He was only off the rostrum twice more, in France and Japan, and both times he finished sixth after falling and remounting. Sandro wasn't happy after the Japanese race, won by his KTM team-mate Danny Kent. The German had to wait for Malaysia, a race he won on the last corner to become champion. Sepang was especially noisy thanks to the performance of local hero Zulfahmi Khairuddin, who took the first pole position by a Malaysian rider and came within an ace of adding the win.

1 – QATARI GP

Last November Maverick Viñales made history by becoming the last winner of a 125 GP. At Qatar the 17-year-old Spaniard made history once more, winning the first Moto3 GP – and what a win it was. Viñales ran away with the race, heading home remarkable rookie Romano Fenati by four seconds.

The pace of the two FTR Honda men must have been a worry for the rest of the pack. Pole-sitter Sandro Cortese won a thrilling seven-way contest for the final place on the podium, but at the end of the 18-lap race he was 18 seconds behind Viñales.

Fenati got a blistering start and it took Viñales five laps to catch up. Once ahead it seemed like he couldn't shake off Fenati, but in fact he was just looking after his motorcycle. With five laps to go Viñales pulled the pin and that was that.

Cortese crossed the line just ahead of Luis Salom, Miguel Oliveira, Zulfahmi Khairuddin and Red Bull team-mate Arthur Sissis.

2 – SPANISH GP

The first race of the day started on a patchy track which claimed no fewer than 20 crashers. The treacherous conditions were of the kind that should benefit older, more experienced warriors, but the fastest survivor was actually 16-year-old rookie sensation Romano Fenati, who took his first GP victory – at only his second attempt – by an amazing 36 seconds.

Fenati bided his time and let his rivals make the early mistakes. Jakub Kornfeil set the early pace, only to fall foul of the conditions. Then Alex Rins took over, only to run off the track. Fenati finally grabbed the lead from Louis Rossi, who also joined the fallen.

Qatar winner Maverick Viñales also slid off but remounted to finish sixth.

3 – PORTUGUESE GP

KTM won its first Moto3 victory at Estoril, the Austrian factory's 23rd GP success and its first with a four-stroke. The win went to former 125 winner Sandro Cortese, who used his superior top speed to hold off brilliant teenager Maverick Viñales. The KTMs had a crucial 3mph advantage on the track's long main straight.

Luis Salom finished a distant third, just ahead of Malaysian Zulfahmi Khairuddin.

4 – FRENCH GP

Louis Rossi won a fairytale maiden GP victory in the crash-ridden Moto3 race. The Frenchman – who lives just a few miles from the Le Mans circuit – made a brilliant start from 15th on the grid to complete the first lap in sixth.

By half-distance Rossi had moved into third place. Then race leader Miguel Oliveira crashed, putting Maverick Viñales into the lead, but a lap later Viñales was also down. Now Rossi was in front, with a 20-second advantage over Estoril winner Sandro Cortese.

Cortese also fell in the final laps, remounting to finish sixth, leaving Rossi with a 27-second victory over runner-up Alberto Moncayo and Oliveira's team-mate Alex Rins.

5 – CATALAN GP

Maverick Viñales crushed the opposition in the Moto3 race, at one point leading the rest of the pack by more than ten seconds. The Spanish teenager was in the thick of the leading battle in the early stages, then checked out at half-distance. While his rivals argued over the same piece of tarmac, Viñales made the best use of the clear road and rapidly built a ten-second advantage. He slowed at the line to finish 7.7 seconds ahead.

The skirmish for second was just like a 125 race, with up to eight riders ducking and diving past each other at every other corner. Points leader Sandro Cortese won the fight, despite a hand injury that required a final painkilling injection on the grid. He crossed the finish line a tenth ahead of podium first-timer Miguel Oliveira. Less than six-tenths of a second separated second place from ninth.

6 – BRITISH GP

Maverick Viñales won a breathtaking Moto3 battle. At one point in the second half there were 11 riders in the lead group. In the final laps, however, Viñales upped his pace and only Luis Salom and Sandro Cortese were able to go with him.

Spaniard Salom got in front on the penultimate lap but Viñales always seemed able to find a way past his compatriot. Cortese also found his way past Salom on the last lap but Salom counter-attacked at the final chicane to grab the runner-up spot. Viñales's third win of the year moved him back into the World Championship lead, two points ahead of Cortese.

7 – DUTCH TT

The race was the closest so far in this new class, with the lead group consisting of half the grid at one-third distance and plenty of particularly vicious passes. In the closing stages it came down to a five-man battle: Maverick Viñales versus factory Red Bull KTM men Sandro Cortese and Danny Kent, with Luis Salom and Louis Rossi also in the mix.

Cortese was the maddest of a very mad bunch, making some brutal passes, especially on team-mate Kent who was lucky to stay on after one high-speed collision exiting Ramshoek. And Cortese was lucky to escape sanction.

The final lap was a heart-stopper. Kent and Cortese led, just ahead of Viñales, who bravely took the lead at Hoge Heide with three corners to go, only to lose it to Salom, who then messed up the final chicane. Viñales came through to win, followed by Cortese and Kent.

8 – GERMAN GP

Sandro Cortese grabbed the championship lead with a brilliantly judged victory over Alexis Masbou.

In the early laps, when the track was soaking, the German was way behind but as the surface dried in the later stages he scythed through the pack. All riders started on wets. In the final stages he fought with Masbou, third-placed Luis Salom and Australian rookie Jack Miller, finally winning his second victory of the year by six-tenths.

Earlier points leader Maverick Viñales had a nightmare weekend, qualifying 24th in the rain and finishing outside the points in 17th.

9 – ITALIAN GP

This was a classic Mugello slipstreaming battle. At first there were seven leaders, chopping and changing at every corner. Then at three-quarters distance Maverick Viñales tried to make the break. He immediately left four of his pursuers behind, but title rival Sandro Cortese and Romano Fenati went with him.

The final lap was a real cliff-hanger, with a neck-and-neck drag race to the finish line. Viñales won, inches ahead of Fenati and Cortese, the top three separated by just 0.07s!

10 – INDIANAPOLIS GP

Luis Salom took the first win of his career by 0.056sec from Sandro Cortese after a ferocious last-lap shoot-out that resulted in Maverick Viñales falling at the last corner. He tried an ambitious move, got on the dirty part of the track and slid to earth. That ended a run of four wins in five races for Viñales and with hindsight it is possible to see that this was the point where his championship challenge finished.

On the other hand it was the start of the renaissance of Jonas Folger. The German had been on the uncompetitive Ioda but after the summer break replaced Hector Faubel on Aspar's Kalex KTM. His third place from a midfield start was the beginning of a run of form that would see him secure the ride for the 2013 season.

By Malaysia, Maverick Viñales was in trouble. He had dropped to third in the championship and was so out of sorts with his team that he went home and missed the race. His time will surely come.

British rider Danny Kent on a works KTM suffered from patchy form early on but came good with two last-corner wins at the end of the season. Jonas Folger resurrected his career when he moved to Aspar's team to win on a Kalex KTM, and the similarly mounted Luis Salom took his debut win at Indianapolis. The other winner was Louis Rossi, FTR Honda, to make it a total of seven different victors in the season.

Champion Cortese eventually won by an enormous 111 points with five victories, a reward for consistency. He moves up to Moto2 in 2013.

11 – CZECH REPUBLIC GP

The first race of the day got under way on a damp track. The man who made the most of the treacherous conditions was German rookie Jonas Folger who took the lead on lap four and quickly built an unassailable lead.

'I pushed very hard, took some risks, made a gap and then held it,' said Folger.

Indy winner Luis Salom took second place from series leader Sandro Cortese at the final esses, but Cortese was happy because he finished one place ahead of title rival Maverick Viñales. The Hondas were critically down on power against the KTMs on this fast circuit.

12 – SAN MARINO GP

Sandro Cortese stretched his series lead with his first victory in five races, but the result was in doubt throughout.

This was a breathtakingly close battle, with the top seven covered by just 1.3 seconds at the flag. Cortese grabbed the lead with three laps to go and only looked safe when he made a break half-way through the final lap.

The skirmish for runner-up spot was won by Luis Salom, ahead of early leader Romano Fenati and Maverick Viñales. Viñales may have won five races to Cortese's three, but he left Misano trailing the German by 46 points.

13 – ARAGON GP

Luis Salom gritted his teeth to win a dogfight of a Moto3 race, beating title rival Sandro Cortese and keeping his slim championship hopes alive.

Salom was his usual aggressive self – no-one could have guessed he'd had two big crashes in practice, including a nasty highside in morning warm-up. Throughout the 20 laps there were up to a dozen riders in the lead group, chopping and changing positions every other corner.

In the end it became a three-way KTM dash to the flag, the Hondas totally outgunned in Aragon's long straight which leads into the final corner.

14 – JAPANESE GP

Danny Kent won his first GP victory following a crazy last lap which started with title hopeful Luis Salom taking out leader Jonas Folger. That left Kent, team-mate Sandro Cortese and Alex Tonucci fighting for the win, with Maverick Viñales just behind.

At the end of the back straight Kent grabbed the lead from Cortese, who then had Tonucci come past him. At this point the German rider lost his cool, riding into Tonucci and crashing, just three corners from sealing the world title. Kent took the victory from Viñales and Tonucci while Cortese remounted to finish sixth, but he then remonstrated with Kent on the slow-down lap. Cortese later apologised for his outburst.

15 – MALAYSIAN GP

Zulfahmi Khairuddin came within 0.3 seconds and a few hundred yards of becoming Malaysia's first GP winner. Instead, he had to be content with becoming the first Malaysian podium finisher after Sandro Cortese took him at the final turn to secure the first Moto3 world title.

Khairuddin spent the early stages of the race chasing Jonas Folger before moving into the lead with seven laps to go. For a while the pair disputed the lead, swapping places five times in just one lap, before Folger slipped back and Cortese took up the fight with Khairuddin.

Cortese took the lead at the penultimate corner but Khairuddin got back in front on the final straight, only for the German to sneak past again for the win. 'When I saw I could win the championship with a victory, then I had to do it,' said Cortese.

Moto3

OPPOSITE, LEFT
Zulfahmi Khairuddin attracted a record crowd to the Malysian GP and he rewarded them with pole and a rostrum

ABOVE Danny Kent stood on the rostrum three times, twice on the top box. He even had time to help the new champion Sandro Cortese with his coiffure

OPPOSITE, RIGHT
Sandro Cortese was the first German champion in the lightweight class since Dirk Raudies in 1993

CHAMPIONSHIP STANDINGS

	Rider	Nat	Team	Motorcycle	Points
1	Sandro Cortese	GER	Red Bull KTM Ajo	KTM	325
2	Luis Salom	SPA	RW Racing GP	Kalex KTM	214
3	Maverick Viñales	SPA	Blusens Avintia	FTR Honda	207
4	Danny Kent	GBR	Red Bull KTM Ajo	KTM	154
5	Alex Rins	SPA	Estrella Galicia 0,0	Suter Honda	141
6	Romano Fenati	ITA	Team Italia FMI	FTR Honda	136
7	Zulfahmi Khairuddin	MAL	AirAsia-Sic-Ajo	KTM	128
8	Miguel Oliveira	POR	Estrella Galicia 0,0	Suter Honda	114
9	Jonas Folger	GER	Mapfre Aspar Team Moto3	Kalex KTM	93
10	Efren Vazquez	SPA	JHK t-shirt Laglisse	FTR Honda	93
11	Louis Rossi	FRA	Racing Team Germany	FTR Honda	86
12	Arthur Sissis	AUS	Red Bull KTM Ajo	KTM	84
13	Alexis Masbou	FRA	Caretta Technology	Honda	81
14	Niccolò Antonelli	ITA	San Carlo Gresini Moto3	FTR Honda	77
15	Jakub Kornfeil	CZE	Redox-Ongetta-Centro Seta	FTR Honda	71
16	Hector Faubel	SPA	Mapfre Aspar Team Moto3	Kalex KTM	63
17	Alberto Moncayo	SPA	Andalucia JHK t-shirt Laglisse	FTR Honda	52
18	Alessandro Tonucci	ITA	Team Italia FMI	FTR Honda	45
19	Niklas Ajo	FIN	TT Motion Events Racing	KTM	40
20	Alex Marquez	SPA	Ambrogio Next Racing	Suter Honda	27
21	Brad Binder	RSA	RW Racing GP	Kalex KTM	24
22	Alan Techer	FRA	Technomag-CIP-TSR	TSR Honda	21
23	Jack Miller	AUS	Caretta Technology	Honda	17
24	Adrian Martin	SPA	JHK t-shirt Laglisse	FTR Honda	16
25	Ivan Moreno	SPA	Andalucia JHK Laglisse	FTR Honda	10
26	Jasper Iwema	NED	Moto FGR	FGR Honda	9
27	Luca Gruenwald	GER	Freudenberg Racing Team	Honda	8
28	Isaac Viñales	SPA	Ongetta-Centro Seta	FTR Honda	8
29	Giulian Pedone	SWI	Ambrogio Next Racing	Suter Honda	7
30	Toni Finsterbusch	GER	Cresto Guide MZ Racing	Honda	7
31	Philipp Oettl	GER	HP Moto Kalex	Kalex KTM	5
32	Juan Francisco Guevara	SPA	Wild Wolf BST	FTR Honda	4
33	Marcel Schrotter	GER	Mahindra Racing	Mahindra	4
34	Kevin Hanus	GER	Thomas Sabo GP Team	Honda	3
35	Kevin Calia	ITA	Elle 2 Ciatti	Honda	2
36	Josep Rodriguez	SPA	Moto FGR	FGR Honda	1
37	John McPhee	GBR	Caretta Technology	KRP Honda	1
38	Michael Ruben Rinaldi	ITA	Racing Team Gabrielli	Honda	1
39	Simone Grotzkyj	ITA	Ambrogio Next Racing	Suter Honda	1

16 – AUSTRALIAN GP

Newly crowned world champ Sandro Cortese dismissed a strong challenge from Portuguese youngster Miguel Oliveira to take his fifth victory of the year. The pair ran away at the front, leaving a ferocious six-man battle for the final podium position, which went to Aussie teenager Arthur Sissis, a top-three first-timer.

Cortese's job was made easier when several riders, including recent winners Luis Salom and Jonas Folger, were penalised for jump starts.

17 – VALENCIAN GP

Danny Kent took his second Moto3 win at the very last corner of the season, diving inside World Champion and Red Bull KTM team-mate Sandro Cortese.

The race was another Moto3 thriller with the top four – Kent, Cortese, third-placed Zulfahmi Khairuddin and Brad Binder crossing the line separated by just four-tenths of a second.

Cortese led most of the way but somehow left the door open for Kent. 'I pushed a little extra on the last lap,' said Kent. 'I'd already seen that Sandro wasn't so strong into the last corner.'

Moto3
BIKES

The first year of the new lightweight class, Moto3, the replacement class for 125s, showed that a well-conceived rulebook can generate good racing.

The rules allow factories to participate but only on strict cost and competition terms. Engines must cost no more than €12,000, and they must be available to at least eight riders should there be that level of demand.

Any modifications carried out to these engines also have to be made available to all the customers who have taken the engine. The same goes for all engine parts. There is a control ECU with limited functionality and a common rev limit of 14,000rpm. The effect is twofold- to keep the playing field level, and to force costs down.

Two factories and two engine development companies started the year, but by the end only the two factories remained. Honda built a 'production racer', a €20,000 250cc four-stroke single, elegantly packaged with a rearwards-tilting cylinder and a reversed head in a strengthened 125 GP chassis. KTM built bikes as well, and these were far more conventional in shape and with a much more top-end-style engine. Honda had to tune their bike for GP use, in accordance with the rules.

Geo Technology, HRC's appointed GP representative, duly supplied engines at a cost of €12,000 to at least eight different riders, equipped

ABOVE AND LEFT The factory KTMs used good old-fashioned tubular steel for their frames

FAR LEFT KTM customer teams got a conventional twin-beam aluminium chassis by Kalex

with high-compression pistons, longer-duration cams and oil coolers. These bikes made enough power to beat the KTMs for the first half of the year.

Several different chassis solutions were available, ranging through keeping the standard one, building one, or buying an FTR or Suter rolling chassis. The standard Honda chassis was perfectly capable of taking a podium in the right hands, but the peach was generally considered to be the FTR.

For KTM the problem was different. They had to find more mid-range performance to beat the Honda's grunt, and then they had to develop their signature (but unproven) steel tube chassis. By

Estoril they had a new engine tune, and the first strengthened frames were being used. The faster circuits at the end of the year favoured the KTM slightly, but there's no doubt that the KTM and the Honda were well matched.

Oral Engineering, owned and run by ex-Ferrari engineer Mauro Forghieri, built an engine too. It was entered as a Mahindra in that company's own bikes and separately as an Oral in some converted Aprilia RS125 chassis. Ex-Aprilia racing team boss Giampiero Sacchi went into partnership with Robby Moto to build their own engine, the EMIR. Both projects suffered big problems with reliability, and neither was expected to return in 2013.

ABOVE Most Honda engines were housed in an FTR chassis

FAR LEFT Some teams stuck with the standard Honda frame – Caretta was one and put Alexis Masbou on the rostrum

LEFT The Ioda team's EMIR engine – a brave attempt to compete with the big boys

RED BULL ROOKIES
PETER CLIFFORD

weekends, in Rookies Cup, it seemed that 20 riders out of the 24 on the grid might do it.

The ever-increasing intensity of competition and the raising of standards as the Cup went through its sixth season were confirmed by the performance of ex-Rookies in the GP classes. Not only did 2012 see Luis Salom become a genuine Moto3 title contender with a string of podium places and two GP wins, but Danny Kent won his first GP in his second season after graduating from the Cup and finished impressively in the title standings. Red Bull KTM team-mate and fellow-alumni Arthur Sissis scored consistently in his first GP season, particularly in the latter half of the year.

It took Alt three years of riding in the Cup to become champion, but the pace of advancement seems to be accelerating, with newcomers like 16-year-old Czech Karel Hanika and 15-year-old Belgian Livio Loi winning races in their first seasons. Hanika was on the pace even during the pre-season test at Estoril, and on the podium with two thirds when the series returned there for the third and fourth races of the season. By then Alt had already set about his winning ways, taking race one at the opening weekend in Jerez and only having another good result taken away from him in race two by a technical failure. His enthusiasm to make up for the lost points led to his only real mistake of the season when he fell in race two at Estoril after taking second behind Scott Deroue in the first race.

Deroue laid claim to being the find of the season, even though he had been a Rookie in 2011. In that, his first, year he had started off trailing the field at Jerez but improved strongly to be fighting at the front by the end. In 2012 the 16-year-old Dutchman's orange helmet became a pretty permanent feature of the lead group, a battle that often included up to 15

Florian Alt, the 16-year-old German, was a worthy winner of the 2012 Red Bull MotoGP Rookies Cup, but boy did he have a fight on his hands every weekend. In no way should the fact that he only won four of the 15 races be taken as a denial of his ability, merely a reflection of the great depth of talent and the closeness of competition. Sandro Cortese had more wins on his way to the Moto3 World Championship, as did Marc Marquez in Moto2 and Jorge Lorenzo in MotoGP, but in those classes only a handful of competitors seem to have a chance of winning. Most

FLORIAN ALT, THE BRIGHTEST OF MANY STARS

LEFT The number 66 bike of Florian Alt leads the pack at the Grand Prix of the Netherlands

LEFT INSET Florian Alt being interviewed by Peter Clifford following his win at Assen

riders, all with a chance of crossing the line first. The way that Deroue had an uncanny ability to work his way towards the front when it counted was a joy to watch. With three wins, a second and a third through the year, Deroue was a title candidate for sure, his campaign only coming off the rails late in the season when he made some errors under pressure. If he continues to progress he will be one of the strong favourites in 2013.

Deroue will not have to deal with Livio Loi, however, because the Brno race two winner has been snapped up by a MotoGP team – even though he will have to miss the start of next season because he is too young. His attraction was clear to see after he overcame a difficult start to the year, when he did not really gel with the machine, to improve so rapidly in the second half. He romped away from the pack in race one at Brno only to be hunted down and beaten by a wonderfully determined home-town hero in the shape of Karel Hanika.

Hanika's early fall in race two left Loi clear to take the victory, and he might have backed that up by winning the last three races of the year. However, his nemesis Hanika robbed him two corners from home in Misano, upsetting him enough to allow Lukas Trautmann through into second. Then, at the final weekend at Aragon, Loi had race one won when an electrical failure stopped him on the last lap. Trautmann took the win that time and then became the unwitting cause of Loi's demise in race two when the pair touched and Loi was left with a broken exhaust.

Austrian 16-year-old Trautmann really came into his own in the second half of the year after a frustrating beginning when he struggled to get into the top ten. He turned it all around with a win at the Sachsenring and was then in the hunt every weekend. After fifths in both races at Brno he followed up with that second at Misano and the race one win at Aragon.

It was fitting that the final victory of the season, and most probably the last two-stroke win at a GP, went to Hanika. Even though he was one of the bigger Rookies he found ways to minimise that disadvantage. Despite suffering the early-season frustration of leading races at any time apart from when he crossed the finishing line, netting him four third places before his first win in Brno, he never pointed the finger at anyone but himself. Following his second win in Misano and then a third victory in Aragon, he gave the credit to rider coach Gustl Auinger and his mechanics.

In a season filled with so much talent and so many sensational performances even winners can be disappointed by season's end. Rookies Cup sensation and title-holder in 2011, Lorenzo Baldassarri won race two in Jerez but otherwise the 15-year-old Italian was denied places on the podium. Being taller and the man to beat proved tough, yet he was usually in the pack and had certainly not lost his ability.

Both Baldassarri and 16-year-old German Philipp Oettl suffered because they raced four-stroke Moto3 machines in the Spanish Championship between their Rookies Cup events. Swapping back to the two-stroke Rookies KTMs cost them dear. Oettl was very much a title challenger with a victory, two seconds and a third in the first half of the year, but as things became more intense the bike-swapping handicap kept him off the podium. They will doubtless go on to great things as the world concentrates on Moto3 and other four-stroke formulae. They must count themselves unlucky to have been caught in the only split season, as Rookies Cup runs Moto3 machinery in 2013. KTM will continue as technical partner, building a close brother to their 2013 factory Moto3 racer, so that the Rookies Cup will continue to provide a step to a Grand Prix career.

WIN TWO GOLD & SILVER PASSES TO A EUROPEAN 2013 MotoGP™ RACE OF YOUR CHOICE. WORTH UP TO £1000. TO ENTER, VISIT:

www.facebook.com/haynesbooks

Visit Haynes Books on Facebook and follow the instructions there on how to enter our free prize draw. No purchase is necessary. The draw closes on 1 March 2013.

The fabulous prize will allow you to experience the excitement of a MotoGP race from the most exclusive location in the finest style.

A Gold Pass gives you access on Sunday/Race Day and a Silver Pass on Saturday/Qualifying practice day.

Our lucky prize winner will receive a full Gold & Silver package for two people for a European race on the 2013 MotoGP calendar.

Subject to availability – excludes Italian GP at Mugello – no travel or hotel costs or other expenses are included.

Best Location and Exclusive Privileges

Situated at the heart of the action, either directly above the Pit Lane or in a smart village area, MotoGP VIP VILLAGE puts you as close as you can get to the world's top motorcycle racers.

Privileged Parking, excellent views, race coverage on closed-circuit TV, Pit Lane Walk, Paddock Tour, Service Road Tour and complimentary Official Programme on Sunday.

The MotoGP VIP VILLAGE Game will offer all guests the chance to win the possibility to view races from the pit wall, a service road tour and one of the many licensed MotoGP products.

Best Service and Excellent Cuisine

Hospitality is of the highest quality, from the buffet breakfast in the morning to gourmet lunch and afternoon petit fours, with a complimentary bar all day.

RIDERS FOR HEALTH

BARRY COLEMAN

riders

WHAT ALVARO SAW

LEFT Alvaro Bautista and Randy Mamola in Zambia on Riders' Experience Africa adventure

Alvaro Bautista has a funny view of the world. The boy's horizon veers wildly and repeatedly, tipping so completely and so dramatically from side to side that he might be expected just to slide gracefully off the surface of the Earth. At times there seems to be a pattern: for anything up to a hundred times in any given weekend, the slide and the vertigo follow a remarkably consistent path. And then, the next weekend, something completely different happens. The professors would conclude that the patient has a balance problem, perhaps something wrong with his inner ear.

Well, he has a new problem now, and in a way it does have something to do with balance. Alvaro has been to see Riders for Health's programme in Zambia. He was a special guest of the Riders' Experience Africa adventure, which means riding through rural Zambia with a small group that happens to include Randy Mamola at speeds of anything up to 55mph. Motorcycling, but not as Alvaro knows it.

When Alvaro now speaks of experiencing Africa he still looks a bit shocked, even though he enjoyed his time there very much indeed. Well, he would do. Zambia, as it happens, is a particularly welcoming country and the Experience Africa route is a very beautiful and absolutely fascinating one. He did not experience the worn-out old media scenario, so effectively popularised by Bob Geldof, of gazing upon acres and acres of fly-covered, starving children while looking a bit bothered about it. No, what he experienced was a country populated by self-possessed, self-managing people who just happened to have found themselves stranded in a century that

is somewhat technologically removed from the one the rest of us fly around in. So riding through Zambia, even if it is immediately apparent that it is not the same as riding through Belgravia, is an encouraging experience.

Alvaro and the team arrived in Zambia's capital, Lusaka, early one morning and were transferred (which is New English for 'taken in a bus') to a very pleasant lodge on the outskirts of town where they could have a rest and become familiar with their waiting motorcycles: Yamaha AG200s. I particularly like that bit: Alvaro Bautista becoming familiar with a 55mph motorcycle. Next day, it was away through the countryside, through villages, past farms, stopping to eat, stopping to chat: fascinating and beautiful. That night they were under canvas. Alvaro is afraid of spiders. There had to be something. Next day it was on to a jaw-dropping nature reserve, then down to a camp on the shores of Lake Kariba … and so on. Visiting clinics, talking with Zambian nurses and clinicians about how the ability to use a motorcycle that actually works has transformed their own impact on health care. Then came more off-road riding, more breaktaking scenery, followed by the slightly irritating tarmac ride to Livingstone.

Is the tarmac ride worth it? A whole three hours?

So what's in Livingstone? Well, the Riders' Southern Province office and workshop, and then – oh yes, I remember – Victoria Falls. That is to say, one of the most startling places on the face of the Earth.

So Alvaro has experienced Africa, and what seems to haunt him somewhat is that, as he puts it: 'Those people, they have nothing. Nothing. And we have everything.'

It's a good point. But it's a less good point because of him. Because every year he shows up for Day of Champions and for Dia de los Campeones in Valencia. It's a less good point because for 25 years his own sport has been working on the question of how health care can consistently be delivered to the rural poor. We're working on that in Southern Province and in Zambia as a whole. And we are not alone. We are working there now with the Bill & Melinda Gates Foundation, the (very prestigious) Stanford University, the Zambia Ministry of Health and with several other technical and financial supporters. Once we worked alone, but now we work with a coalition of the smart, the determined and the willing. That's a change of viewpoint, and a swing and swirl of horizon every bit as dramatic as the one Alvaro sees every time he goes to work. Motorcycle racing has changed health-care delivery in Africa for ever. Get your head round that without causing it to spin.

'WHAT A MAN CAN DO, A WOMAN CAN DO'

Riders for Health's reliable motorcycles and skilled technicians are improving access to health care for 12 million people across Africa. Our programmes are run entirely by local people so our work is also having a positive social impact, such as empowering women through training and employment.

'It is very rare to see a woman riding a motorcycle,' said Linet Wanga, a community health worker for Support Activities In Poverty Eradication and Health (SAIPEH). 'So it has also added me some prestige in the community. Many young ladies are also wishing to train and ride the motorcycles.' Based in western Kenya, SAIPEH is a grassroots organisation. Their activities focus around the support of women, orphans and vulnerable children.

Before being trained by Riders for Health, Linet said her work was very challenging. She had to rely on an old bicycle to reach remote rural communities. 'One; it was cumbersome to reach the community because of the bicycle, because sometimes as you go the bicycle breaks down. Two; it was very expensive because we used a lot of resources. Three; we were unable to reach the target people because of the limited transport.'

Part of Linet's role is to monitor orphaned children that SAIPEH support through school, and they also identify guardians to look after them. Now that she is mobile, Linet is free to carry out her vital work without interruption. 'Now we are visiting a total number of a thousand people a month and above. We have 522 students we visit in school and, because of the motorbikes, we are reaching these students in time so that is a very big achievement.'

Riders for Health teaches health workers like Linet to ride a motorcycle safely and confidently in the difficult African terrain. Linet has also learnt how to carry out daily maintenance checks on her bike so that it doesn't break down. With reliable transport, a health worker in Africa is able to help up to five times more people than before with vital health care and education. And less time spent travelling between rural villages means they can stay longer in the communities attending to patients too.

'We aim to build a long-lasting solution for health-care delivery in Africa,' explains Riders' co-founder and CEO, Andrea Coleman, 'and crucial to this is the training of local men and women. Skills developed with Riders provide local employment and can be passed on for future generations, benefiting the whole community.'

Linet Wanga wears a skirt over her protective clothing because, in some of the more remote homesteads she visits, the men will not accept her into their homes if she is wearing trousers

'MY MOTORCYCLE HAS REALLY CHANGED MY LIFE AS A WOMAN IN THE COMMUNITY. I AM NOW RESPECTED. WHENEVER THEY SEE ME RIDING THE MOTORCYCLE THEY TURN TO LOOK AT ME AND WONDER THAT WOMEN TOO KNOW HOW TO RIDE MOTORCYCLES.'

AISHA ISSA, HEALTH WORKER, KENYA

Since 2010, one in four trainees at our International Academy of Vehicle Management (IAVM) in Zimbabwe have been women.

Our programme leaders in five out of seven countries – the Gambia, Lesotho, Kenya, Zambia and Malawi – are all women.